TIMOTHY GREEN BECKLEY, EDITOR

Illustra

LEGACY OF THE SKY PEOPLE

The Extraterrestrial Origin Of Adam And Eve;
The Garden Of Eden; Noah's Ark And The Serpent Race

**Ancient Astronaut Photos From The Private
Collection Of Brad and Sherry Steiger.**

BY...
THE 8TH EARL OF CLANCARTY
AND NICK REDFERN
WITH SEAN CASTEEL,
AND TIM SWARTZ

The Legacy Of The Sky People

From The Original Source Material By Brinsley Le Poer Trench
With Additional Material by Timothy Green Beckley;
Nick Redfern; Tim Swartz, and Sean Casteel

This edition Copyright © 2012 by Timothy Green Beckley

All rights reserved. No part of these manuscripts may be copied or reproduced by any mechanical or digital methods and no exerpts or quotes may be used in any other book or manuscript without permission in writing by the Publisher, Timothy Green Beckley, except by a reviewer who may quote brief passages in a review. If you are the legitimate copyright holder of any material inadvertently used in this book, please send a notice to this effect and the offending material will be removed from all future printings. The material utilized herein is reproduced for educational purposes and every effort has been made to verify that the material has been properly credited and is available in the public domain.

ISBN 13: 9781606111277
ISBN: 1606111272

Published by Timothy Green Beckley
Box 753 · New Brunswick, NJ 08903
Printed in the United States of America

Staff Members
Timothy G. Beckley, Publisher
Carol Ann Rodriguez, Assistant to the Publisher
Sean Casteel, Associate Editor
Tim R. Swartz, Cover Graphics and Editorial Consultant
William Kern, Editorial and Art Consultant

Sign Up On The Web For Our Free Weekly Newsletter
and Mail Order Version of Conspiracy Journal
www.ConspiracyJournal.com

Order Hot Line: 1-732-602-3407
PayPal: MrUFO8@hotmail.com

TABLE OF CONTENTS

MEN ARE FROM MARS! MEETINGS WITH THE REMARKABLE BRINSLEY LE POER TRENCH, 8TH EARL OF CLANCARTY
—By Timothy Green Beckley—Page 1

ALIEN SECRETS ON THE MOUNTAIN
—By Nick Redfern—Page 4

**ANGELS OR ALIENS—
ANCIENT CONTACTS WITH THE SKY PEOPLE**
—Tim Swartz—Page 26

"WE HAVE MET THE MARTIANS AND THEY ARE US!"
An Interview With Brad And Sherry Steiger
—By Sean Casteel—Page 32

**ANCIENT ALIENS
AND THEIR TRUE RELATIONSHIP
WITH GOD ALMIGHTY**
An Interview With Giorgio Tsoukalos
—By Sean Casteel—Page 39

THE SKY PEOPLE
—By Brinsley Le Poer Trench—Page 51

CONTRIBUTING AUTHORS BIOS—Page 211

STATES WILLIAM KERN, ANCIENT ASTRONAUT THEORIST:

The Sky People, by Brinsley LePoer Trench, is an indictment of religions, priests, lawyers and politicians and the strictly controlled, destructive, antagonistic society these fearful, paranoid lower life forms (Adam-II) have forced upon us all to compensate for their lack of higher mental abilities—most notably, telepathy—and their complete dependence upon vocal speech to convey their destructive and deadly ideas.

Beyond that, however, *The Sky People* is a comprehensive, well researched and educated revelation of our man/hu-man origins (Adam-I and Adam-II) as created by space beings we mistakenly call "gods."

The author makes a convincing case for the presence of two races of space beings, Jehovans and Elohim—The Sky People—on earth for literally millions of years, and, although we observe them in their physical forms but rarely and briefly, they are among us this very moment; the Elohim guiding the *Galactic Man*, Adam-I, changing him, molding him into a being who will one day rule galaxies of his own, while the Jehovan Adam-II hu-man—a wholly brute animal being—will eventually fade from the galactic record forever.

LEGACY OF THE SKY PEOPLE

MEN ARE FROM MARS!
MEETINGS WITH THE REMARKABLE
BRINSLEY LE POER TRENCH, 8ᵀᴴ EARL OF CLANCARTY

By Timothy Green Beckley

I am one of the few Americans ever-so-humbly honored to have been invited to speak on the subject of UFOs before a private member organization of the House of Lords, the upper arm of Great Britain's Parliament. While having no official "power of authority" to take matters into their own hands, the members of the House of Lords UFO Group tried for over a decade to pressure Her Majesty's Ministry of Defense to release its Top Secret findings on a subject that has fascinated, titillated and provoked a sense of controversy on both sides of the international pond.

Brinsley Le Poer Trench

As a teenager back in the 1960s – long before the internet existed of course – I began corresponding with UFO researchers from all over the world. Having started publishing a widely read, mimeographed newsletter when I was just 15, we exchanged our Interplanetary News Service Report with similar publications and affiliated organizations all over the world, even inside the Soviet Bloc nations where there was said to be great censorship and hostility toward the subject, although it turns out later this was probably overplayed by naïve American UFOlogists.

Among the liaisons I established was with British bloke Brinsley Le Poer Trench, whose interest in UFO-related matters garnered him the rather atypical job of editor of the world's most prestigious publication on unexplained aerial phenomenon. "The Flying Saucer Review" was the only magazine of its type in the world, with an international readership of several thousand UFO stalwarts. Among its "celebrity" subscribers was Prince Philip, as well as Lord Hill Norton, a five star Admiral of the British Fleet. What made "The Flying Saucer Review" so provocative was the fact that it did not shy away from publishing a host of challenging essays on the possible paranormal aspects of the UFO mystery as well as relying heavily on the increasing quantity of encounters with any number of weird appearing occupants said to steer these ostensibly intergalactic craft.

As divinity would have it, Trench had been born into the British aristocracy through Dutch nobility, and with the passing of his brother he became the 8th Earl of Clancarty, a position that comes with a prestigious seat in the House of Lords whose lineage goes back to the wealthy land barons. They are not the elected officials who hold public office in Great Britain, but those who have a "right to govern" by virtue of their noble birth. Actually, as we know, the Lords and Ladies of today are mostly penny-strapped and make due like the rest of mortal men these days.

Yet, being the *"Earl of anywhere"* does come with a few perks – mainly that the person is usually taken a bit more seriously. Luckily for Brinsley, because he had some pretty outlandish ideas he was trying to get across. For you see, Brinsley Le Poer Trench has to be placed in the Ancient Astronaut hall of fame as one of the originators of the theory that visitors from the stars – or "elsewhere" – have been popping in from time immemorial to keep a watchful eye on humanity, either because they are just blatantly curious or because – as some theorize – they actually created us and we are the lab experiments of this group of cosmic voyagers. There are various offshoots of this hypothesis, but it's the basic theory that we have never been alone.

Ancient Astronauts pop star Eric von Daniken popularized this concept for the masses, but Brinsley preceded von Daniken by a number of years with the notion that ancient aliens were still lurking about the planet. Brinsley went a step or two further, in fact, by coming up with the hypothesis that the human race itself – in one form or another – actually came to Earth from elsewhere in space and that this is not our original habitat.

"The Sky People" by Brinsley Le Poer Trench was originally published in the UK in the 1960s and went through several printings. It was even issued in the United States in hardback by my late friend Ray Palmer, who headed up Amherst Press and was one of the original publishers of "Fate Magazine" (still being put out today by Phyllis Galde). Brinsley, the 8th Earl of Clancarty, had quite a career as a writer and author, though he has virtually been forgotten amongst the dozens of ancient astronaut theorists who populate the press and television airways these days. Most fascinating is the fact that, while the Earl came before the "many others," his conclusions and ideas were fresh and perhaps a bit more "far out" than those of his soon-to-be contemporaries.

What did Trench believe, in a nutshell, about the ancient astronauts he called

LEGACY OF THE SKY PEOPLE

The Sky People?

According to Trench, in his book *The Sky People*, Adam and Eve, Noah and many of the other characters from the Bible originally lived on Mars. Trench believed that Adam and Eve were the experimental creations of extraterrestrials. His claim was that the Biblical description of the Garden of Eden was inconsistent with what was on Earth, and, as Mars contained canals, that the Garden of Eden must have been located on the Red Planet (or perhaps inside of it). He further claimed that the north polar ice cap melted on Mars, and this caused the descendants of Adam and Eve to move to Earth. The vehicle they arrived in would have been, without a doubt in Brinsley's mind, Noah's Ark, making the great Noah a "Martian" – obviously an opinion that takes some getting used to and which will have fundamentalists lining up to burn this edition of Brinsley's thesis like they would most definitely have done with the original Sky People book if they had known it existed.

Personally, I don't think the good Earl would object to our "tacking on" some very pertinent new material which expands upon his general theme as well as enhances his contribution to the entire ancient astronaut realm. I know from personal experience that he was a sharing and caring individual. He shared his papers with others and even had a branch of his organization that catered to teenagers called the International Sky Scouts, with thousands of members, but centered mainly, it seems, in Japan, where the organization was headquartered for a while.

It was unfortunate that I only got to meet Brinsley once but I did spend two full days with him as he introduced me to members of Parliament and hosted a dinner for me at his flat in London. His library, very extensive, was housed on the fourth floor of the brownstone he occupied while carrying out his duties as a member of the House of Lords.

Recently, the MOD released over a period of time thousands of files on Britain's UFO encounters. I can't help but believe that Brinsley was partly responsible for this new "sharing of information" with the public. It started with his research into the Legacy of the Sky People and his later pressuring of the government to "come clean" about UFOs.

We need more like the 8th Earl of Clancarty in power today.

Unfortunately, such men and women are difficult to find in service to their country on and off the UFO playing field.

mrufo8@hotmail.com

www.ConspiracyJournal.Com

LEGACY OF THE SKY PEOPLE

ALIEN SECRETS ON THE MOUNTAIN

By Nick Redfern

Folklore, Floods and a Man Named Noah

If one takes a look at the *Book of Genesis* as contained in the *Holy Bible*, one is confronted with the following memorable words:

"God looked upon the earth, and, behold, it was corrupt; for all flesh had corrupted his way upon the earth. And God said unto Noah, 'The end of all flesh is come before me; for the earth is filled with violence through them; and, behold, I will destroy them with the earth.'"

It was not quite everyone who was going to be exterminated by God's powerful wrath, however. According to the old book, God had selected one man and his family not only to survive the disaster that he had in mind, but also to help kick-start life again, once the cataclysmic event had finally subsided. That man was Noah, revealed in the pages of the *Bible* as the grandson of Methuselah, supposedly the oldest person to have ever lived. God, we are told, made his stark and stern orders very clear to Noah:

"...make thee an Ark of gopher wood; rooms shalt thou make in the Ark, and shalt pitch it within and without with pitch. And this is the fashion which thou shalt make it of: The length of the Ark shall be three hundred cubits, the breadth of it fifty cubits, and the height of it thirty cubits. A window shalt thou make to the Ark, and in a cubit shalt thou finish it above; and the door of the Ark shalt thou set in the side thereof; with lower, second, and third stories shalt thou make it."

As for why God specifically chose Noah to build such an immense vessel, that becomes clear when we study the next words attributed to the Christian deity: "And, behold, I, even I, do bring a flood of waters upon the earth, to destroy all flesh, wherein is the breath of life, from under heaven; and every thing that is in the earth shall die."

LEGACY OF THE SKY PEOPLE

Fortunately for Noah, he and his family were destined and determined by God to survive the looming, planet-wide disaster that was to decimate the population and even re-sculpt the very landscape of the Earth itself. God thundered at Noah:

"But with thee will I establish my covenant; and thou shalt come into the Ark, thou, and thy sons, and thy wife, and thy sons' wives with thee. And of every living thing of all flesh, two of every sort shalt thou bring into the Ark, to keep them alive with thee; they shall be male and female.

"Of fowls after their kind, and of cattle after their kind, of every creeping thing of the earth after his kind, two of every sort shall come unto thee, to keep them alive. And take thou unto thee of all food that is eaten, and thou shalt gather it to thee; and it shall be for food for thee, and for them."

As a result, the now legendary saga of the Ark of Noah – that saw the man of the moment and his family surviving the almighty deluge within the giant ark for a period of forty turbulent days and nights – was born. It was also a saga that saw the massive boat in question come to a final resting place very high on the precarious, ice and snow covered slopes of Mt. Ararat, Turkey. But, it was not just

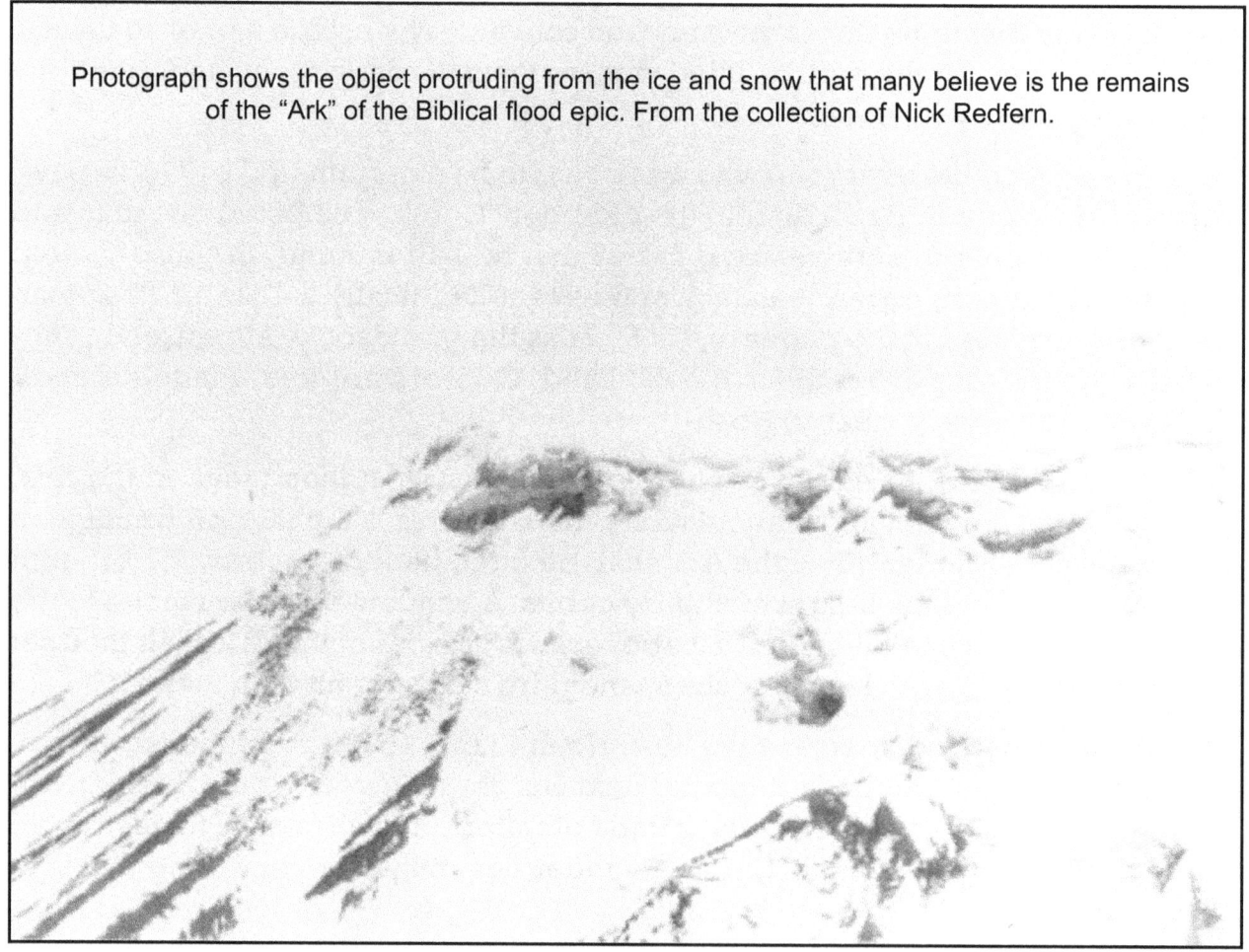

Photograph shows the object protruding from the ice and snow that many believe is the remains of the "Ark" of the Biblical flood epic. From the collection of Nick Redfern.

LEGACY OF THE SKY PEOPLE

Noah and Co. who survived.

There were also those many animals too that God had wisely ordered Noah to take on-board. Thus, the process of starting over could now begin in earnest. Of course, as history has shown, a great deal of controversy exists – even within Christian circles – regarding the true nature of the old legend, and even if Mt. Ararat was the correct location when it comes to trying to define the final resting place of Noah's Ark.

Further Floods, Further Folklore

That there almost certainly were massive, deluge-style, floods in times long gone seems a matter of little doubt. Indeed, one can take even the most cursory examinations of the fables, legends and stories of numerous countries worldwide and find that they, too, all told of gigantic, nation-destroying floods and warnings from God – or a near-army of gods – to prepare for the very worst scenarios possible.

In fact, such legends can be found in the cultures of Native American Indians and the Aborigines of Australia, as well as the people of Argentina, Scandinavia, the British Isles, China, Greece, Korea, Peru, and Bolivia. And that many of these stories are eerily and chillingly similar in nature strongly suggests a common point of origin, or thread, running through each and every one of them. For those who think the story of Noah's Ark amounts to the first and last word on such matters, it's time to think again.

Hindu culture speaks of the mighty Manu, the premier Brahman ruler of our world, and one that rescued our species from total obliteration in the very earliest years of human evolution. But, according to Hindu texts, the ship that Manu built did not come to rest on Turkey's famous Mt. Ararat. Its last port of call was none other than the Malaya Mountains, which aren't even in Turkey. Rather, they – today known as the Western Ghats – are situated in western India.

Then there is the Sumerian *Epic of Gilgamesh* – which is most deeply detailed on twelve impressive tablets from the equally impressive library of an Assyrian ruler named Ashurbanipal, who was a major force to be reckoned with in the 7th Century BC. *Gilgamesh* also highlights a story of a huge, devastating flood. And although the tablets date from roughly 650 BC, the tale they tell – scholars suggest – is likely much older; in fact, way, *way* older.

It must be stressed, however, that despite the clear and undeniable differences in terms of deities, locations, cultures and religions, all of the stories have remarkable parallels and similarities. *Gilgamesh* introduces us to Utnapishtim, who creates a gigantic ark, inside which he and his wife and family – along with countless examples of animal life – survive the water-based destruction that is unfolding all around them on a massive, planet-pummeling scale.

As for the Native Americans legends, they reveal how, when the actions of the human population of the Earth were deeply frowned upon by one Gitche Manitou – a creator character in Native American lore – the response was death on a massive scale, all thanks to a massive, worldwide deluge courtesy of Gitche Manitou.

In other words, while we do, of course, have to be careful when it comes to taking any of these stories, legends and tales literally, they all suggest inherited knowledge and significant data on the part of the ancients on several important matters:

★ That a cataclysmic disaster of a flood nature was bearing down on the human populace at some point in the fog-shrouded past.

★ That supreme deities – all over the world – chose to warn specific people of how they might survive the looming disaster.

★ That the world was to be rebooted by those lucky few who had been selected to be spared death by drowning as the waters of the Earth rose to near-unimaginable levels.

Science Tackles the Deluge

Fortunately, we do not have to simply rely on old legends and tales that, in all probability, have been massively distorted via time and repeated translation from language to language. Science has helped us to have an understanding of those long gone, turbulent, flood-filled eras.

Back in 1997, a professor emeritus and a geophysicist based at Columbia University named Walter Clarkson Pitman III, along with William Ryan, a geologist, theorized that the saga of the flood as specifically described in the pages of the *Bible* was actually an account of a very real – and very large - flooding of the Black Sea; maybe as much as 7,500 years ago. That the sea in question borders Turkey – which just happens to be home to Mt. Ararat – makes matters all the more intriguing.

Moving on, we have the discoveries of a man named Bruce Masse, an environmental archaeologist operating out of the New Mexico-based Los Alamos National Laboratory. Masse suggested that, at a point around 7,000 years ago, a gigantic comet possibly slammed into our world, with terrible force, into the waters off Madagascar, resulting in truly gigantic tidal waves, a massive number of fatalities, and, as an inevitable result, the birth of never-forgotten flood legends that were ascribed to the work of a god or gods, rather than a comet.

LEGACY OF THE SKY PEOPLE

There is, however, one matter that stands out with regard to the saga of Noah's Ark that is very different from the tales of Gilgamesh, the Native Americans, the Europeans, or the South Americans.

That difference is as intriguing as it is mysterious: for decades, elements of the U.S. Government, Air Force, Pentagon, and CIA have taken a deep, secret and clandestine interest in what may very well have come to rest high on Mt. Ararat. As for why, well, the answers push us far away from tales of a large, old, wooden ark, and far closer to tales of a crashed ark from another world.

Noah's Ark, 1949: The Government First Takes Note

It was early one particular morning in mid-June of 1949 when a USAF spy-plane took to the air from its home-base in mainland Europe. The crew was on a secret mission to photograph what, intelligence-gathering assets had suggested, was a new military installation being constructed by the Soviets near the Turkish border. So, with the mission underway, the captain quickly bound the plane for Turkey and the troublesome Reds.

As it transpired, and as luck would have it, to get to the specific area where the Soviets were reportedly hard at work and flexing their military muscles – and also to avoid detection by the Russians - the crew had to fly very close to the 17,000-foot peak of Mt. Ararat. Actually: *extremely* close. None of the crew, surely, had any inkling of what they would find as they closed in on that mighty, imposing

The government takes notice. USAF overflight photograph of Mount Ararat. From the collection of Nick Redfern.

mountain. They were very soon to find out, however.

It was when the crew approached Mt. Ararat at a height of about 3,000-feet short of its peak that one of the men on board the plane cried out that he could see something deeply strange protruding out of the thick sheets of ice and snow. It looked, said the amazed man, like an aircraft wing, but one that – rather astonishingly – was around 500 to 600 feet in length. Hardly the sort of thing you would expect to see anywhere, never mind at the top of Mt. Ararat! Yet, there it was.

Wasting no time, the crew contacted base, explained what they had stumbled upon, and asked permission to briefly break off from the planned mission and photograph the strange device. Not surprisingly, permission was immediately given to do exactly that. But that was scarcely the start of things.

As the chief photographer on board quickly snapped off a reel of film, from the other side of the plane a shout came from another of the crew: he could see a near-identical wing, and of near-identical size, sticking out of the ice from another part of the mountain. If these really were wings, then their overall combined width would have been somewhere in the order of 1,000 to 1,200 feet. It scarcely needs to be said that no one is flying aircraft of such size even today, never mind as far back as 1949. Or, at least, no one from around here is flying any such incredibly huge aircraft.

So, after taking shots of the first anomaly, the crew then maneuvered the aircraft to secure photos of the other whatever-it-was. It was then on with the original mission, followed by a flight back to base, at which point the priceless and mysterious photos taken over Mt. Ararat were forwarded to the Pentagon for analysis. No one should be surprised to know that they vanished into decades-long oblivion. This would not be the only occasion upon which these mountain-based curiosities were encountered by U.S. military personnel, however.

Witnesses Speak

In 1952, one William Todd, while in Turkey with the military, was yet another figure fortunate enough to encounter the curious structure, or structures, high on Mt. Ararat. According to Todd, the vehicle he saw looming out of the dense, icy, snow-dominated mountain was gigantic, oblong-shaped and of a dark color, not unlike that of slate.

Two years later, it was the turn of a man named Lieutenant Colonel Robert Livingston to become immersed in the puzzling matter of what was really going on atop Mt. Ararat. At the time, Livingston was on an assignment of the temporary kind at Wright-Patterson Air Force Base, Ohio – an installation with a long history of ties to UFO sightings, extraterrestrial encounters, and rumors of dead alien bodies deep below the base in cryogenic storage. Livingston, while at Wright-

LEGACY OF THE SKY PEOPLE

Pat, was attached to a sub-office of what was then designated the Topographic Engineering Center, which operated from within the confines of Fort Belvoir, Virginia.

Livingston worked at Ft. Belvoir from the late 1940s until the early years of the 1970s – retiring as Chief of Field Office – and was an old man indeed when he chose to go public with a story of how, on one particular day in 1954, at Wright-Pat, a USAF captain ordered him to provide analysis of a single picture that had made its way to the base via the Turkish Embassy.

It had reportedly been taken by the crew of a U.S. military aircraft at some point earlier which may very well mean it was one of the priceless photos secured back in 1949; although, admittedly, that is speculation. The important fact is, however, that Livingston saw, handled and analyzed the photo – regardless of when, exactly, it was taken.

Livingston went on record that the picture displayed what appeared to be a lengthy object that was somewhat rectangle-like in design and dark in color, and partly obscured by thick ice –all this, of course, closely echoing the words of William Todd. Livingston and his team were told to study the photo and come to some form of conclusion regarding what it showed.

Aside from confirming that the picture seemed to reveal some sort of large, structured thing, not much could be ascertained at all. Evidently, however, this was all fine, as the captain thanked Livingston and his men and went on his way. Livingston never saw the captain – or the intriguing photo – again.

A year on – records released under the terms of the Freedom of Information Act by the CIA show – a French explorer named Fernand Navarra stumbled on a large section of ancient wood, that seemed to have been fashioned by human hand, only a short distance from where the USAF secured its photos back in 1949. Whether or not this indicates a connection between the two remains unknown; but that the CIA, of all people, chose to note for posterity Navarra's findings demonstrates that someone at an official level was clandestinely following the Frenchman's work in relation to the saga of Noah's Ark.

Let's now focus on the words of Gregor Schwinghammer, also of the USAF. Although the precise date has been lost to the fog of time, it was during the 1950s, when he was at Adana, Turkey, that Schwinghammer was also exposed to the curious structure atop Mt. Ararat. He, too, described it as oblong-shaped and huge.

Interestingly, Schwinghammer heard that, at some point, a U-2 spy-plane had been utilized to photograph the anomaly. More significantly, the U-2-secured imagery suggested the thing on the mountain displayed evidence of having moved at some point – no doubt as the ice-banks shifted and changed – thus strongly suggesting that this was some sort of independent object, rather than a large chunk of rock attached to the mountain.

From Britain to the Smithsonian

It was not just the United States that was addressing the Noah's Ark controversy during this post-Second World War era. The Brits were doing likewise. In the 1950s, British Intelligence and American Intelligence began to share data on their respective findings on the curious phenomenon atop Mt. Ararat. As far as the U.K. material was concerned, the vast majority of it was focused upon what Her Majesty's Government had learned about Adolf Hitler's secret attempts to find the Ark back in the latter stages of the Second World War.

Precisely why the Nazis had such an obsession with locating the Ark of Noah is not known; but that Hitler spent considerable time trying to find it – even to the extent of flying secret, balloon-based missions over the old mountain to photograph the very same area that intrigued the USAF so much in 1949 - is a clear indication that something significant had piqued his interest.

Moving on from the fragmentary data on Noah's Ark that has surfaced out of the vaults of the British Government, let's now see what secrets of the Ark variety may be hidden deep within the bowels of the Smithsonian. For those answers, we need to turn our attentions towards a man named David Duckworth. It was only two years before the dawning of the 1970s when Duckworth, who was employed at the Smithsonian at the time, witnessed a number of crates brought into the Smithsonian under somewhat covert and stealthy circumstances.

Quite understandably, pretty much everyone wanted to know what they contained. According to Duckworth, he was quietly told by one of the staff that they contained nothing less than fragments of what was believed to be the legendary ark of Noah.

And, perhaps of relevance to the British Government's data on attempts by the Nazis to locate the ark via balloon, Duckworth recalled that the stash of material brought to the Smithsonian also included photographs taken by balloon. Whether or not these were new photos, or ones found in the vaults of the Nazis when the war came to a close, is a matter that remains unresolved.

Evidently, however, all this whispered talk and gossip about what was hidden in the crates reached the eyes and ears of senior personnel at the Smithsonian, and everyone was ordered to cease all discussion of the matter – something that coincided with the material evidence being secretly shipped out to destinations unknown. Area 51, perhaps? Maybe Hangar 18?

Although all those who had been exposed to this story were ordered not to discuss what they had seen or heard with anyone, David Duckworth did exactly the opposite: portions of his story surfaced in 1982, in a book titled *Has Anyone Really Seen Noah's Ark?* The book – penned by Violet Cummings – outlined Duckworth's experiences at the Smithsonian, something which led to a curious, and somewhat ominous, development.

Although 1982 was practically a decade and a half after Duckworth's memorable and very unusual experience at the Smithsonian, it seems someone still had the affair set firmly in their sights. When Cummings' book hit the bookstores, Duckworth got a visit from the FBI. Suggesting in tones that weren't exactly threatening, but that were certainly to the point and very clear, the visiting agents told Duckworth it would be a very good idea for him to not say anymore about the Ark, the Smithsonian, and anything he saw and heard on such matters all those years earlier.

Now, with the background and witness testimony to the secret saga of government interest in Noah's Ark detailed and described, let's take a look at what has surfaced on this enigmatic issue via the terms of the Freedom of Information Act.

Secret Files and the Ark of Noah

It's intriguing to note that while we have countless witness reports from the 1950s and 1960s that clearly demonstrate U.S. officialdom's interest in Noah's Ark throughout that very period, the fairly limited number of files that have surfaced via the Freedom of Information Act on this matter only date from the early 1970s onwards.

This surely begs two important questions: (a) what has happened to that earlier documentation? And: (b) why has none of it, at all, reached the eyes and ears of the public and the media? Unfortunately, there appears to be no clear cut answer to those questions – at least, not right now – but that does not mean that the post-1960s data is without any merit. It most certainly is.

The vast bulk of the data that has been successfully obtained on Noah's Ark via FOIA has come from the Central Intelligence Agency. The earliest declassified memo dates from May 1973 and reveals that on the 13th of that month William Colby, who was then the CIA Director, approached the CIA's Directorate of Science and Technology – as well as a man named Sayre Stevens, who was a former deputy director of intelligence – and advised them that a Lt. Col. Walter Brown of the U.S. Air Force Academy was asking questions about Noah's Ark and what the U.S. Government might know about it. Notably, Brown had apparently heard rumors that the Ark had been clandestinely photographed by U.S. intelligence sources at some point in the past.

LEGACY OF THE SKY PEOPLE

We still don't know how Brown acquired such data – that, as we have seen already, was right on target – but he got a response from the CIA that, yes, the CIA did secure aerial photography of Mt. Ararat, in September 1957, but none of the pictures showed anything unusual that even remotely resembled anything like a huge, ancient ark. Nevertheless, when attempts were made to have these allegedly innocuous photographs declassified, the CIA – perhaps inevitably and unsurprisingly – flatly refused.

As for the next development in the story – or, perhaps more correctly, the next development that we have been able to uncover information on – that all began one week into August 1974. On the 6th of the month, Congressman Bob Wilson contacted the CIA and asked if one Dr. John Morris, the son of Dr. Henry Morris – at the time, the head of the Institution of Creation Research of San Diego, California - could be given clearance to view and study the CIA's aerial pictures of Mt. Ararat, with a view to determining if they displayed any evidence – large, small, or somewhere in between – of Noah's Ark on the mountain.

The CIA's press-liaison, a man named Angus Theurmer and someone who did not want to rock the boat with a U.S. Congressman, admitted that, yes, the CIA did possess such photos. But, no, they could not be shared with anyone outside of Langley. That was not quite the end of the matter, however.

Five months later, Dr. John Morris contacted Congressman Wilson and advised him that additional informants had told him that aerial pictures of what was believed to be Noah's Ark had been taken only months earlier! Exactly who told Morris this amazing story remains tantalizingly unknown; however, it most certainly caught the attention of the CIA, as it strongly – and almost certainly correctly – demonstrated that someone on the inside was leaking secret Ark-themed information to the outside. Once again, however, there was an absolute refusal on the part of the CIA to reveal, or share, any data or imagery with Morris or Wilson at all.

Spying on Ark Authors

To demonstrate the sheer, and astonishing, extent to which the CIA kept a careful and secret watch on pretty much each and every development in the matter of the enigmatic thing, or things, atop Mt. Ararat, we have to turn our attentions to something else. That "something else" collectively amounted to the published books on the subject, which Agency personnel spent a great deal of time analyzing behind the closed doors of their Langley headquarters.

As a prime example of this: when any author has a book published, this is generally followed by a period in which the author publicizes his or her book on TV, radio, at lectures, etc. And that was certainly the case with Fernand Navarra –

whose Ark-related work has been noted earlier. From the last week of March to the first week of April 1975, Navarra was busy publicizing his then-recently published book, titled *Noah's Ark: I Touched It* at a stall that had been created for that specific task at the Iverson Mall in Washington, D.C.

Declassified CIA memoranda shows that agency personnel took far more than a passing interest in Navarra's book. In fact, and somewhat amazingly, plainclothes operatives from the CIA's National Photographic Interpretation Center (NPIC) stealthily checked out Navarra's book display, and even engaged him in conversation about his findings on the matter. Clearly, this is highly indicative of deep CIA interest in Noah's Ark. After all, one does not send out personnel to secretly check out a new book on Noah's Ark if one has no interest in the matter!

And Fernand Navarra was not the only author with a fascination for Noah's Ark that the CIA kept its beady eyes on. The same situation applied to Thomas Nelson, also in 1975, when his book *The Ark of Ararat* appeared. Of major concern to the CIA, Nelson had heard and published data in his book on the thorny matter of the CIA's aerial photographs of Noah's Ark.

Quite obviously, data was leaking like a sieve out of the Agency on this matter. And only a couple of months after getting all bent out of shape by Nelson's revelations, the CIA opened a file on a group – from Frankston, Texas – called the Holy Ground Mission that claimed to have photographic evidence of Noah's Ark in their possession. Clearly, then, something was afoot on the mountain that had got the CIA interested – and maybe worried, too.

An Astronaut Asks Questions

There is a glaring absence of available CIA files from 1976 to 1981, but come 1982, we see some notable developments. In February of that year, none other than the man that piloted NASA's Apollo 15 Lunar Module - astronaut James B. Irwin – made a telephone call to a man named Dino Brugioni on the matter of the mystery of Mt. Ararat.

It turns out that Brugioni worked for the CIA's National Photographic Interpretation Center (NPIC), and Irwin – who had a deep, personal interest in Noah's Ark and took part in a number of quests to find it on Mt. Ararat - had heard the stories suggesting the Agency knew quite a bit about the Ark and wanted answers. That the call to Brugioni came to his home, rather than his office, put him on the spot for a moment or several. Nevertheless, he denied to Irwin that the CIA had ever found the remains of anything on the mountain. We will return to Brugioni shortly, as the story takes a bit of an intriguing twist years later.

LEGACY OF THE SKY PEOPLE

A Decade Onwards...

Rather oddly, and maybe even conspiratorially, no further 1980s-era documentation on Noah's Ark has surfaced from the CIA. The next entry in the declassified stash of documents originates in 1992. It was in that year that a man named Charles P. Aaron – who had a strong interest in the controversy surrounding Noah's Ark, was friendly with James B. Irwin and had his support, and worked for a group called the Tsirah Corporation – contacted the CIA and inquired if they would be interested in helping him to find the Ark, once and for all, and clear up the mystery of the mountain.

After a bit of internal debate on the matter of Aaron's letter of inquiry, the CIA basically replied "No" to his request for assistance, which is hardly surprising. But it was not so much Aaron's approach to the CIA that bothered its staff. Rather, it was Aaron's revelation to the CIA that he had been told – by unidentified sources - of new technology developed by the U.S. Government that allowed powerful and sophisticated cameras to actually penetrate through sheets of ice – which would, of course, have been ideal when it came to trying to determine the real nature of the strange object semi-buried in the ice and snow of Mt. Ararat.

That the CIA spent a good deal of time trying to decide how to tactfully respond to Aaron's words on this specific matter suggests that he may actually have been given good, solid data on a very real, clandestine program involving ice-penetrating photographic technology.

Historic Photos Finally Surface

March 1995 was a historic period in the quest to understand what the CIA in general, and the U.S. Government in particular, knew about Noah's Ark. It was in that month that a Professor Porcher Taylor III of the University of Richmond successfully obtained from the Defense Intelligence Agency at least some of the old photographs taken by the USAF back in 1949. This was a major development. However, the DIA did all that it could to play the matter down. In their own words:

"The anomaly is located along an unstable precipice near the edge of the permanent glacial ice cap atop Mt. Ararat. The accumulated ice and snow along the precipice obviously fall down the side of the mountain at frequent intervals, often leaving long linear facades. It appears that the anomaly is one of these linear facades."

The DIA's distinctly skeptical approach did not prevent others from commenting, however. And those additional comments suggested the DIA was very wrong in its conclusions. That the object appeared linear, and seemed to have slid down the mountain, led many to question the observations of the DIA.

LEGACY OF THE SKY PEOPLE

More importantly, when the photos reached the eyes and ears of the mainstream media, it opened the floodgates to even more revelations. Take, for example, Dino Brugioni, who, in 1982, had said on the telephone to Apollo astronaut James Irwin that at no time did the CIA ever find Noah's Ark.

Well, when the interest in the Ark saga took on new proportions as a result of the DIA disclosures, Brugioni gave a further statement. He confirmed that, during the Yom Kippur War that began in October 1973, the CIA used a spy-satellite to photograph Mt. Ararat. And while Brugioni still stood by his statement that they never found Noah's Ark, the pictures did show, well...something.

An Ark of the Aliens

The biggest question that needs to be asked with regard to this entire controversy of what the U.S. Government does or does not know about Noah's Ark is this: why on earth (or, perhaps, off it!) is officialdom even interested in the matter anyway? Wouldn't a quest to resolve the truth behind the legend be something more in line with the research of students of the *Bible*? Yes, it would. After all, why would the remains of a huge old boat occupy some of the finest minds in the Pentagon and the CIA?

Well, the answer is simple: it wouldn't. That is, however, unless the Ark of Noah is actually not an ancient ship that sailed the high seas, but something very different entirely – like an alien spacecraft. With that admittedly, and undeniably, controversial thought in mind, it's time to focus our attentions on a curious character that, decades ago, attracted the attention of the FBI for discussing such possibilities and theories.

Noah's Ark: A Contactee Speaks

Having grown up in the heart of Jefferson County, Ohio, it wasn't too long before a man named George Wellington Van Tassel got antsy for somewhere new and moved onto pastures very different: specifically the scalding-hot California desert. And, it was here – specifically in an area known as Yucca Valley – that, in the early 1950s, Van Tassel claimed his face to face encounters with very humanlike extraterrestrials kicked off in earnest.

The bizarre bones of Van Tassel's first claimed experience with aliens from a world far away surfaced in the same month as the encounter itself: August 1953. But, so dramatic and eye-catching were they, that none other than the much-feared FBI Director, J. Edgar Hoover, got in on the alien action. Indeed, FBI agents kept a close and secret watch on Van Tassel for an astonishing two decades, and all because of his claimed encounters with aliens, which included receiving revelations of the Noah's Ark variety.

LEGACY OF THE SKY PEOPLE

The FBI Pays a Visit or Several

For a year or so after Van Tassel's initial encounter, the FBI's interest was somewhat irregular. But, by late 1954, the surveillance had increased dramatically. Indeed, Bureau agents – on more than several occasions – actually, and quite openly, visited the Van Tassel home and requested that Van Tassel tell them all about his experiences – which he was more than happy to do.

Giant Rock, Landers, California
The fabled Giant Rock had attracted the first native nomads hundreds of years before settlements rose from the dusty ground. The granite stone and surrounding ground had been held as holy ground by the Native Americans. It is reported that the Hopi knew of this rock and joined other tribes across the desert to convene and celebrate the coming seasons. Shaman drew spiritual strength for the tribes through this rock. It is also said that the magic in the rock represents the heart of Mother Earth. It is also thought to be the world's largest freestanding boulder — at about seven stories high and covers 5,800 square feet of ground. From the collection of Nick Redfern.

Unlike many, who might find a visit from the FBI massively intimidating, Van Tassel practically basked in the attention. By now, the man of the hour was living out at Giant Rock, Landers – so named after a huge rock that, to this day, sits out in the desert like some huge meteorite from afar.

FBI agents scrupulously recorded Van Tassel's every word as he told them how, on the night in question, when he had his first encounter, he received a visitation from a very humanlike, male alien who was dressed in an outfit very similar to that of a military pilot. But this man wasn't flying anything with wings.

Nope: he was none other than the captain of a literal flying saucer that, Van

LEGACY OF THE SKY PEOPLE

Tassel genially told the bemused FBI agents, offered him a tour of the UFO. He eagerly accepted the challenge. After all, how often is it you get the opportunity to take a stroll around a spaceship built on, and flown from, another world? Not often at all, that's when!

Van Tassel further added that the whole experience was somewhat surreal, as the aliens never spoke a word to him, but conversed by what, today, we would likely call telepathy. And they were aliens with a mission: to try and convert the Human Race into peace-loving people that would lay down their atomic weapons and live alongside each other in never-ending bliss and happiness. Some chance of that happening.

But, this was no mere suggestion. The commander of the craft reportedly told Van Tassel that if we, as a species, did not follow the wise words of the aliens, either we would end up wiping ourselves out...or...the aliens would intervene and obliterate us themselves. Admittedly worried to the core by the prospect of the Human Race being exterminated, or the planet destroyed, Van Tassel duly began to spread the cosmic word just about anywhere and everywhere possible.

Preaching for the Aliens

As the early 1950s became the mid 1950s, Van Tassel elected to put on a regular once-a-year conference at Giant Rock, to which the flying saucer devotees flocked in – quite literally – their thousands. And: the FBI, albeit in plainclothes rather than typical Men in Black-type outfits, were invariably there, too. Guess what: it was Van Tassel's comments on the *Bible* and Noah's Ark that attracted the most interest on the part of the FBI, and which also led them to share their files on the man with several other U.S. Intelligence-based agencies.

As a prime example of this, midway through April 1960, Van Tassel was invited – by the Denver Unidentified Flying Objects Investigative Society - to give a lecture to an impressively large audience in Denver, Colorado. The location was the Phipps Auditorium, and as well as the saucer-seekers, the FBI was there, too, faithfully and secretly recording Van Tassel's every word.

A section of the report at issue states of Van Tassel's presentation:

"The program consisted of a 45 minute movie which included several shots of things purported to be flying saucers, and then a number of interviews with people from all walks of life regarding sightings they had made of such unidentified flying objects. After the movie George W. Van Tassel gave a lecture which was more of a religious-economics lecture than one of unidentified flying objects."

The FBI agents in attendance continued:

"The major part of [Van Tassel's] lecture was devoted to explaining the oc-

LEGACY OF THE SKY PEOPLE

currences in the Bible as they related to the space people. He said that this is due to the fact that man, space people, was made by God [sic] and that in the beginning of the world the space people came to the earth and left animals here. These were the prehistoric animals which existed at a body temperature of 105 degrees; however a polar tilt occurred whereby the poles shifted and the tropical climates became covered with ice and vice-versa."

Van Tassel, FBI agents advised J. Edgar Hoover, reported that as a means to ensure that life – animal and human – survived the devastating Ice Age, massively advanced alien entities came up with the idea of creating huge arks, on which all manner of terrestrial life-forms could be saved and preserved for the day when the re-seeding of the planet could once again begin.

Van Tassel also claimed that this action occurred on several occasions, the most recent being after a huge, worldwide flood. Thus, in Vas Tassel's world, it was the aliens' actions during these various planetary cataclysms that led to the legend of Noah's Ark – when, in reality, the truth revolved around dozens and dozens of space-arks saving the day, and the Human Race.

The FBI also noted: "Van Tassel said that this race [of extraterrestrials] then intermarried with 'intelligent, upright walking animals,' [us, in other words]. Then when the space people came back in the supply ships they saw what had happened and did not land; but ever since due to the origin of ADAM, they have watched over the people on Earth."

And the FBI continued to watch over Van Tassel, often coming back to his theories and ideas pertaining to the Ark controversy.

Noah's Ark and a Secret Project

The most remarkable aspect of the alien angle as it relates to Noah's Ark came from Don Riggs, whose father worked in the field of photographic analysis for the National Reconnaissance Office in the late 1970s.

According to Riggs, just before his death in 1997, his father revealed to him a startling story concerning records and imagery on Noah's Ark that had been referred to the NRO for analysis by a small group of people stationed at Wright-Patterson Air Force Base, Dayton, Ohio, and who were attached to an operation called Project Moon Dust, about which we will now learn a great deal.

If some UFOs are indeed alien spacecraft and a small percentage of those same craft have crashed to Earth, then among the most important questions currently facing the UFO research community are surely:

LEGACY OF THE SKY PEOPLE

★ Who within the official world is responsible for coordinating the retrieval of such craft?

★ How are those tasked with the recoveries seemingly able to secure UFO crash-sites with such apparent speed and ease?

★ Where, exactly, are the recovered extraterrestrial materials and debris taken to?

★ Can we identify the key and integral players that have been implicated in this particular controversy?

To try and answer at least some of those particularly important questions, we have to turn our attentions to an official United States military-intelligence project named Moon Dust that – from the 1950s onwards – was housed at Fort Belvoir, Virginia, and whose mandate, according to officially-declassified documentation, was to recover and exploit foreign and exotic technologies.

While it is apparent that the bulk of the work of Project Moon Dust was directed towards the careful capture and analysis of crashed Soviet space satellites and rocket debris, there are strong indications that Moon Dust's work may have extended into far stranger – and possibly even extraterrestrial – realms, too, some of which had a major bearing upon the story of Noah's Ark.

A November 1961 Air Force Intelligence document pertaining to the activities of – and guidelines for – Moon Dust personnel, specifically at their base of operations within the 1127th Air Activities Group at Fort Belvoir (known in other incarnations as the 4602nd Air Intelligence Service Squadron; and the 1006th Air Intelligence Service Squadron), carefully outlined the nature and the scope of Moon Dust.

Titled *AFCIN Intelligence Team Personnel*, the document revealed that with respect to the 1127th Air Activities Group: "In addition to their staff duty assignments, intelligence team personnel have peacetime duty functions in support of such Air Force projects as Moon Dust, Blue Fly, and UFO, and other AFCIN directed quick reaction projects which require intelligence team operational capabilities."

The author of the document added:

"Unidentified Flying Objects (UFO): Headquarters USAF has established a program for investigation of reliably reported unidentified flying objects within the United States. Blue Fly: Operation Blue Fly has been established to facilitate expeditious delivery to Foreign Technology Division of Moon Dust or other items of great technical interest. Moon Dust: As a specialized aspect of its overall material exploitation program Headquarters USAF has established Project Moon Dust

LEGACY OF THE SKY PEOPLE

to locate, recover, and deliver descended foreign space vehicles" (Ibid.).

Secret Revelations

But what of the Noah's Ark connection to Project Moon Dust? According to Don Riggs, just before his death in 1997, his father had revealed to him a startling story concerning records on Noah's Ark that had been referred to the NRO for analysis by a "small group of people" stationed at Wright-Patterson Air Force Base, Dayton, Ohio.

Riggs adds that his father told him that the file referred to Project Moon Dust – an organization that Riggs' father was not previously aware of – and how Moon Dust personnel had begun to take an interest in the Noah's Ark controversy during the late 1960s. Riggs states that his father had discussed with him his knowledge of seven photographs that appeared to show the strange craft at very close quarters.

He further explains that two of the photographs displayed what was, beyond any shadow of a doubt, a "very large, metallic-looking, rectangular object sticking partly out of the ice. No way was this wood, he said, like an ark would be made of," says Riggs.

Riggs goes on to say that the photographs had been immediately classified after they had been taken "at some point around '59 by a U-2 plane [sic]," and had "been circulated" to various elements of American Intelligence in an effort to try and determine what it was that was partially buried under the thick ice and snow of Mt. Ararat.

"My dad said that the pictures on their own didn't really answer much at all, because of the mountain being so inaccessible – apart from by spy-cameras. No one was able then to get to the exact right place on-foot to check it out." says Riggs.

Significantly, however, he maintains that his father revealed that at some point in the summer of 1975 a covert mission was initiated that saw a "team" of what Riggs describes as "Delta-Force-type guys, I suppose, or something like that," covertly "dropped" in the area late one night and "found their way to the site." Riggs says that his father was given access to these latter photographs for analysis some time after the initial, earlier batch was supplied to him.

Riggs elaborates and says: "This is what my dad told me; so I can only go on that." With that, Riggs says that a lengthy report was filed by the team-leader that was duly sent to a group "that my dad says was called the Moon Dust."

Riggs claims that his father did not know too much of the true nature of the object that has come to be referred to by U.S. Intelligence as the Ararat Anomaly.

However, he says that his father made it clear to him that the Anomaly was extensively damaged, appeared to be very old, was deeply embedded in the ice, "was vacant inside as if it had been trashed, and was just a shell of metal," and was certainly not "just a big, old, wooden boat."

Reportedly, Riggs divulges, the documentation "had its home at Wright-Patterson and a courier was told to take it to my dad, who was asked to look at the photographs to see if anything could be seen that would give clues to this thing."

"Everything," he adds with much significance, "had a Moon Dust stamp – on each page."

Riggs concludes:

"There was no history of the Ark or whatever it was, and nothing that was background information for my dad to work with - apart from the description of the object and the photos, and some background on the team that had landed and took the pictures. He was never told what it was: only to make an evaluation of the photographs. But the thing that always stands out for me is that this was not just like a big old boat or ark. My dad said it looked like a huge metal device that had crashed into the ice, probably thousands of years ago."

As the above demonstrates, staff from both Wright-Patterson and Moon Dust appears to have played a central role in the saga of Noah's Ark. Moreover, the fact that the aforementioned Robert Livingston was linked with Fort Belvoir's Topographic Engineering Center is highly significant. At one point in its history, Project Moon Dust personnel specifically had their base of operations within the 1127th Air Activities Group at the same base, Fort Belvoir.

Summing Up

So, having now digested numerous examples of (a) testimony from former and retired military personnel; (b) government files and photographs from the Federal Bureau of Investigation, Central Intelligence Agency, Defense Intelligence Agency, and the U.S. Air Force that have all been declassified via the terms of the Freedom of Information Act, and (c) the words of Don Riggs, what can we say about this most curious puzzle?

Well, first and foremost, as I have noted, government agencies – whether intelligence-based or military-based – have no logical reason for spending decades investigating biblical mysteries just for the sheer hell of it. Such a situation would be manifestly absurd and a complete waste of money. Government agents are neither archaeologists nor historians. So, there has to be a different reason for the interest.

As for what that reason may be, well, the fact that Project Moon Dust got involved in the investigation, that the testimony of Don Riggs offers a possibility that Noah's Ark was actually some type of ancient alien vessel, and that the CIA was even classifying its photographs of the mountain is highly suggestive of the probability that there is far more to Noah's Ark than merely an old boat.

Perhaps, for all the criticism that many of his claims provoked back in the 1950s – and still provoke today – George Van Tassel's theories on Noah's Ark being some huge space-ark, piloted by extraterrestrials, and involved in a mercy mission to preserve numerous examples of terrestrial life as a flood-driven cataclysm loomed, may not be too wide of the mark.

Something strange, huge and deeply enigmatic lies buried on the harsh, cold, icy, frozen slopes of Mt. Ararat, Turkey. The U.S. Government – even if it doesn't have all the answers – knows it. And, now, so do you!

Sources:

Berlitz, Charles. *The Lost Ship of Noah*. New York: Fawcett Crest, 1987.

Campbell, Roland. *Noah's Ark - Select Rumours from the Front*. Secret Intelligence Service, November 28, 1948.

Central Intelligence Agency."Noah's Ark 1974-1982."

http://www.foia.cia.gov/docs/DOC_0000728028/DOC_0000728028.pdf

Defense Intelligence Agency. "Analysis of 'Anomaly' on 1949 Mr. Ararat Imagery and response to FOIA taker 95-007122, July 21, 1995."

Defense Intelligence Agency."Imagery of Mt. Ararat, Turkey (1949)."

http://www.dia.mil/public-affairs/foia/pdf/mt_ararat.pdf, 2011.

Federal Bureau of Investigation files declassified under the terms of the Freedom of Information Act. *George W. Van Tassel, Unidentified Flying Objects*, April 26, 1960.

"Flood Legends from Around the World,"

http://www.nwcreation.net/noahlegends.html, 2011.

Gerig, Bruce L. "Searching for Noah's Ark."

http://epistle.us/articles/noah.html, 2003.

Gertz, Bill. "CIA spy photos sharpen focus on Ararat Anomaly." *Washington Times*, November 18, 1997.

Goldwater, Senator Barry. Letter to CIA Director Stansfield Turner, September 1, 1978.

Kneisler, Matthew. "Noah's Ark: United States Government." *http://www.arksearch.com/nausgov.htm*, 2010.

Lamb, Andrew. "The Ararat Anomaly." *http://creation.com/the-ararat-anomaly*, March 2001.

Lorey, Frank, M.A. "The Flood of Noah and the Flood of Gilgamesh." *http://www.icr.org/article/noah-flood-gilgamesh/*, 2011.

Maier, Timothy W. "Anomaly or Noah's Ark?" *http://findarticles.com/p/articles/mi_m1571/is_43_16/ai_72274814/pg_2/*, November 20, 2000.

Navarra, Fernand. *Noah's Ark: I Touched It*. Plainfield, NJ: Logos International, 1974.

Redfern, Nick, and Andy Roberts. *Strange Secrets*. New York: Paraview-Pocket Books, 2003.

Redfern, Nick. "Is This Really Noah's Icy Tomb?" *Western Daily Press*, July 3, 2001.

Redfern, Nick. "Project Moon Dust: How the Government Recovers Crashed Flying Saucers," the *Fifth Annual UFO Crash Retrieval Conference Proceedings*. Broomfield, CO: Wood & Wood Enterprises, 2007.

Ryan, William, and Walter Pitman. *Noah's Flood: The New Scientific Discoveries About The Event That Changed History*. New York: Simon & Schuster, 1997.

Theoferrum. "Adam's Body in Noah's Ark." *http://theoferrum.hubpages.com/hub/Adams-Body-in-Noahs-Ark*, 2011.

LEGACY OF THE SKY PEOPLE

25

LEGACY OF THE SKY PEOPLE

ANGELS OR ALIENS—
ANCIENT CONTACTS WITH THE SKY PEOPLE

Tim Swartz

The idea that there could be life on other planets is nothing new. Popular science fiction from the 1920s and 30s were full of swashbuckling tales of intelligent alien life forms whizzing around the galaxies and interacting with humans, usually as a hostile invading force. However, no one really took these stories seriously, that is until people started actually seeing strange objects buzzing around in the sky. Then, the thought that there really could be extraterrestrial beings visiting us seemed not so far-fetched after all.

However, the belief in strange beings coming down from the stars to intermingle with humanity can be traced back to the earliest days of mankind. The current notion of UFOs and their extraterrestrial pilots is simply a modern version of the myths and legends contained within almost every ancient culture and civilization.

The Ancient Astronaut hypothesis has gained in popularity over recent years. Eric von Daniken popularized the concept of space visitors coming to Earth in antiquity in the late 1960s with the publication of his bestseller "Chariots of the Gods?" But in fact, there were a few authors who were knocking around the idea several years before. They were both British authors, W. R. Drake and Brinsley Le Poer Trench. Trench's "Sky People" received a fairly warm reception when it first came out in the U.K. circa 1960. It was published in various languages, but has been to some extent forgotten in recent times, thus the need for the volume you are now digging into either in the conventional printed form or a techno e-book edition. Could be the ancient astronauts had their own laptops "way back when" and we are just reinventing the wheel (or the hard drive).

PAINTINGS ON ROCKY WALLS

Carved on cave walls and rocky cliffs is the silent testimony of ancient man's

LEGACY OF THE SKY PEOPLE

views of the world around him. These petroglyphs often display crude representations of the daily activities of the people and animals that inhabited this archaic time. Other drawings are not so easily interpreted. Cave paintings from Tanzania, estimated to be up to 29,000 years old, depict several disc shaped objects that appear to be hovering over the landscape. Another painting shows four humanoid entities surrounding a woman while another entity looks down from the sky inside some sort of box.

Going back as far as 17000 -15000 BCE are images from inside the cave of Pech Merle near Le Cabrerets, France, of early humans gazing upon UFOs - or are the UFOs gazing down upon them?

Inside the French cave of Pech Merle near Le Cabrerets are paintings from around 17000 – 15000 BCE that show landscapes full of wildlife with a number of saucer shaped objects. One painting actually shows the figure of a man looking up at one of the overhead saucers.

In northern Australia there are a number of cave paintings, possibly more than 5,000 years old, that show strange beings with large heads and eyes, wearing spacesuit-like garments. The Aborigines call these creatures Wandjina, and according to legend, Wandjina came down from the stars in the Milky Way during the Dreamtime and created the Earth and all its inhabitants.

Archeologists dismiss these paintings as abstract depictions of birds, clouds or stars. The strange beings are interpreted as detailing ritualistic activities where shamans would dress up as spirits to insure a good hunt or weather. It is impossible to know what these drawings were actually meant to represent. But, as man learned to write down his thoughts, it became clear that there existed a rich tradition of myths and legends that told of gods and star people who came

Not hard to see why ancient astronaut theorists think these Aborigine figures known as the Wandjiina were visitors from the stars.

LEGACY OF THE SKY PEOPLE

down to Earth to bring civilization to an infant humanity.

GODS FROM OTHER WORLDS

Even the briefest of examinations of ancient civilizations will find stories of strange beings that came down from the heavens to interact with mankind. These visitors were considered to be the bearers of mankind's wisdom, religion, knowledge and technology. Evidence for this theory comes from a variety of sources, including ancient scriptures, unexplained archaeological artifacts and a seemingly advanced knowledge of engineering by some ancient cultures.

The Philistine deity, Dagon, who was one of the four sons of Anu, the lord of heaven, was said to have a human face and hands, but a portion of his body resembled a fish. Dagon flew down from the sky in a ball of fire and taught mankind the ways of the plow and agriculture.

Clay tablets inscribed around 2600 BCE by the ancient Sumerians detail a 400,000 year history that included visits by creatures called Annunaki who flew in vehicles called Shems, or Mu. These celestial craft were described as being tall rocket-like "rocks" which emitted fire. The visitors stayed in human-built temples and were waited on hand and foot. The detailed descriptions of everything from who shakes hands with the gods first, to what food is served, and how the gods are carried back to their Shems imply that the Sumerians were not speaking of spiritual visitors, but actual physical beings from the sky.

The Sumerians never called the Anunnaki, gods. They were called dingir, meaning "righteous ones of the bright pointed objects." The Annunaki are sometimes depicted as humanoid. At other times they are bird-headed with wings. Often they are Reptilian in appearance, especially when depicted as warriors.

In addition, a history of Mesopotamia written in the third century BCE by Berossus, a Babylonian priest, states that ancient man lived in a lawless manner like the beasts of the field. In those days there appeared a creature whose name was Oannes, or Ea, meaning the "fish of heaven." Oannes body was like a fish, and "under the fish's head he had another head, and connected to the fish's tail, he had feet similar to those of a man."

Oannes taught mankind writing and math, and

The Sumerians depicted the Anunnaki or Dingir gods as being bird-headed with wings..

28

he is credited by the Sumerians for giving civilization to man. Oannes was said to stay in the sea every evening, but when he departed for the last time, he flew up into the sky and returned to the heavens.

What are modern looking-aircraft doing being depicted on the walls of the Egyptian pyramids going back to the days of the great Pharaohs?

Ancient Egyptian legends tell of "Tep Zepi," or the First Time. This is described as an age when "sky gods" came down to Earth and raised the land from mud and water. They supposedly traveled through the air in flying "boats" and brought laws and wisdom to man through a royal line of pharaohs.

A passage from *The Egyptian Book of the Dead* tells of contacts with glowing beings that fly the heavens in their disks: "Behold, oh ye shining ones, ye men and gods....I speak with the followers of the gods. I speak with the disk. I speak with the shining ones."

In Tibet there is a book called the Kantyua, which means "the translated word of Buddha." It tells of flying "pearls in the sky" and of transparent spheres carrying gods to visit man. Kantyua speaks of the belief of being reborn time and time again and not just to Earth, but to other planets in the universe. The Royal Pedigrees of Tibetan Kings dates back to the seventh century and states that the first seven Tibetan kings came from the stars and that they eventually returned to the stars.

Five thousand years ago, when the Shamanic Turks started their journey from Central Asia towards today's Turkey, they brought with them a belief that intelligent beings can be found on other worlds. The original Turks were called "GökTürk." Gök means sky, Türk means human or people – "Sky People." Their earliest creation stories started with the existence of flying gods called Kara-han, who created the world and allowed their brethren from the stars to populate it.

Coptic Gnostic texts that were written around the first and second centuries C.E. contain passages that describe ancient encounters with alien-like beings called the Archons. A passage from The First Apocalypse of James (NHC V, 3) states: "A multitude of Archons may turn on you, thinking they can capture you. And in particular, three of them will seize you, those who pose as toll collectors.

LEGACY OF THE SKY PEOPLE

Not only do they demand toll, but they take away souls by theft. They are not entirely alien, for they are from the Fallen Sophia, the female divinity who produced them when she brought the human race down from the Source, the realm of the Pre-Existent One. So they are not entirely alien, but they are our kin."

It is interesting to note that the actions of the Gnostic Archons bear a close resemblance to modern reports of UFO abductions, and the mysterious Men-In-Black, who supposedly travel in threes and pose as authority figures.

Scott Corrales, in his article *Unvoiced Testimony - Visitors in the Dawn of Times*, relates the legends of Brazilian natives and their experiences of gods or travelers from the sky. These visitors descended to earth when humans were little more than animals to instruct them in agriculture, astronomy, medicine, and other disciplines. One being in particular, Bep-Kororoti, a space warrior worshipped by the tribes of the upper reaches of the Xing River, possessed a flying vehicle capable of destroying anything in its path. Bep-Kororoti terrified the natives until he stepped out of his "raiment" and revealed himself to be fair-skinned, handsome, and kind. He amused the natives with his "magic" until he grew restless for his land in the sky and returned there.

Bep-Kororoti, a space warrior worshipped by the tribes of the upper reaches of the Xing River, in Brazil.

In North America there is a Native-American chronicle of contacts with unearthly beings that reaches back into a mysterious past. Along the Mississippi river in Illinois are the remnants of the mound-building Cahokian civilization. At its apex, around 1050 CE, the city of Cahokia had more than 15,000 residents.

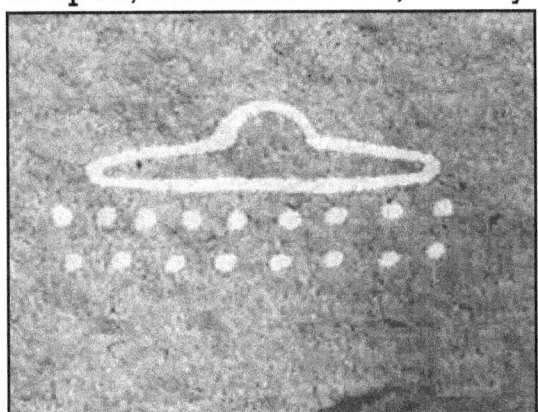

Those darn UFOs are in the neighborhood again - in the neighborhood of antiquity. For thousands of years they have been seen and images left behind.

Legend has it that around 720 C.E. the struggling Cahokian tribes, who were made up of many other tribes, including the Illiniwek Indians, were in danger of being wiped out due to famine and disease. On the brink of collapse, they were visited by numerous robed beings from the sky. These beings offered them the knowledge and technology to save their civilization from extinction, as well as allow them to prosper and become one of the most powerful cultures on the continent.

It is impossible to detail the numerous

historical accounts of the ancient sky-beings in one volume. However, there are some excellent books for those wishing to undertake further study, this as well as the History Channel's currently popular "Ancient Aliens" series.

The late Zecharia Sitchin, who was an expert in Sumerian cuneiform, wrote six scholarly books of the "Earth Chronicles" series detailing 20 years of study of ancient contacts with other worldly beings. Meanwhile, Brinsley Le Poer Trench's *The Sky People*, and Erich von Däniken's *Chariots of the Gods?* are just a couple of examples of the many books that have been written on the subject.

Despite many diverse civilizations sharing a common understanding of non-humans from the sky bringing knowledge and enlightenment to mankind, historians tend to assume that these ancient legends are simply myths. However, considering modern stories of UFOs and the alleged contacts with the non-human pilots, there are startling similarities between UFO encounters over the last 60 years and ancient accounts that are thousands of years old. The only difference is that early man had no real concept of the realities of the universe and life on other planets. To them, strange beings coming down from the sky in glowing chariots had to be gods, angels or demons. Thus, ancient encounters were put within a religious or spiritual framework.

Today, in the view of a society brought up on images of moonwalks and robotic rovers on Mars, UFOs and their bizarre inhabitants are seen as extraterrestrial visitors. A thousand years from now, who knows what changes in science and culture will do to the perception and understanding of this strange phenomenon?

Whether we think of this phenomenon as originating from aliens or gods, better understanding it is also the key to better understanding our past, the true origins of man and the ultimate mysteries of our existence.

LEGACY OF THE SKY PEOPLE

"WE HAVE MET THE MARTIANS AND THEY ARE US!"

Brad And Sherry Steiger

By Sean Casteel

★ World-renowned author Brad Steiger offers his praise for Brinsley Le Poer Trench, calling him a groundbreaking researcher who is unfairly neglected today. Would we even have an ancient astronauts theory without the pioneering work of Trench, the Eighth Earl of Clancarty?

★ "We have met the Martians and they are us," says Steiger. Why? Was the great Ark of Noah really a spaceship from Mars on a mission to save a remnant of early human life?

★ Brad Steiger says there is new evidence to suggest that life on Earth was first planted in South America and spread out from there. Learn the reasoning behind this theory.

★ Are we hardwired as a species to seek a higher intelligence or even the God who created us? If not, why have we had these strange and mysterious encounters with angels, demons and extraterrestrials so consistently down through the ages? The names we give them may change, but the mysterious entities are the same!

*   *   *   *

Brad Steiger is the author of countless books on UFOs, aliens, and nearly any other paranormal phenomena you can think of. While preparing this heady volume on the ancient astronauts known as the Sky People, we spoke to Steiger on the subject of Brinsley Le Poer Trench, the 8th Earl of Clancarty, and his involvement with a topic that has come to fascinate millions over the course of just over half a century. As usual, Steiger does not disappoint as he reveals the theories and beliefs he has constructed along the way.

LEGACY OF THE SKY PEOPLE

TRENCH IS UNFAIRLY OVERLOOKED

"I read Brinsley's book when it came out in the 1960s," Steiger said. "I haven't had the privilege of hanging out with him, the way Brother Tim (Beckley) has, but I certainly am familiar with his work. It's the groundbreaker aspect, which many of us – Tim and I were kind of at the forefront of things and in our own way we each forged certain things ahead, as Brinsley Le Poer Trench did.

Brad and Sherry arriving in Machu Picchu. From the photo collection of Brad and Sherry Steiger.

"Now, when I wrote 'Atlantis Rising,'" Steiger continued, "which has become one of my most long-lived books – it went into eleven printings in just a year and a half – I quoted quite freely from Brinsley Le Poer Trench's work, with his 'hu-man' and 'chemical man' and 'sky gods' and so forth, giving him full credit, of course, for every attribution. This is a field where, when it was very new, there were only a few proponents."

Steiger recalled an Ancient Astronauts conference in the early 1980s at which the main speakers were Erich von Daniken, NASA's own Josef Blumrich, who authored a book called "The Spaceships of Ezekiel," and himself. Brinsley Le Poer Trench was not among the speakers.

"He was probably generally neglected," Steiger said, "because Erich von Daniken was the fair-haired boy at that time and was given a great deal of credit for coming up with the whole ancient astronauts concept.

"It was easier to do then. We didn't have the media that we do now. And a book such as 'The Sky Gods' was read by a few individuals, but the great masses of people then were not interested. Then something comes out and gets a lot of attention, like 'Chariots of the Gods?' As people said, von Daniken just happened to be standing in front of the cosmic slot machine when it paid off.

"There are others," Steiger continued. "Tim has published the work of others who were very prominent at that time. That's one of the great accomplishments of Tim's career, not only his own research but the fact that he is publishing so much work that no one today would have heard of. These books and authors deserve to be republished and the authors deserve to get their credit because they certainly do have their niche in the great totem pole of who's been doing this

LEGACY OF THE SKY PEOPLE

research."

THE SCHOLARLY APPROACH

Steiger feels that Trench stands out from his contemporaries because the late earl's approach was more scholarly and careful in terms of the claims he made.

"Brinsley would present things as a hypothesis," Steiger said. "He would say, 'PERHAPS you find this daring; PERHAPS you find this offensive to your beliefs. But consider that the Jehovah may have been a leader of people who came from the stars.'

"There's a difference," Steiger said, "between presenting things and allowing your readers to ponder them and then make up his or her own mind than just coming out and saying, 'These entities came from outer space and they built the pyramids.' There's a difference between presenting it as a hypothesis and presenting it as fact."

(It should be noted that spokesman Giorgio Tsoukalos defends Erich von Daniken on these same grounds, saying that von Daniken never flatly declared that the aliens built the pyramids as well as the fact that "Chariots of the Gods?" has around 200 question marks scattered throughout the book, serving to indicate that von Daniken was also presenting his evidence hypothetically.)

THE MARTIANS ARE US

Steiger was asked for his opinion about human life originating on Mars, and he had a ready answer.

"In my book 'Gods of Aquarius,' I said, 'We have met the Martians and they are us.' And that's been echoed. I don't know if I was the first to say it. That was in the mid-1970s, but it's certainly been said

On an expedition to the ancient "City of the Giants," Sacsahuaman, high in the Andes of Peru. From The Photo Collection Of Brad And Sherry Steiger.

many times since. And I suppose I was – at least subconsciously, unconsciously – harking back to what I read in Trench.

"That the great Ark, instead of Noah being an ancient Israelite, he was a great leader on Mars and the great Ark was a great spaceship coming to Earth. At the time Trench said it, people weren't prepared. But it's been interesting to see that in most polls the idea of life existing on other planets or in other solar systems is now generally accepted by young people. Whereas back in the 1950s and 1960s it was rejected by nearly everyone. More and more, the idea that life could have existed elsewhere in our solar system doesn't get a door slammed immediately. At least they're open to discussion."

One of the massive building blocks of Ollaytantambo. Many of the blocks are more than 200 tons and appear to be cut with laser precision. From the photo collection of Brad and Sherry Steiger.

Steiger pointed to the recent statements by mainstream scientists that propose that the components of DNA and the human genome may have originated on other planets. The idea was even used in the movie "Star Trek: The Search For Spock."

"It's interesting, isn't it?" Steiger commented. "How any new idea whose time has come filters into society on so many levels. Then the idea becomes a 'meme' and is like a living thing that plants itself in the psyches of those who hear it and perpetuate it."

THE SOUTH AMERICAN CONNECTION

Is there anything new in the ancient world?

"Well, there's a lot new," Steiger answered. "It seems like every day we're finding another temple; we're finding evidence of an advanced civilization. Now for many years, ever since my book 'Worlds Before Our Own,' I've been suggesting – just suggesting now, a hypothesis – that civilization may have moved from South America to the rest of the world, not vice-versa. As we study our history now, of course, we begin with the Sumerians and then we move forward eventually to the Egyptians, then it's the Greeks, the Romans.

LEGACY OF THE SKY PEOPLE

"But we're finding so many ancient civilizations now in South America. We have massive structures and no one knows exactly who built them. One theory after another crumbles as we date these structures farther and farther back. I think if the sky gods came, if the sky people came, they may have landed in and built their first civilizations in South America. Or, if you don't accept that, then simultaneously."

Steiger said he differs from the more mainstream beliefs about evolution, preferring to believe that homo sapiens evolved alongside other hominid species as opposed to a clean chronology from Neanderthal to Cro-Magnon to homo sapiens. Our current species was the Sky People's eventual goal, but that several hominid forms of life coexisted with us and then died out, he said.

Dr. Cabrera believes these petroglyphs were fashioned on hardened volcanic rock by protohumans who lived near what is now present-day Ica, Peru, over 230 million years ago during the Mesozoic Era. He further believes that those prehistoric hominins were genetically engineered by extraterrestrials who first visited Earth as long ago as 400 million years. From the photo collection of Brad and Sherry Steiger.

The petroglyph on the right depicts "the Creator God" holding up a mirror to demonstrate that the ancient astronauts used genetic engineering to create the prehistoric humanlike beings in their own image.

The one on the left shows an ancient alien looking up toward "home." The comet indicates that the extraterrestrial creators arrived before the continents separated.

(A similar theory is presented by Giorgio Tsoukalos elsewhere in this book when he cites the stone blocks of Puma Punku in Bolivia as the "smoking gun" of the ancient astronaut theory and also argues for humankind originating in South America.)

THE MAGICAL NATURE OF THINGS

Steiger said it is impossible to know the precise order of the Sky Gods, whether they were the true Creators of everything or only a group of extraterrestrial scientists who created mankind in a kind of laboratory setting.

"We've had great science fiction writers point out," he said, "that any group that is greatly advanced will be considered great magicians by the more primitive people. Great advances in science would appear magic. We're talking over something that definitely would have been considered magical and had us burned at the stake for if we were to say we could communicate by holding a box to our ears. That would be considered magical. But certainly people who had come flying from the sky would fit the various interpretations."

HARDWIRED TO SEEK GOD

"I think, the more I study," Steiger said, "that we are definitely hardwired to perceive advanced beings as godlike, and I think we are hardwired just to perceive and understand a concept of God. I think that is hardwired into our species. Now, whether that has been hardwired by our progenitors from outer space, or it is just hardwired in terms of our evolution and our DNA, for how we perceive entities greater than we, is a question we could discuss endlessly. But I think it's simply hardwired into us to perceive that we are part of a greater cosmic entity."

Sherry finds handprint imprinted in solid rock in Peru. From the photo collection of Brad and Sherry Steiger.

Steiger reiterated his support of Trench, saying, "I think it's a very viable hypothesis of Trench's, that our ancestors, our creators – that gets a little bit dicey for some people – that our creators came from another world and fashioned us to be the grand experiment that we are today."

Steiger and his wife and working partner Sherry receive dozens of letters and emails every day from people writing about their paranormal experiences. He feels most of the communicants are intelligent, well-educated individuals whose testimony of their strange encounters would hold up in a court of law.

"They believe that these experiences, these interactions – and again I marvel that this idea has become such a living, developing philosophy and even a religion to so many people. Where people would have talked about angels and demons a century ago, or still today, of course, but now we talk about aliens. We talk about reptilians. Again, I'm talking about how a template seems to have been laid down in the human psyche, to interpret whatever we're interacting with, whatever this phenomenon is, to interpret it in the same age-old vocabulary and concepts."

LEGACY OF THE SKY PEOPLE

SHERRY STEIGER WEIGHS IN

Steiger's wife, Sherry, is an ordained minister. When asked how the alien question affects her faith, she said she has no problem entertaining such possibilities because there is so much that dovetails in all religions and myths. But she still believes that there has to be a God who rules over all. We may be created by others, but there is still a supernatural Creator/Spirit that determines the outcome.

Brad Steiger said that pronouncements from the Vatican in recent years seem to indicate an openness to the question. He and Sherry receive correspondence from clergymen who are nominally receptive to the idea.

"I do get letters," Steiger said, "saying, 'Well, I can't openly agree with you, but I do agree with you.'"

There was at one time an organization called "Spiritual Frontiers Fellowship" (Steiger said he doesn't know if it still exists today) made up of clergymen of many different faiths.

"I spoke at their meetings a number of times," he said, "and I found a great openness and agreement with the concepts we're discussing. Now, whether they declared that from their pulpits when they got home, I'm not certain. But I know they did in person and in our continued correspondence they expressed these things.

"I think any of the established religions could accept the basic premise if it's not presented in an offensive way, like 'Boy, you people are stupid to believe this. We've come into a modern age.' That's going to turn everyone off. But if you ask, as Trench did, and certainly as I've tried to do, and Sherry, in our writings, if we present these things as hypotheses, which ask people simply to consider, then I think you would find a great openness among people of all faiths."

A PARTING TRIBUTE

Asked if he had any final comment to make, Steiger said, "I'd like to pay tribute to all the groundbreakers like Brinsley Le Poer Trench, who had the courage, in a very intellectual, non-offensive, hypothetical manner, to bring up ideas that caught fire in my psyche, Tim Beckley's psyche, and the psyches of now hundreds of thousands of people who are at least entertaining the concept of what has become popularly known as 'ancient astronauts theory.'

"I know that Tim, Sherry and I say that the UFO mystery, whatever it is – none of us claim to know precisely what it is – but we all accept that it is an integral part of our lives that we have yet to fully grasp."

LEGACY OF THE SKY PEOPLE

ANCIENT ALIENS AND THEIR TRUE RELATIONSHIP WITH GOD ALMIGHTY

By Sean Casteel

★ In an exclusive interview, Erich von Daniken spokesman Giorgio Tsoukalos carefully makes a distinction between the ancient aliens and the true Creator God. Do the aliens have the same imponderable questions as we do about life, death and religion? Are the aliens superior in technology only? Are we on an equal footing spiritually?

★ Do we insult the true Creator of the Universe when we call mankind the pinnacle of creation? Tsoukalos says that allowing for aliens in the mix makes reality all the more rich and wonderful, no matter one's religious beliefs.

★ Tsoukalos discusses a location in Bolivia that is home to ancient stone blocks cut so precisely that we could today duplicate the process only with huge stone-cutting machinery and diamond-tipped saws. How did the ancient Bolivians create the painstakingly measured stone blocks? It would have been impossible given what we know about the tools of ancient man, who likely had only copper hammers at the time. Did they have help from ancient astronauts?

*   *   *   *

Giorgio Tsoukalos has been a world traveler from a very early age. His parents took him on journeys throughout the planet and always made sure to visit the museums and ancient monuments, often leaving young Giorgio to explore some of the locations by himself. When he and his family returned from their visits to faraway locales, Tsoukalos' grandmother would remind him that there were ways to view the ancient sites that differed from the mainstream history taught by the tour guides and reference books.

LEGACY OF THE SKY PEOPLE

"At a very early age," Tsouklalos said, "I was introduced to the work of Erich von Daniken, David Childress and Zechariah Sitchen. It was pretty much dinner table conversation growing up, even though I grew up in a Catholic household. And, being a child of the 1980s, we have to remind ourselves that the two biggest box office hits back in the day were the 'Star Wars' trilogy and the 'Indiana Jones' trilogy. Looking back, I can definitely say that I have been greatly influenced by both to do what I do today."

What Tsoukalos does today is to serve as Erich von Daniken's spokesman for the English-speaking world, as well as publishing "Legendary Times Magazine" and directing Erich von Daniken's Center For Ancient Astronaut Research, not to mention appearing regularly on the History Channel series "Ancient Aliens."

Which makes Tsoukalos more than worthy to voice an educated opinion about the primary author of the book you are now reading, the late Brinsley Le Poer Trench.

"Brinsley Le Poer Trench's books," Tsoukalos said, "have been quoted in many classic ancient astronauts works. An argument definitely can be made for the points that he has written about, especially because he based a lot of his research on more ancient texts that are not available as readily as they were back when he was alive. I do think he is one of the founders of the modern-day ancient astronauts theory."

ARE THE "GODS" TRULY GOD?

The position held by Tsoukalos and von Daniken is very specific on this point: ancient man called the ancient astronauts "gods" mistakenly and inadvertently. The true Creator is another matter entirely.

"Let's say you and I create an intelligent species in the lab," Tsoukalos said. "That does not make you and me God. The whole 'God question' transcends the extraterrestrial presence. The extraterrestrials that Erich von Daniken and I talk about are not ethereal beings. They were flesh and blood, physical people consisting of the same atoms and molecules and particles that every single human being and every single thing has here on Planet Earth.

"That is also why the extraterrestrials look like us," he continued. "The whole idea that extraterrestrials look like something out of the movie 'Aliens' or 'Independence Day,' that's a Hollywood stereotype. But both Erich and I do think that there is an all-encompassing force in this universe. But you can't really put your finger on it. You can't really touch it. It's most certainly not what is referred to as a 'personal God.' Nobody should regard those extraterrestrials as 'gods' at all."

The only reason ancient man regarded the aliens as gods was that primitive mankind simply didn't understand the mechanical or technological aspects of the aliens' visits, which were made, Tsoukalos firmly declares, in nuts-and-bolts spaceships.

"So even though we are proposing," Tsoukalos reasoned, "that mankind would not exist without this extraterrestrial intervention with our genes, this artificial mutation of our genes, which took place thousands of years ago in a lab, even though we are 100 percent convinced that this is what happened, we are still not saying that whoever did this are truly our God, that we worship, that God for whom we would go down on our knees."

Tsoukalos made reference to the 2012 blockbuster sci-fi movie "Prometheus," in which the ancient creator aliens are called "the Engineers."

"Even those 'engineers,'" he explained, "were created by someone else, by other potential extraterrestrials, and then you can spin backwards this game to the very beginning when that first species or that first intelligent extraterrestrial life came into being. Whoever or whatever gave that initial species its intelligence was, in my opinion, God."

We all belong, along with the extraterrestrials who "made us," to the same universe. We are part of the fabric of that universe.

"Even the extraterrestrials," Tsoukalos said, "have the exact same questions about life, death, God and religion and all those different things that we are struggling with today. To suggest that the extraterrestrials have all the mysteries solved about life, death, religion and God – I think it's not that easy."

AN INSULT TO CREATION

Tsoukalos is also quick to adamantly deny that his beliefs about ancient astronauts make him an atheist. He says he continually struggles with that false and "bizarre" charge. People will often say to him, "Oh, you're the one who believes in aliens. That means you're an atheist."

"I cannot express," Tsoukalos said, "how unnerving that statement or observation is because it's anything but true. Personally, I think the fact that intelligent extraterrestrials exist makes creation or God even more magnificent than we've thought of so far. Because right now, if we are to subscribe to all the stuff that the theologians are saying, that we are the pinnacle of creation – if you step back for a moment and look at the greater picture of all this, of that statement or idea, then that's an insult in the face of creation. Because that means that God couldn't do any better than us.

"That is an insult in the face of God," he went on, "when comments like that are made. So the fact that extraterrestrials exist makes creation or God even more magnificent than we think of it because it means we're not alone and that not all hope is lost for the universe. I welcome the day when hopefully we'll make contact within our own lifetime, but I don't think it will happen for at least 50 years from now."

LIFE ON MARS?

What about the notion that life began on Mars, in some Martian Garden of Eden?

"It's certainly an interesting idea," Tsoukalos replied, "especially if we look at the biorhythms of our bodies. Our biorhythms, or the circadian cycles of our bodies, are not configured to the nighttime and daytime cycle of Earth, but they apply to Mars. So there have been theories out there that Mars at some point was a lush planet with water and an atmosphere and everything, just like Planet Earth. Then some kind of a catastrophic event took place on Mars or thereabouts, and that's why we have the asteroid belt within our solar system. Some people have suggested that some planet or planets collided into Mars, and before this destruction took place, some quote, unquote 'Martians' rescued themselves to Planet Earth. Therefore, in theory, we are actually Martians."

But there is still a hole in this theory, according to Tsoukalos.

"When the ancient peoples asked those visitors, 'Where did you come from?' they never said, 'Hey, we come from across the mountains or we come from another continent or we come from Down Under or whatever.' They always, always pointed to the sky and said they came from far away. 'We come from out there.'

"And Brinsley Le Poer Trench leaves out the fact that in none of the ancient descriptions do the visitors say they that they come from Mars or that they come from a planet within our own solar system. That text passage, as far as Erich von Daniken and I know, does not exist.

"Therefore I have to be a little bit more cautious about embracing the whole Mars-was-civilized-and-then-they-came-over-here. Do I think it's an interesting idea? Do I think it's worth looking into? Absolutely. The world needs more thinkers like Brinsley Le Poer Trench, for sure. I think it's wonderful that a guy like that, at the time he wrote those books – that was pretty courageous to come forward with a book like this and propositions like this in the late 1950s and early 1960s."

AN INTERGALACTIC PEACE CORPS

Tsoukalos also doesn't suffer gladly those who oversimplify his and von Daniken's message.

"One of the greatest misconceptions," he said, "next to the whole atheist

LEGACY OF THE SKY PEOPLE

thing, which is nonsense, the second one is, 'Oh, the ancient aliens theory. You guys are the ones who say the pyramids were built by aliens.' I challenge anyone to find a passage where I have written or spoken that the pyramids were built by aliens. The same goes for Erich von Daniken. He never wrote in 'Chariots of the Gods?' that the aliens built the pyramids. What he wrote was that the Egyptians had help, had assistance, and therein lies the great difference. That we had help, that there was some kind of an intergalactic Peace Corps that saw there is potential for advanced life here. 'This is very precious in the universe, so let's make sure that we can put them on the right path.' So it's certainly not 'Oh, look at the pyramids and that right there proves alien life.'"

THE SMOKING GUN OF ANCIENT ALIENS

"In my opinion," Tsoukalos said, "the smoking gun of the ancient alien theory is this one tiny place in South America. It's called Puma Punku, and it's in Bolivia. There we have perfectly cut stones made out of granite, giant stone blocks that we today would have great difficulty to replicate. Now we today absolutely, without question could and can replicate what we see at Puma Punku, but in order to do so we would use the most gigantic of rock-cutting machines. They are these humongous pieces of machinery that have these giant saws. You have to have a water supply line to it because otherwise, if you cut stone and don't have water you're going to melt the blade and things like this.

Puma Punku is one of the most mysterious locales thought to be evidence of the arrival of extraterrestrials.
Photo from the collection of Giorgio Tsoukalos.

LEGACY OF THE SKY PEOPLE

"They're very sophisticated, advanced machines," he continued. "And mainstream archeologists, they want us to believe that Puma Punku, these granite stone blocks, were cut with chicken bones or copper chisels. That's a physical impossibility. If you would like to argue against raw physics, be my guest. But in the end, raw physics will always win over using chicken bones and copper tools."

Tsoukalos bases his own argument on a density scale created by a 19th century German mineralogist named Friedrich Mohs, which places a diamond, the hardest, at number ten, the highest point in the scale. The granite found at Puma Punku rates around seven on the scale, while copper tools come out at around a three or four. Tsoukalos said he feels the theory that lasers were used was thoroughly disproved on an episode of his own "Ancient Aliens" History Channel program. Lasers simply melted the stone into a form of glass, which, Tsoukalos said, makes the mystery of how the stone blocks were cut all the more intriguing.

The ancient Bolivians must have used some kind of diamond-tipped tool, he believes, but the questions remains: Were human hands responsible at all? The answer continues to elude us.

The granite stone blocks in Bolivia would be difficult to duplicate even with modern technology.
Photo from the collection of Giorgio Tsoukalos.

LEGACY OF THE SKY PEOPLE

WHAT ARE THE PUMA PUNKU BLOCKS FOR?

Given that the mysterious stone blocks at Puma Punku were not made by human skill alone, what are they for?

"Puma Punku is certainly not an altar," Tsoukalos said. "Yes, our ancestors did build things that were intended for worship, for rituals. But those places usually contained or featured some type of hieroglyphics or glyphs or some wonderful ornamentation that's been carved into the rock, or faces or flowers. Just beautiful carvings.

"Puma Punku, on the other hand, is one hundred percent anonymous. Not a single glyph has been found, not a single carved flower or carved ornamentation. The blocks that we find there, some of them up to 85 tons, are all very technical in nature. You've got a whole lot of little inside boxes that have been cut out. Every block at Puma Punku looks as if it was the counterpart to another block. Like a female piece and a male piece fitting together and vice-versa.

There are some who theorize that the blocks - some of which are exact duplicates of each other - were constructed in one night while a spaceship hovered overhead. Photo from the collection of Giorgio Tsoukalos.

LEGACY OF THE SKY PEOPLE

"Another interesting thing is also the fact that it's as if only master stonemasons were allowed to work there, because nowhere do you find any mistakes. Nowhere is there a place where a guy slipped while he was cutting a stone. It's all perfect."

All of this leads Tsoukalos to conclude that Puma Punku is, by far, the most "inexplicable" site in the world.

"I would venture to say," Tsoukalos declared, "that Puma Punku is the only place in the world that was not built by human hands, that that place was, in fact, built by extraterrestrials using some kind of machinery. Nobody knows the purpose, but I theorize that Puma Punku might have been one of the base camps of the extraterrestrials. It was basically THEIR place."

ARE THE GODS STILL HERE?

Tsoukalos is often asked, "Okay, so how come the ancient aliens were here in the past but they're not here in the present?"

He answers by saying, "Nobody's ever claimed that they have left. I think this planet has been under observation since times immemorial, since before recorded time that we're aware of. I think that's how far back the extraterrestrial presence goes. Now, obviously my field is more into the ancient realm of extraterrestrial visitation, but that does not mean that all of a sudden, thousands of years ago, that that was the last time [they appeared] and then they showed up again in 1947 with Roswell.

"The difference as to why the extraterrestrials are not showing themselves today publicly, meaning that they don't land on the White House lawn or something crazy like that – because in the past, that's what they used to do. They used to have quite public appearances with a lot of people seeing what was going on. Today, if extraterrestrials were to show themselves by hovering above Los Angeles or Paris or of all the world capitols around the globe, none of us – or at least I hope so – none of us would drop to our knees and start praying. Why?

"Because the moment they would show themselves we would know immediately, 'Oh, here they are, the extraterrestrials, in their nuts-and-bolts spaceships, which were built using technology.' They're not 'gods' in that sense. They're 'godlike,' but they're not 'gods.' Being godlike doesn't make you a god. You don't become an ethereal being at one with the universe. So an extraterrestrial coming here with a spaceship is as disadvantaged as we are. The only advantage an extraterrestrial has is that he has an advantage technologically speaking. But that's about it. As I said earlier, I think even an extraterrestrial would have the same questions about life and death."

LEGACY OF THE SKY PEOPLE

In ancient times, according to Tsoukalos, the extraterrestrials knew we would misperceive them as gods and used this much to their advantage, instructing ancient man to carry out various tasks and to worship the visitors from afar. Today, however, we would not be so naïve.

"But they're here," Tsoukalos affirmed. "Otherwise why would we have all these abduction stories and UFO sightings and things like that?"

EVERYTHING IS GOD

As the interview drew to a close, Tsoukalos said, "Both Erich von Daniken and I are proponents of the nuts-and-bolts ancient aliens theory. But that does not negate the idea that ethereal beings or beings that are not physical, but are just 'souls' or something like that, that those beings do not exist. But at the same time, if also those types of beings are here with us today or are helping us, they're still not God. Because everything is God. We're all part of this universe, which makes us all inherently divine. It sounds more complicated than it really is."

LEGACY OF THE SKY PEOPLE

"Galactic Man Has Arrived," Says The 8th Earl of Clancarty, Brinsley Le Poer Trench.

LEGACY OF THE SKY PEOPLE

Pictograph of Early Man Holding His Hands Toward The Sky As If Protecting Himself.

LEGACY OF THE SKY PEOPLE

LEGACY OF THE SKY PEOPLE

SENSATIONAL NEW EVIDENCE ABOUT ANCIENT ASTRONAUTS!

FOR THE MILLIONS HELD SPELLBOUND BY CHARIOTS OF THE GODS

THE SKY PEOPLE

BRINSLEY LE POER TRENCH

PROOF THAT EXTRA-TERRESTRIAL BEINGS HAVE VISITED THE EARTH FOR MILLIONS OF YEARS—THAT THEY ARE AMONG US NOW!

DON'T TRY TO DENY THE AMAZING FACTS UNTIL YOU'VE READ THIS BOOK.

LEGACY OF THE SKY PEOPLE

The Sky People Were Here Millions Of Years Ago... They Are Here Now!

In this astounding but scholarly book you will find proof that visitors from other planets exist—and have existed since ancient times.

You will be shocked to learn that.....

. Apollo and other Greek "gods" were actually visitors from outer space

. The Garden of Eden was on another planet

. Virgin birth is attributed to extraterrestrial beings

WE ARE ALREADY HERE, AMONG YOU.

"Some of us always have been here with you.

"Now, however, our numbers have been increased in preparation for a further step in the development of your planet: a step of which you are not yet aware . . .

"We have been mistaken for the gods of many world religions, although we are not gods, but your own fellow creatures—as you will learn . . ."

In this fascinating report, an acknowledged expert brings forth an astounding new theory on outer space that explains the inexplicable.

Throughout recorded time, beings from other planets with superhuman powers-mistaken for gods-have guided men on earth through critical periods in history.

Now the earth is about to undergo another period of crisis. The warnings are here and so are *THE SKY PEOPLE!*

"Let brotherly love continue. Be not forgetful to entertain strangers; for thereby some have entertained angels unawares."

—Hebrews XIII: 1-2.

THE SKY PEOPLE

Brinsley Le Poer Trench

LEGACY OF THE SKY PEOPLE

LEGACY OF THE SKY PEOPLE

Obituary—Page 56

Acknowledgements—Page 58

Foreword—Page 59

Prologue—Son of the Sun—Page 62

I—Man and Hu-man—Page 66

II—Where was the Garden of Eden?—**Page 75**

III—Enter Cross-Man—Page 87

IV—Quarantine—Page 98

V—Celestial Chariots—Page 111

VI—Unusual Childbirths—Page 121

VII—The Real Cross—Paage 129

VIII—Three Glorious Suns—Page 139

IX—Space Ships Galore—Page 144

X—The Problem of Adam-II—Page 156

XI—Communication—Page 168

XII—Tektites and Silicon—Page 176

XIII—The Serpent People—Page 184

XIV—This World Will Not End Tomorrow—Page 188

XV—What Colour Are Space People?—Page 195

XVI—One Duty—Page 200

Last Song (Poem)—Page 206

Bibliography—Page 207

LEGACY OF THE SKY PEOPLE

Brinsley Le Poer Trench: 1911 - 1995

In the introduction to ***The Sky People*** (1960) Brinsley Le Poer Trench – the 8th Earl of Clancarty – wrote: "Understanding is a gradual process. It cannot be forced, but far more people today all over the world than is generally realized have got wider horizons and greater acceptance levels than hitherto. By greater acceptance levels, I do not mean they are more gullible. Far from it. Although there are still scientists with dogmatic, crystallized views among us, there are also many others with wider and more open ones. An acceptance level is the level at which concepts, views and data can be allowed to flow into your mind without being rejected at the outset as being impossible. It does not necessarily mean you accept the facts or concepts coming to you as total truth, but that you are prepared to give them house room in your mind…"

Clancarty was a major figure in British ufology and frequently pursued the subject in Parliament through his House of Lords All-Party UFO study group and among his fellow peers. He was a world-renowned UFO author and one of the first to espouse the ancient astronaut concept that life on Earth had arrived here from some point in space, perhaps the planet Mars, and that an ancient alien race has been continuing to visit throughout antiquity right up until modern times.

One of these peers, who also edited the prestigious ***Flying Saucer Review*** after Brinsley stepped down from his esteemed post, Gordon Creighton, had this to say about his chum: "On May 18th, 1995, at the age of 83, my old friend and colleague, the Earl of Clancarty, departed from this life... Exactly 40 years ago, in the Spring of 1955, and known then of course as the Honourable Brinsley le Poer Trench, he recruited me as one of the very first subscribers to the new journal, **Flying Saucer Review**, which, according to British press reports, he and some associates were about to launch. It was a bi-monthly in those days, and the first eight issues were edited by a former RAF pilot, Derek Dempster, who is still around and, interestingly enough, only made contact with us again recently. Thereafter, Brinsley ran the journal for the next 20 issues (from Volume 2/4 in 1956 to Volume 5/5 in 1959), when he handed the reins over to the third of our Editors, Waveny Girvan. (My own material, including translations from Chinese, Arabic, Russian, German, Dutch, French, Italian, Spanish, Portuguese and Croatian, had begun to appear in **FSR** from issue No. 3 onwards).

"One evening, when Brinsley knew he was about to become the eighth Earl, he phoned me and said he planned to talk 'of our subject' in his maiden speech in the House of Lords. I told him that if he did so he would be a b.f. [bloody fool]. However, he did so, and in 1979 he introduced **FSR** into the libraries of both the House of Lords and the House of Commons and he set up the so-called House of Lords UFO Study Group, whose members I was myself invited to meet and address on two separate occasions. Whatever one may think about some of his particular theories, it remains a fact that the Earl of Clancarty was a brave man who throughout the years stuck to the highly unpopular opinion that we Earthlings are not alone."

LEGACY OF THE SKY PEOPLE

ACKNOWLEDGMENTS

I wish to express my deep appreciation and thanks to Mrs. Millen Belknap, of Fallbrook, California, for permission to include the poem, Last Song, and for her untiring researches into Genesis, which have made this book possible.

I also wish to thank the Misses Mary and Agnes Kouroussidis, of London, for their invaluable and enthusiastic research and notes in the field of Greek mythology.

My grateful thanks go to Mrs. Rosemary Decker, of Vista, California, and Mrs. Gillian Boyd, of London, for additional research on Genesis; Dr. Bernard E. Finch, of London, for notes on Tektites, and to the Editor of Flying Saucer Review for permission to quote from that magazine.

Finally, my thanks go to Mildred Alleyn Spong, who encouraged this enjoyable exercise and wanted a book.

LEGACY OF THE SKY PEOPLE

FOREWORD

Some of the concepts advanced in this book are of a completely revolutionary nature and the very opposite to those handed down to us by the priests and the scientists.

For thousands of years men have had persistently instilled into them the idea that the earth was the centre of the universe.

The notion that there could possibly be a race outside the earth which might have a wisdom and technology superior to their own was thought both amoral and heretical.

During the last thirteen years people all over the world have been seeing what are popularly termed 'flying saucers'. Thousands of men and women in every country, many of them trained observers, have spotted these strange craft, and reports of their out-of-this-world behaviour have been published in the world press, magazines and in over a hundred books. They have been photographed, filed and tracked on radar screens. Governments have set up special projects to investigate this Phenomenon.

People everywhere are beginning to awaken to the idea that something is behind it all. Ideas themselves, however, are not negotiable. They are not transferable. One cannot put an idea into another mind. One can only awaken and, perhaps, draw out the ideas already there; ideas that have been covered up by blindness, forgetfulness or deliberate burial.

This is education, from a Latin word meaning 'to lead out'—which rather goes to show the old Romans knew more about it than we do. If somebody holds up one of his ideas for you to see, and you say, 'Yes, I like that idea!' It is because, in your own mental files you have one similar to it. If you cannot find any such similarity, you will reject the idea as impossible or invalid.

The mind is the man and the man is individual. Communication as an act of Love is done with mirrors.

Challenge-and-Proof is an act of Combat, and proves only which is stronger, which ran out of data first and, so was wrong! Proof proves nothing more. In short, so-called proof does not really settle anything.

One of the greatest obstacles to the advancement of humankind is the stubbornly held notion that knowledge is transferable, that it can be taken out of one head and put into another. It cannot.

Every individual has his own potential connection to the source of knowledge and truth, and he can know and comprehend only so much as the strength of that connection will transmit—and no amount of words, or proof or demonstration will bring him one whit more.

But, in subtle and sometimes undetected ways, an educator may open channels, strengthen connections and allow knowledge, data and truth to flow.

Facts, as presented in textbooks, and physical laws as they are explained by scientists, may not be the product of complete understanding. These facts and laws may have been proved by scientists, but that does not mean they are necessarily true.

A pair of stubbornly inventive young men named Orville and Wilbur Wright went out to a flat spot in the Kitty Hawk Dunes, Carolina, one day in 1903, and proceeded to destroy a well-known fact that had survived for thousands of years. They were the first men on earth (in this civilisation) to fly a heavier-than-air machine powered by an engine.

Recently, some persistent scientists of Chinese extraction, disposed of the Law of Parity.* And the whole, well established theory of colour perception, which everybody knew to be gospel, has suffered a similar fate. It has been scientifically proved too, that aerodynamically, the Bumble Bee's wings will not enable it to fly.

Understanding is a gradual process. It cannot be forced, but far more people today all over the world than is generally realised have got wider horizons and greater acceptance levels than hitherto. By greater acceptance levels I do not mean that they are more gullible. Far from it. Although there are still scientists with dogmatic crystallised views among us, there are also many others with wider and more open ones. An acceptance level is the level at which concepts, views and data can be allowed to flow into your mind without being rejected at the outset as being impossible. It does not necessarily mean you accept the ideas or concepts, coming to you as total truth, but that you are prepared to give them house room in your mind. That is what I hope you will do with the perhaps novel and strange ideas advanced in this book. I do not ask you to believe in them. I do ask you not to reject them outright but to let them have the hospitality of your mind for a while.

Here is a little fable to illustrate my point.

Once upon a time in a far country nobody ever visits any more, a man walked

LEGACY OF THE SKY PEOPLE

down a little lane, carrying a very large fish. He met another man. This other man had never seen a fish, of any size, large or small. Neither had he ever seen a body of water larger than the pail his wife washed their communal bowl in after he had eaten his porridge.

'What is that?' he demanded of the man who was carrying the fish.

''Tis a fish,' the man replied.

'What does it do?'

'It swims.'

Puzzled, the inquiring one asked further:

'So? What's to swim?'

'It's done in the water, so . . .' replied the man with the fish, making a waving motion with one hand.

The inquirer looked at the size of the fish with an expression of grave skepticism. 'There don't be that much water all in one spot.'

'Over the hill there is.'

'Show me how he swims!' demanded the skeptic.

'Come with me over the hill to the lake, and I will,' said the man with the fish agreeably, and set off.

'Wait!' shouted the skeptic. 'Show me here! Show me right here in the lane where we met face to face. If you cannot show me right here, I will never believe you!'

But the man with the fish was over the brow of the hill, and he didn't hear.

***

It is my sincere hope that those who take up this book will not stick in the lane. Why not join in a very unusual adventure and come with me over the hill?

Brinsley LePour Trench, London, May 1960.

Law of Parity: Extract from the article on Physics, World Book Encyclopedia: '... two Chinese-born American physicists, Tsung Dao Lee and Chen Ning Yang, startled the scientific world in 1956 when they disproved the thirty-year-old law of the conservation of parity. This law states, in part, that matter would retain its same basic physical properties if the direction of motion of the particles within the atom were reversed. The work of Lee and Yang opened new fields of research in physics.'

LEGACY OF THE SKY PEOPLE

PROLOGUE
SON OF THE SUN

This article, written under the pseudonym of 'Alexander Blade' originally appeared in the November 1947 issue of Fantastic Stories (U.S.A,), and was reproduced in the August-September 1958 edition of Round Robin, published by the Borderland Science Research Associates (BSRA), San Diego, and more recently in the November-December 1958 number of the London Flying Saucer Review. While the author of this book was Editor of the latter magazine this article created more interest and impact than any other published during the three-year tenureship of that office.

We are already here, among you. Some of us have always been here with you, yet apart from, watching, and occasionally guiding you whenever the opportunity arose. Now, however, our numbers have been increased in preparation for a further step in the development of your planet: a step of which you are not yet aware, although it has been hinted at frequently enough in the parables of your prophets, who have garbled whatever inspiration they have been able to receive. Sometimes they were ignorant. Sometimes they were unable to translate clearly the concepts implanted in their minds. Sometimes they were cautious and to ensure the preservation of the information they wished to place upon the record in the world, they spoke in metaphors and symbols.

We have been confused with the gods of many world-religions. Although we are not gods, but your own fellow creatures, as you will learn directly before many more years have passed. You will find records of our presence in the mysterious symbols of ancient Egypt, where we made ourselves known in order to accomplish certain ends. Our principle symbol appeared in the religious art of your present civilisation and occupies a position of importance upon the great seal of your country. It has been preserved in certain secret societies founded originally to keep alive the knowledge of our existence and our intentions toward mankind.

We have left you certain landmarks, placed carefully in different parts of the globe, but most prominently in Egypt where we established our headquarters upon the occasion of our last overt, or, as you would say, public appearance. At that time the foundations of your present civilisation were 'laid in the earth' and the most ancient of your known landmarks established by means that would appear as miraculous to you now as they did to the pre-Egyptians, so many thousands of years ago. Since that time the whole art of building, in stone, has become symbolic, to many of you, of the work in hand—the building of the human race towards its perfection.

Your ancestors knew us in those days as preceptors and as friends. Now, through your own efforts, you have almost reached, in your majority, a new step on the long ladder of your liberation. You have been constantly aided by our watchful 'inspiration', and hindered only by the difficulties natural to your processes of physical and moral development, for the so-called 'forces of evil and darkness' have always been recruited from among the ranks of your own humanity—a circumstance for which you would be exceedingly grateful if you possessed full knowledge of conditions in the universe.

You have lately achieved the means of destroying yourselves. Do not be hasty in your self-congratulation. Yours is not the first civilisation to have achieved—and used—such means. Yours will not be the first civilisation to be offered the means of preventing that destruction and proceeding, in the full glory of its accumulated knowledge, to establish an era of enlightenment upon the earth.

However, if you do accept the means offered you, and if you do establish such a 'millennium' upon the basis of your present accomplishments, yours will be the first civilisation to do so. Always before, the knowledge, the techniques, the instructions, have become the possessions of a chosen few: a few chose themselves by their own open-minded and clear-sighted realisation of 'the shapes of things to come'. They endeavoured to pass on their knowledge in the best possible form, and by the most enduring means at their command. In a sense they succeeded, but in another sense their failure equalled their success. Human acceptance is, to a very large extent, measurable by human experience. Succeeding generations, who never knew our actual presence, translated the teachings of their elders in the terms of their own experience. For instance, a cross-sectional drawing much simplified and stylised by many copyings, of one of our travelling machines became the 'Eye of Horus', and then of the eyes of other gods. Finally, the ancient symbol that was once an accurate representation of an important mechanical device has been given surprising connotations by the modern priesthood of psychology.

The important fact is, however, that we are here, among you, and that you, as a world-race, will know it before very much longer! The time is almost ripe but, as with all ripening things, the process may not be hurried artificially without danger of damaging the fruit. There is a right time for every action, and the right time for our revelation of ourselves to your era is approaching.

Some of you have seen our 'advance guard' already. You have met us often in the streets of your cities, and you have not noticed us. But when we flash through your skies in the ancient traditional vehicles you are amazed, and those of you who open your mouths and tell of what you have seen are accounted dupes and fools. Actually you are prophets, seers in the true sense of the word. You in Kansas and Oklahoma, you in Oregon and in California, and Idaho, you know what you have seen: do not be dismayed by meteorologists. Their business is the weather. One of you says, 'I saw a torpedo-shaped object'. Others report 'disclike objects', some of you say 'spherical objects', or 'platter-like objects'. You are all reporting correctly and accurately what you saw, and in most cases you are describing the same sort of vehicle.

The 'golden disc'—now confused with solar disc and made a part of the parcel of religion—even in your own times. The 'discus', hurled sunward by the Grecian—and your own athletes. The 'eye of Horus', and the other eyes of symbology, alchemical and otherwise. These are our mechanical means of transport.

Now that the art of manufacturing plastic materials has reached a certain perfection among you, perhaps you can imagine a material, almost transparent to the rays of ordinary visible light, yet strong enough to endure the stresses of extremely rapid flight. Look again at the great nebulae, and think of the construction of your own galaxy, and behold the universal examples of what we have found to be the perfect shape for an object which is to travel through what you still fondly refer to as 'empty' space.

In the centre of the discus, gyroscopically controlled within a central sphere of the same transparent material, our control rooms revolve freely, accommodating themselves and us to flat or edgewise flight. Both methods are suited to your atmosphere, and when we convert abruptly from one to the other, as we are sometimes obliged to do, and you are watching, our machines seem suddenly to appear—or to disappear. At our possible speeds your eyes, untrained and unprepared for the manoeuvre, do make mistakes—but not the mistakes your scientists so often accuse them of making. We pass over your hilltops in horizontal flight. You see and report a torpedo-shaped object. We pass over, in formation, flying vertically 'edge-on', and you report a series of disc-shaped, platterlike objects, or perhaps a sphere. Or we go over at night, jet-slits glowing, and you see an orange disc.

In any event you see us, and in any event we do not care. If we chose to remain invisible, we could do so, easily, and, in fact, we have done so almost without exception for hundreds of years. But you must become accustomed to our shapes in your skies, for one day they will be familiar, friendly, and reassuring sights. This time, it is to be hoped that the memory of them, passed on to your children and their children, will be clear and precise. That you will not cause them to forget, as your ancestors forgot, the meaning of the diagrams and the instructions we will leave with you. If you do fail, as other civilisations have failed, we will see your descendants wearing wiring-diagrams for simple machines as amulets, expecting the diagrams to do what their forefathers were taught the completed article would accomplish. Then their children, forgetting even that much—or little— would preserve the amulet as a general protective device—or as an intellectual curiosity, or, perhaps as a religious symbol. Such is the cycle of forgetfulness!

Tuzigoot National Monument
Brad Steiger ponders who the inhabitants might have been about 1,000 years ago. The Hohokum, the Anasazi, and then the Sinagua appear to have all called this home.

From the private collection of Brad and Sherry Steiger.

Tuzigoot National Monument
Sherry comments on how very different this ruin is from Montezuma's and others. Situated in a 120 foot limestone ridge, the Tuzigoot ruins in Arizona appear to have been a hill town overlooking the Verde Valley.
From the private collection of Brad and Sherry Steiger.

LEGACY OF THE SKY PEOPLE

CHAPTER I

MAN AND HU-MAN

'The universe is but a great city, full of beloved ones, divine and human, by nature endeared to each other.'

—Epictetus.

This is the story of the Sky People who have been coming to Earth for millions of years. Countless legends and myths in the folklore, mythologies and sacred books of races everywhere refer to a period—a Golden Age—when the gods came down and mingled with mortals. The myths themselves are but the fairy story coverings these true happenings of a bygone age were wrapt up in to preserve them for posterity.

At times of crisis the Sky People have assisted in establishing a new civilisation after a period of cataclysm and have brought much needed light and wisdom to the remnant who had to build anew. After giving this tonic shot in the arm the visitors would withdraw to see what humanity did with its newly acquired knowledge. While on Earth, some of the Sky People were elected rulers. For instance, Osiris became one of the earlier divine pharaohs of Egypt. Subsequently, after their withdrawal, and Osiris is a case in point, they were worshipped as gods.

Nobody really knows when the Sky People-Galactic Men were first created. This signal event is lost in the starry mists of an antiquity so vast our own planet is no more than a little child in it. Genesis i refers to the establishment of the Golden Age and to the creation of Galactic Man.

So God created man in his own image, in the image of God created he him, male and female created he them.

It is interesting to note that both males and females were created in Genesis i, long before Adam was made from the dust of the ground—Chemical Man—in Genesis ii. It is also worth considering that Eve was not made until a long time after Adam.

C. Kerenyi, in his book **The Gods of the Greeks**, referring to the Golden Age, wrote:

LEGACY OF THE SKY PEOPLE

...the whole earth was a paradise where sun and showers made a lasting spring. The trees bore their fruit and flowers of every hue filled the air with perpetual fragrance. The tribes of living creatures preyed not on each other, none as fierce,—the lion gamboled with the kid, and the serpent was guileless as the dove.

Hesiod, celebrated Greek poet who lived in the eighth or ninth century B.C., described five ages of mankind who had successively inhabited earth down to our own times. These were the Golden, Silver, Bronze and Iron ages, as well as the Age of the Heroes, which came between those of Bronze and Iron. Each age unhappily degenerated—with the exception of the Age of Heroes—and got steadily worse. We are now living in the Iron Age, or what the theosophists term, Kali Yuga.

According to Greek mythology, Kronos, the Titan who had ruled over the world during the long Golden Age, was overthrown by his youngest son, Zeus, through force and cunning. The era of the Olympian gods now dawned. Zeus was soon involved in a terrific struggle against his elder brothers, the Titans, who wished to regain their kingdom. The Titans belong to a far distant period and appear to have had a strong connection with the divinity of the sun. They launched a great onslaught upon the stronghold of Mount Olympus. Zeus descended into Tartarus and freed the Cyclops who had only one eye in the middle of their foreheads, and also the Hedatoncheires, monsters each with one hundred invisible arms and fifty heads attached to their backs. Zeus made them his allies and with their help vanquished the Titans.

In his book **Road in the Sky,** George Hunt Williamson wrote:

The Cyclopeans were the immortals of our legends, the God Race or Elder Race that preceded hu-man beings.

Zeus had hardly put down this dangerous revolt when he had to combat with new opponents. The Giants were supposed to have sprung from the blood of mutilated Uranus, the father of Kronos. They attacked in force, but the gods around Zeus stood firm. Apollo disposed of Ephialtes. Poseidon chased Polybutes over the sea, finally flinging the Island of Nisynos on top of him.

Who were those divine Beings around Zeus on Mount Olympus? The chief gods and goddesses apart from Zeus himself were Apollo, Artemis, Hermes, Hera, Athene, Hephaestus, Aphrodite, Poseidon, Hestia, Ares and Demeter. There were also many lesser gods at the Olympian Court, including Helios, Selene, Dionysus, Themis, Eos and Leto.

Many people believe that the gods were not really based on that magnificent peak—Mount Olympus—in the Thessalian mountains. Indeed Walter Otto in **The Homeric Gods** wrote:

LEGACY OF THE SKY PEOPLE

But these glimpses present no clear and consistent picture. Nor does it really matter, for though the memory of the Thessalian mountain of the gods never faded and was kept alive by the very name of the 'Olympian' gods, men were nevertheless convinced that these gods had their dwellings on no peak, majestically as it might tower heavenward, but on high in the lofty heaven. Even in the sanctuaries which men instituted for their worship they lingered only briefly. They came down to earth from heaven's ether, and thither returned; it was there that the gaze and uplifted hand of the petitioner sought them...

The whole concept of Greek mythology—tales of gods and goddesses who came down from the sky and mingled with mortals—lends itself to the hypothesis that they were indeed actual Sky People. All races everywhere on earth have their own legends and myths—the Greeks are not unique in this respect—and many of these tell of gods coming down from the heavens. The Red Indians of North America relate of white gods who came down from the sky in an age long past. Although the stories in Greek mythology are but the fairy tale wrappings placed round them to preserve them for other ages, some of the tales have less coating than others. Furthermore, it will be seen that several stories in Greek mythology parallel those in Genesis to an amazing degree. The writer of the Pentateuch and those who passed on the tales of Greek mythology, in many instances, appear to have been relating similar events.

In the Old Testament there are many examples of divine messengers—Angels—meeting, walking, and talking, with mortals. These divine messengers also consistently appeared to mortals in the tales of Greek mythology. It is interesting to note that the Greek word for 'Messengers' is 'Angelos'. The similarity to the Biblical word 'Angels' is strikingly obvious.

The Bible has numerous accounts of fiery chariots coming to Earth. And Greek mythology, too, has its complement.

It is well known that Zeus gave his son, Apollo, a chariot with swans. It is also interesting to see how Thomas Bulfinch in ***The Age of Fable***, has the Goddess Ceres commuting between Olympus and Earth in a chariot.

... So saying, she wrapped a cloud about her, and mounting her chariot rode away, and turned her chariot towards heaven, and hastened to present herself before the throne of Zeus.

Incidentally, take careful note of the word 'cloud' in the above quotation. We shall come across clouds in connection with spacecraft from other worlds many, many times before the end of this book.

Most countries today are proud of their hospitality to visitors, but the modern Greeks especially have an inborn sense of hospitality to strangers and also an innate curiosity to know something new. These traits in them are very marked indeed. Do they derive from those far-off times—those days when they received the very gods themselves in their homes who brought them wonderful knowledge? Surely there is food for thought here.

Numerous people are inclined to dismiss Greek mythology out of hand as a collection of nonsensical fairy tales and, in any case, consider it all rather pagan. Those same people would be perhaps a little put out to learn that the Hebrew version of the Old Testament uses the word Elohim instead of God in Genesis, and that Elohim means Gods. If you search enough, it is still possible to find even in the English King James version of the Bible many references to the plurality of Gods.

Come let us go down, and there confound their language...

Woe unto us! Who shall deliver us out of the hand of these mighty Gods? These are the Gods that smote the Egyptians with all manner of plagues in the wilderness.

—I Samuel iv. 8.

And the king said unto her, be not afraid: for what sawest thou? And the woman said unto Saul, I saw Gods ascending out of the earth.

—I Samuel xxviii. 13.

There are many more quotations like these from the King James version of the Bible which could be given, but it is suggested that a direct translation from the Hebrew version would be even more illuminating, for in many instances where the King James version uses the word God, the Hebrew uses the word Gods.

It can also be shown that the word Jehovah can be used in the singular or plural and, as masculine or feminine. In the Hebrew version some of the Jehovahs mentioned include: Jehovah, the God of Israel; Adonai (His Lords); Jehovah (plural); the name-Jehovah; the Voice-Jehovah; Jehovah of Hosts (the 'Man of War'); Jehovah-El-Shaddai (who covenanted with Abraham).

To say that all these are simply the names of one Jehovah is to miss the whole point. The Hebrew language, particularly in its literary form, is very carefully and intricately constructed so as to show subtle differences in meaning by the structure and form of the words used. After all, the scholars wrote by hand upon a very expensive substance, very difficult to prepare, and they carried their economy to the extent of boiling everything down into what amounts to a system of codes.

So, when Jehovah speaks and says 'Jehovah' will do or say something, it refers, according to the structure of the language used, to *another* Jehovah, otherwise the form 'I will do' or 'I will say' would have to follow.

The God who addressed Noah, spoke to him as a female, as is understood from the words:

... For yet seven days more, I (anochi) will cause it to rain upon the earth forty days and forty nights. ...

—Genesis vii. 1-4.

The word Anochi was used, whereas Ani would be the masculine form.

The God who spoke to Abraham likewise spoke as a female in the feminine gender, as is understood from the words:

After these things the word of Jehovah came unto Abram in a vision, saying, Fear not, Abram, I am (anochi) a shield to thee, thy reward shall be exceedingly great.

—Genesis xv. 1.

Ezekiel is filled with references to Adonai Jehovah. The meaning of the Hebrew word Adonai is 'My Lords!'. Sometimes not only does Jehovah come but the family arrives too.

And the angel Jehovah spoke to Gad to say to David, that David should go up, to erect an altar unto Jehovah on the threshing floor of Ornan the Jebusite. And David went up by the word of Gad, which he had spoken in the Name of Jehovah. And when Ornan turned back he saw the angel, and his *four sons with him hiding themselves*. Now Ornan was threshing wheat.

—I Chronicles xxi. 18-20.

Again, I could give many more quotations to support the contention that the Jehovah are indeed a family or even a race of Gods.

Some of the famous Biblical characters are written of as though they were members of the Jehovah. Moses, David, Noah, and Jacob for instance. Let us consider the case of Moses. He could well have been one of the Jehovah. This is actually 'concealed' and revealed in the Tikuneh ha-Zohar, Tikuna 13, page 48, as well as in references and in the language of Biblical descriptions of Moses, his acts and experiences.

Robert Graves, in his excellent book **The White Goddess**, referring to Essenes, adds weight to my comments on Moses.

... they refrained from worshipping at the Jerusalem Temple, perhaps because the custom of bowing to the East at dawn had been discontinued there, and exacted the penalty of death from anyone who blasphemed God or Moses.

LEGACY OF THE SKY PEOPLE

Since among the Jerusalem Pharisees, Moses as a man could not be blasphemed, it follows that for the Essenes he had a sort of divinity.

The Essene initiates, according to Josephus, were sworn to keep secret the names of the Powers who ruled their universe under God.

The fact that there may be many gods need not alter anyone's belief in one universal God or Spirit who created everything and both sustains and nourishes all life now and eternally. I am merely postulating that there are, indeed, many godlike beings in an ever expanding scale of grandeur on the stairways of evolution to the stars.

Now, one important point should be understood and brought forward at this stage. Nowhere, except in commentaries written by interpreters and scholars, is the Jehovah called or referred to as the Universal Spirit or the One Supreme God, as contemporary religious people now believe him to be.

Here is a footnote from the **Secret Doctrine** (Vol. II, pp. 214-15, Adyar Edition) which explains the circumstances clearly and concisely (whatever you may think of its author, Madame Blavatsky, or of what her followers have done with her ideas).

If we are taken to task for believing in operating 'Gods' and 'Spirits' while rejecting a personal God, we answer to the Theists and Monotheists: Admit that your Jehovah is one of the Elohim, and we are ready to recognise him. Make of him, as you do, the Infinite, the ONE and the Eternal God, and we will never accept him in this character. Of *tribal* Gods there were many; the One Universal Deity is a principle, an abstract Root-Idea, which has nought to do with the unclean work of finite Form. We do not worship the Gods, we only honour them, as beings superior to ourselves. In this we obey the Mosaic Injunction while Christians disobey their Bible-missionaries foremost of all. 'Thou shalt not revile the Gods,' says one of them. Jehovah, in Exodus xxii 28 but at the same time in verse 20 it is commanded: 'He that sacrificeth to any God, save unto the Lord only, he shall be utterly destroyed.'

Now in the original texts it is not 'God' but Elohim and Jehovah is one of the Elohim, as proved by his own words in Genesis iii. 22, when 'the Lord God said Behold the man is become as one of us.'

Hence both those who worship and sacrifice to the Elohim, the Angels, and to Jehovah, and those who revile the Gods of their fellowmen, are far greater transgressors than the Occultists or than any Theosophist.

Most of the difficulties encountered by theologians in explaining and understanding the personality of Jehovah as it appears in the Bible become a lot less mysterious (because more reasonable) if it is understood that while he is a 'god' from our human point of view, he is not, nowhere pretends to be, and nowhere is pretended to be the Universal Spirit.

* * * * *

Few people realise that the first two chapters of Genesis contain two separate creation stories. The majority consider these are two different reports of the same creation. There are a few enlightened people in the world who have not dared to more than hint at the truth. The time of revelation had not come.

Indeed, it is hardly advisable to speak too openly about such matters even today. The idea smacks too strongly of blasphemy in a world that has tangled up its creation stories so completely that the name applied to the second creation has been moved up to apply to the Universal Spirit. Blavatsky, for instance, writing in the nineteenth century, only dared let drop a hint here and there that far enough back in the arcane traditions. Jehovah equates with Satan—hints that appear briefly and then are as quickly covered up again, in reams of irrelevant material.

The first creation story in the Book of Genesis refers to the establishment of the Golden Age. Creation story number two as related in Genesis ii is the creation of human with an earth-animal chemical body—the creation of a second Adam by 'Jehovah'.

It was the sin of that Great Angel who said: 'I will be like God'—and who, in punishment for his temerity was given charge over the effects of his unauthorised experiments until such time as matters could be straightened out satisfactorily for all entities concerned.

Of course this is not to say that God and the Devil are the same. Far from it. The Universal Spirit has been called by many names in many times, in many places, by many different peoples. Right now, Christian people refer to IT as though it were essentially male and give IT the name of the creator of Adam-II humanity, as it is given in their sacred scriptures, which they borrowed from the Jews. This is, basically, a confusion of terms and ideas otherwise separate and distinct.

The creation of compulsively or necessarily solidly animal man was an illegal act. It was done without permission, in a specially chosen, isolated place.

Adam-II humanity was not intended to be as long-lived as his creators. He was invented and built to be their servant and they had no intention of allowing him to become as one of them.

Now it is possible to trace, in esoteric literature, the reaction of Galactic Man to this whole idea, and its resulting train of circumstances.

The creation of Animal Man is a relatively recent occurrence. It may even be that Earth-scientists are right when they maintain that his particular form of protoplasmic life exists naturally nowhere else in the Universe.

This may, in the final analysis, turn out to be a good thing. On the other hand, it may have been a cosmic necessity or it would not have happened.

However, it appears not to have been done at the appointed time, or by those who ought to have done it, had events been allowed to mature and to pursue their natural course.

Therefore, it was an illegal act. By its bad timing, the formation of animal-mankind, where and when it happened, threw a spanner into the cosmic years. Whoever performed this illegal and premature act of creation did not find favour with his equals and contemporaries.

They judged that its creator's duty was to finish what he started, to see through to its end the chain of events he had set in motion—he and those who had worked with him.

The experiment got out of hand, failed, and he and his assistants were put in charge of the resulting confusion until such time as some kind of order could be brought out of it. This in no way diminishes, or even reflects upon his inherent grandeur as compared to them, and it in no way lessens the respect and honours they should pay him at all times to define his functions in the greater picture of the Universe as a whole, of which we are only a very small part.

That whoever created animal man was, at the same time and in the same act, the author of the difficulties that beset him, would seem to be fairly evident. That's what is meant by the 'Satan' aspect of Jehovah. It is an esoteric statement of events, and has nothing whatever to do with that modern theological invention, 'the Devil'.

Confusion of the 'Devil' idea with the Satan aspect is just another instance of muddling concepts that have already been muddled enough.

Before we consider the question: Where was the Garden of Eden? We must have this idea firmly and clearly in mind.

Let us look for a moment at Adam-II man's search for something edible that will prolong life, and the possibility apparent in the scriptures that he can find it if he looks in the right place.

In Genesis that something—a tree, or a plant—was said to be growing in the Garden of Eden that Adam-II man's creator made. So we have it, on what we accept as good authority, that at one time at least this plant did exist somewhere.

Man's use of drugs, narcotics, stimulants and magical plants in general is all a part of his search for this lost tree. Anything that loosens the connection with the animal body has been used somewhere by some people or other to go where God is, to communicate with the Gods, or to travel to or see whatever heaven went along with their concepts of religion.

Just what the original Edenic tree of life may have been is a good question for pure conjecture, particularly since the Garden of Eden was probably not even located on earth.

Humanlike footprint in strata 125 million years old.
From the Brad and Sherry Steiger collection.

LEGACY OF THE SKY PEOPLE

CHAPTER II

WHERE WAS THE 'GARDEN OF EDEN?'

Where was the Garden of Eden? Scholars have argued the point for centuries and they seem to have made very little progress toward settling the question.

In all likelihood several Gardens of Eden will be found in the process of unraveling the much-collapsed legend as it has become entangled in the histories of a variety of peoples. Stories coming down to us from such very early times have degenerated and have suffered much reinterpretation to fit them into known historical events. Even the names of some of the principal characters have been changed, either in reference or in meaning, or in both. Names of whole peoples are now taken to be names of patriarchal individuals who furnished the patronyms of the tribes they founded. Events involving times and peoples in the very remote past have been brought down in time and associated with different places, and so made to refer to much later occurrences. At first glance, the whole collection of legends would appear to be hopelessly confused. But is it? Not necessarily.

The scribes who attempted to put together the encyclopaedia of history we call the Bible made some progress in their own way and according to their own understanding, toward a sorting out of the old stories. This is particularly noticeable in the book of Genesis.

Unfortunately, later interpreters have stubbornly refused to read that book the way it is compiled, and have insisted upon recombining the stories the early scribes laboured to differentiate.

The result is a religion now flourishing in this world and maintaining that there was only one Cycle of Creation, when anybody capable of reading the first chapters of its Holy Book in any good translation quite literally falls over two.

The elevation, or promotion, by the churches of Jehovah (an individual Jehovah) to the rank of Universal Creator by the simple expedient of transferring his name to a more developed idea of Godhead that finally came along with a better idea of the nature of our Universe itself, has done nothing to help the situation.

In order to make the idea that the Garden of Eden may have been located on another planet seem a little less like a fairy tale and a little more like cold sober, scientific fact, it will be necessary to go back a bit and consider that other somewhat startling idea that Type-II Adam Man's Creator could have made a mistake.

The thought that any being so exalted and knowing that he could animalise the race of human beings successfully, could also err, may be just a little bit hard for some people to swallow at first. It is definitely indicative of wishful thinking to hope and to believe that everybody higher on the so-called 'scale of evolution' is absolutely perfect. This just cannot be true.

So he made his animal man, and at the same time he made his Great Mistake. In the Galactic Code there is no provision for capital punishment. However, banishment, quarantine and other restrictions of personal liberty and, enforcement of obvious duty, are adequately provided for.

When Adam-II man was turned out of the Garden of Eden and forbidden to return, Genesis does not come right out and say that his creator went along with him. This would have been obvious to the writers of the document and to its expected readers,

In the very next chapter, we find that creator still watching over the people he had made, so we learn by inference that he did remain in charge of them. After all, the story of Adam-II man's creation and subsequent tribulations is written from the Adam-II viewpoint, and we must look elsewhere for more definite word of what happened to his creator.

One need not be an esotericist to know the story of how he who would be like God—was 'cast out of Heaven' for his temerity—and all his Host with him. Their destination? The world 'under the Heavens' from the point of view of those who wrote the story: our own planet, Earth. A world 'down' from the point of view of the Solar System, too, i.e. one nearer the Sun.

It is very plainly put in arcane literature that Jehovah was originally a Lord of Mars. He is also a god of battles. It is interesting, too, that both the Greeks and the Romans (to name two peoples) have the same significance attached to Mars and to the Lord, or, as some say, 'god', connected with it. Mars and its Lord are somehow deeply associated with the strife and violence, affecting and afflicting that type of humanity inhabiting the Earth.

As indicated in the previous chapter, in the same way that Elohim is a plural word and means gods, so too, can Jehovah be plural, and it can be used to mean both male and female.

Like many another name in that old document, Genesis, it represents not just one individual, or even four individuals (two male and two female) but refers

LEGACY OF THE SKY PEOPLE

basically to a race of beings or, to use the word most frequently applied: a Host.

Jehovah then is a name adopted quite recently as such things go, to designate the People from Somewhere Else in space who deliberately created, by means of their genetic science, a race of hu-man beings peculiarly adapted to perform certain definite and predetermined functions. In addition to their adapting human life-forms to their own ideas they probably also made special adaptations of plant and animal forms. They achieved all this in an artificial environment prepared in what was, at the beginning of their project, a desert area. The exact location of this place has always puzzled Biblical students. By means of irrigation they turned this land into a veritable garden. It was an enormous agricultural project. In this garden area they placed the new animal hu-man type, specifically (we are told in the Genesis story) to till the ground, care for the vegetation and to guard the area. The Garden of Eden on Mars? There was a time when total concealment of such a wild idea was absolutely necessary. Being burned for heresy is hardly a desirable end. (Neither, come to think of it, is insulin, or electric-shock therapy.) Nevertheless, many writers up to and including Blavatsky and the Chevalier Ramsay managed to mark the trail. Blavatsky scattered hints all through the Secret Doctrine.

Actual conditions and circumstances always precede symbols. Symbols are distilled from disappearing (evaporating) history. If Mars symbolises primitive or initial generative powers for the purpose of human procreation as Blavatsky says (Secret Doctrine, Vol. III. Footnote, p. 55), and if Adam-Jehovah, Brahma and Mars are, in one sense identical (ibid.) as she states, an objective interpretation demands a very close connection with the Garden of Eden.

How does Genesis describe the four rivers that flowed from Eden? The Smith-Goodspeed version reads: There was a river flowing out of Eden, to water the garden, and leaving it divided into four *branches*.

But the King James version reads: And a River went out of Eden, to water the garden; and from thence it was parted, and became four heads.' (Genesis ii. 10.).

The latter version appears to be correct—head is the correctly used word according to the Hebrew original, the definition of Head being: Prime Source. This means that four prime sources flowed in four directions. Nature demonstrates that rivers don't flow this way. But canals do!

If such a canal system as described in Genesis ever existed on this earth, there is no trace nor record of it.

Dr. William F. Albright, the renowned archaeologist who contributed a fifty-page Appendix on recent finds in Bible lands to Young's Analytical Concordance to the Bible, quoted Hebrew, Babylonian and Egyptian sources as having placed

LEGACY OF THE SKY PEOPLE

The Garden of Eden in the Under World. Not underground. Under world.

Well.., if the sun was to the Ancients, as to us, 'above' any neighbouring world outside our orbit might easily be *under*.

And our next-door neighbour on the 'under' side is Mars. And Mars is netted with canals! There is, too, a quotation from an ancient Akkadian poem about the River of the Garden of Eden:

Thou art the River which created everything when the great gods dug thee.

Whoever dug a river? We dig canals.

In the midst of Thee, Ea, King of the *Under World*, built his abode....

From internal evidence in the words of the story about this creation, Adam-II type of man was thoroughly chemical and Earth-animal in a way that made him very different from the original Adam-Galactic Man-created by the Elohim ages before. The words used to describe him, when legitimately and according to accepted usage in such matters, reduced to their numerical forms, reveal the very chemical constituents of his animal flesh. They provide, again close approximations for the atomic weights of these elements, and they reveal, further, that the Host of Jehovah is intimately connected with the Age of Iron, or Kali Yuga, and that the Lord Jehovah is the Administrator (for the planet Earth) of that Age.

This specialised secondary type of humanity created by the Jehovah was made of the dust or very small particles, of the Earth itself, and these particles became a permanent feature of his physiology in a strictly animal way.

This was something new and different and it did not happen until ages after the first type of Mankind was well established.

The time of this accomplishment is referred to as a day apart from and following the other days of creation. It is called 'the day of making Jehovah God's earth and heavens'.

Adam-II was formed on the eighth 'day'. So Adam-II hu-man being was placed in an artificially prepared park or garden, every plant and tree of which was suitable for his food, and all of which he was free to use except for two prohibited varieties. Somehow, this has the earmarks of a commercial venture or at least a situation approaching such an arrangement.

Animal man was put into this garden to keep it and to guard it (to use the original word as it is given to us in the Book of Genesis). Two of the 'trees' or crops were reserved for the owners of the garden, and the death penalty was established for any gardener who diverted them to his own use. (See Genesis ii. 17.)

If such an ordinance seems a little extreme, especially in view of earlier

LEGACY OF THE SKY PEOPLE

remarks that in the Galactic Code there is no provision for capital punishment, it must be realised that this second creation, the gardeners, were a new and untried type of creation about whom nothing much could be known except in theory. In addition, they were probably low-rated by their creators to the level of the animal that went into their physical composition. Animal-man was indeed made 'lower than the angels'.

This is further indicated by the related circumstances that when they became lonely, their creators introduced animal forms at that physical level, apparently in the belief that association with them would relieve their boredom and keep them happy. (Genesis ii. 18-20.)

However, even though Adam-II became friendly enough with all the animals to give them names, he was still dissatisfied.

So the creators 'built' (to translate directly again) the Adam-II woman, using (according to the tale) tissues taken from the already successfully created animal man.

This complicated performance would seem to indicate again that the creator was, in reality, a group or even a race, rather than the individual later scribes credit with the events in question, and that they possessed a very advanced technology capable of some of the miracles, of tissue culture our own scientists are working toward-already with some notable success.

Up to this point in the story, the people of the garden were living in it at an animal level, unclothed and without a culture. They had certain duties to perform, and they reported to the creators of the garden who made periodic tours of inspection.

All this is in the story as we have it in Genesis.

The people who lived outside the confines of the garden were part of the original races of Mankind, and they belonged to the Galactic Race created by the Elohim. These people have been known from time immemorial, as the Serpent People, or People of the Serpent. That the ancient Gods were individuals connected with human history has been ably—but not adequately—pointed out by many scholars.

Outstanding people often assume the proportions of godhood within a few generations after their death. But very little remains to us of the ancient Galactic Religion of the space people.

However, here and there in ancient cultural relics, and here and there in cultural fossils still in use in our own time, there appears the ancient symbol of the serpent, and the concentric figure we call the sun but which, in reality, represents

LEGACY OF THE SKY PEOPLE

much more, including quite another star.

The serpent has been made the symbol of many concepts and ideas, which is the reason for its present great importance. Primarily (for one thing) it is a representation of the two major arms of the spiral galaxy in which we live, and is, therefore, the symbol of Galactic civilisation as well as the sigil* of the Great Creator. At another level, it is a symbol of the waveform of energy. At still another level it is a sperm-symbol and therefore representative of life in bodily form, particularly animal-bodied. It was a seal of the Serpent Kings who are said, by old cultures all round the world, to have come from the sky to establish the beneficent and civilising rule of the Sons of the Sun, or the Sons of Heaven, upon Earth.

These people became curious as to what was going on inside this reservation, and in between visits of its creators they, too, walked in the garden and made a few inspection tours of their own. Very probably the Adam-II men dutifully drove them out whenever they found them intruding, since one of their purposes was to guard the garden.

However, the women fraternised with the trespassers, talked to them, and there was an exchange of information.

It will be recalled that when the second Adam's race (we will call him here Adam-II to distinguish him from Adam-I, originally created by the Elohim) was made, it was for the sole purpose of guarding and tilling the garden. They were not expected to reproduce. For a long time they were on their own; then animals were introduced and finally women (Eve) were made through tissues taken from the male folk. During the whole of their long stay in the agricultural preserve they did not have children. You will find that nowhere in Genesis are they told to reproduce in Eden.

This condition of sterility was accomplished at least in part, by restricting their diet. There were certain things they were not allowed to eat under pain of the death penalty.

When the women broke the general rule of isolation, fraternised with the people from outside the 'garden' (the 'Serpents' or Wise Ones), they learned that the deadly quality was not inherent in the forbidden foodstuffs, but was simply an imposed penalty for disobedience.

So the women, who may well have been in charge of preparing the meals, then as now, served the men the 'forbidden fruit'.

They learned, too, that people wear clothes. Up till this time Adam-II man went about unclad.

Adam-II man has a built-in compulsion to report on events that is still with his descendants, even in our own time. In the beginning this was reinforced by frequent visits from his creators (Jehovah), who talked with him about the affairs of the garden.

Not caring to admit to his creators his nefarious consumption of the forbidden crops, Adam-II began to fail to report in, fearing the death penalty for his transgressions. To make matters worse, when he was finally tracked down in the underbrush he was wearing clothes!

One can almost feel the exasperation of his creators when Adam-II is asked point-blank: 'Who told you you were naked?' This exasperation comes out again when the Lord of the Garden curses the serpent for his interfering ways and prophesies the degradation of the serpent's offspring via, as it turned out, the crossing of his kind with the descendants of the people of the garden. (Genesis vi. 2.)

Upon discovering the defection of his servants, the Jehovah foresaw the action he would take in closing down his agricultural operation. He was furious with the Serpent People for informing his servants of their latent humanity, for opening their eyes to their lowly condition, and for awakening the desire in them to live in a manner considered to be good for hu-man beings and to get out of a condition considered bad for them.

The Jehovah is consistently portrayed in the Biblical descriptions of him as a volatile and somewhat irascible character, with a fairly violent temper and given to drastic measures when aroused.

In the fourteenth verse of the third chapter of Genesis, the Jehovah is found cursing the Serpent People. And since he was not actually the Ultimate Being, the Jehovah's curses did not really cause the Sons of God to crawl on their bellies and eat dust. But the Jehovah's fervent expression of his feelings is indicative of their heat and tenor, and their figurative and symbolic meaning turned out to be fairly accurate. It is remarkable how the warlike Jehovah equates with Zeus and the Olympian Gods of Greek mythology. Zeus, as we saw in the last chapter, overthrew Kronos by force and cunning, and usurped the kingdom of his elder brothers, the Titans. Zeus, too, created a race of mortals and is said to have commanded Prometheus to take red clay from a river bank and mix it with water from the river. These things he did and made men, breathing into them the breath of life. This is the race which Prometheus afterwards befriended, and for whom he stole the forbidden fire out of heaven, whereby they became masters of every art that ministers to life. For this he was punished by Zeus and was chained to a rock. There are many things here that parallel the Garden of Eden story, as related in Genesis. It is strange, too, how many similar legends are to be found in different parts of the world. For example, Francis Huxley, in his book, **Affable Savages**, about the Urubu Indians of Brazil, writes:

LEGACY OF THE SKY PEOPLE

The Urubus believe that vultures are shamans, or medicine-men, and that the man who shoots them will surely die. The easiest way of finding out why the Indians believe this is to look at one of their myths, which tells of Mair and the Vulture. Mair is the culture-hero of the Urubus, who gave them their customs, inaugurated their rites, and told them how to plant manioc and prepare it as food. Strangely enough, however, it was not Mair but the vulture who originally owned fire so Mair had to steal it from him, as Prometheus did from Zeus.

The vulture is the original owner of fire in many mythologies. There are obvious reasons for this: the vulture soars high above the world, and is thus the nearest living creature to the sun....

The Urubus, too, in their legends tell of a time when women neither conceived nor bore children. This links with the time when the Adamic-II race in the Garden of Eden did not reproduce, but were 'built' by Jehovah. Huxley writes:

At the beginning of the world, for instance, women neither conceived nor bore children for Mair could make them by himself: He would ejaculate into an earthenware pot, cover it up, and wait till he heard a scratching noise come from inside the pot; then he would know that the child he had made was fully formed and ready to be taken out. This way of making children, however, being a magical one, was only effective if no one peeked into the pot while the child was being made, so he warned everyone not to interfere. One day, however, a woman passed by Mair's hut, where a great pot was standing, and hearing a scratching noise come from it she became curious, lifted the lid and looked inside. The child immediately died, and after a few days began to smell. When he discovered what had happened, Mair flew into a rage, picked the child up and threw it into the woman's belly. 'That'll teach you to be inquisitive,' he said; 'now you'll have to bear children, and when you do it will hurt.'

So the Jehovah foresaw that his people would mix with the original people created by the Elohim to inhabit the galaxy; he foresaw that there would be a crossing of the two stocks, and in the fifteenth and sixteenth verses of the third chapter of Genesis he makes his predictions according to his vision.

And I will put enmity between thee and the woman, and between thy seed and her seed, it shall bruise thy head, and thou shalt bruise his heel.

Unto the woman he said, I will greatly multiply thy sorrow and thy conception; in sorrow thou shalt bring forth children; and thy desire shall be to thy husband and he shall rule over thee.

The first prophecy concerns a fundamental psychological enmity or difference between the two kinds of people—a difference which still appears in the present inhabitants of the earth, because they represent a cross between the two creations.

LEGACY OF THE SKY PEOPLE

The Son of God in our make-up comes directly from the clear-going, lucid, telepathic and spiritually oriented Galactic peoples created by the Elohim.

The Son of Jehovah's Adam in us comes from the solidly chemical-bodied, earth-oriented and derived domestic animal men the Jehovah created to till and guard his farming enterprise. (And yet, it is to this side of our nature, in a mystical way, that the Final Victory is given—it is what makes our sort of humanity the last which becomes the first, the stone rejected of the builders which is become the head of the corner.)

One portion of our heritage is oriented towards the stars and comes to us from the ancient Galactic civilisation of the Elohim. The other part of our heritage is oriented toward the Earth, toward its ownership, its cultivation, and its protection from all comers. In each and every one of us, because of the crossing of the two stocks, both these tendencies are present and are the prime sources of human conflict, individual and social.

The knowledge of Good and Evil referred to in the Book of Genesis refers to a quantitative evaluation of Consciousness. Total Consciousness would be the same as total agreement with Divinity, or God. Life forms, living organisms, exist in the scale of consciousness between total consciousness, Divinity, and total rejection of consciousness. That is: between the highest form of consciousness and the least active form of matter.

Man, as the most conscious of animal-bodied organisms, possesses both the qualities of Divinity and its opposite. He incorporates in his total structure both highest consciousness and some of the lowest forms of matter.

The act of assuming an Earth-animal body is a deliberate rejection of a certain amount of pure consciousness. The first Adamic Galactic Race of the first creation story did not have Earth-animal bodies. They had, and have bodies that are of a somewhat different structure and function. These bodies are chemical bodies, but they are not animal ones.

So he drove out the man; and he placed at the East of the garden of Eden cherubim and a flaming sword which turned every way, to keep the way of the tree of life.

The two Martian satellites could be said to turn every way. A Russian scientist, Dr. L. Shklovsky, announced in 1959 that the two moons circling Mars are artificial satellites that were put into orbit by a civilisation on the red planet aeons ago. The Russian, writing in Komsomolskaya Pravda, stated that the origin of the moons, named Phobos and Deimos, could not be explained by any method found in nature. Deimos is estimated to be only five miles in diameter and Phobos ten miles. The latter is only 5,800 miles from the planet and takes seven hours thirty-nine minutes to go round it. Deimos is 14,600 miles up, in an orbit lasting one day, six hours and eighteen minutes.

They differed from the satellites of other planets, according to Dr. Shklovsky, by their insignificant size and their extreme closeness to their planet. Phobos, moreover, had shown another striking dissimilarity from all other natural satellites in the solar system. In the last few decades it had deviated from its calculated orbit by two and a half degrees and speeded up its movement. This meant that it had come closer to the surface of Mars.

Jonathan Swift knew about these Martian satellites. In Gullivers Travels, published in 1726, he described their sizes, distance from Mars and periods of rotation, almost exactly as finally observed and recorded by Asaph Hall at the United States Naval Observatory 175 years later.

If in truth Phobos and Deimos constitute the cherubim that 'turn every way' and guard the gateway, having been placed East presents no problem, if it is remembered that the term was synonymous to the ancients (and still is to many peoples) with sunward. The cherubim were placed 'toward the sun', that is, in the sky. And, don't our scientists hope to create a manned Earth-satellite which will 'guard the way' for us?

There is no Garden of Eden in the first creation story. Earth-animal man was not created in the Garden of Eden either. He was created elsewhere and placed in the garden, and after his expulsion he was taken back to the place whence he was taken. (Genesis iii. 23.)

Those human entities who accepted the Earth-animal bodies placed in Eden's garden rejected some of the consciousness of life that is proper to mankind, and started themselves on the downward spiral of degeneracy that finally resulted in the Deluge.

Now as a mixed race (after crossing back to the original stock) they are in process of working their way back to total consciousness, through the Cross (which is a genetic cross). This is the doctrine of Salvation or salvage, of those entities who became Earth-animal mankind.

This mingling of the two types of people is the original genetic meaning of the Cross, and through interpretation and reinterpretation we have the Cross as a symbol of generation. On the evolutionary side, this same set of circumstances furnishes us with the spiritual interpretations of that same symbol, and the progress of Cross Man's regeneration can be traced through history in the changing forms of the Cross as it appears in succeeding millennia.

So the Great Experiment failed, the garden was shut down, and its people

LEGACY OF THE SKY PEOPLE

were turned out to fend for themselves, which was not at all easy for them after their comfortable life in a prepared environment. In the garden they had been completely protected from all predatory and annoying forms of animal life. By contrast, they found the Earth a most inhospitable place.

And yet they did not die. Instead, they multiplied and with them multiplied the problems they posed for their creators, the Jehovah.

Their descendants attempted to follow an agricultural way of life based on the original experiences of their kind in the garden, which came to be looked upon as a kind of paradise, as indeed, it truly must have been. It was God (not Jehovah, but the Elohim) who stepped in and commanded Noah to make the Ark. The flood story, again, is pieced together out of two tales, the piecing showing up in Bibles by the alternate use of God and Lord; Elohim and Jehovah. We have already quoted sources that tell us Jehovah was originally a Lord of Mars. Madame Blavatsky, for one, informs us that Jehovah equates with Noah, and we find other references to Jehovah-Noah. How can this be? Working back through the levels of association that have been piled up on the Noah story is like reading a history of mankind in reverse. Everywhere it is found (and it is found in some form literally everywhere there are Adam-II people) it has been brought down in time whenever some major catastrophe has struck any particular nation or group.

So to begin with, we find it in a variety of forms, depending pretty thoroughly on what has been the history of the people we happen to be listening to at the moment. It would take a strong plot with a solid foundation in some cataclysmic fact to survive all this emendation and addition of detail without becoming lost or distorted beyond recognition.

Only one other plot has stood up so well in all the course of history, and that is the related story of a divine being who is 'made of flesh', and who ultimately is taken up from earth and returns to his rightful home in the sky. This one has survived, too, because it is both the whole story of our humanity, in general, and of one member of it, in particular.

These two plots have maintained their basic characteristics, no matter how they have been dressed up, or by whom, or who has tried to interpret all the history out of them. They have survived because they represent the essential history of Earth-animal mankind, and his essential destiny.

When the last remnant of Atlantis went down to destruction, the Noah story was moved along in time to cover the consequences. When the great gate between the Pillars of Hercules was broken and the below-sea-level Mediterranean Valley was swamped, the survivors told the story of Noah over again, with new, and for them personal and immediate meaning. When the Tigris-Euphrates Valley was disastrously flooded, a local Noah made his escape in traditional fashion. And we can discover still other Noahs attached to other civilisations—always the same plot but with different and localised characters.

The mere fact that floods do occur, and people do survive them, is not nearly enough to keep such a main plot intact for such a very long time. Actually, so much repetition would produce boredom unless there was some memory of a similar but vastly more important and significant event to maintain an inner substance and continuing interest. The fact that the main plot has survived all these subsequent disasters is a strong indication of its great antiquity as well as its more universal importance.

Who was the first of these saviours of Earth-animal man and beast?

Esoteric sources inform us that it was Jehovah, the same Jehovah that was responsible for his creation. Blavatsky wrote it down in so many words.

The Ark, in spite of its description handed down to us by a people of later generations in terms they understood, was a spaceship. The people mentioned in the Bible as its passengers were real enough, but their names also covered social entities, as well as the Patriarchal individuals themselves, that is, they were tribes or groups. Just as there are two creation stories in the Bible, so there are two stories of Noah and the Deluge. We find several types of crossbred humanity being loaded aboard a spaceship, along with breeding stock of the Earth-animal forms that had been in the garden (put there, according to the story, by the Jehovah to comfort, accompany and entertain the animal-man—not all the animals of Earth, but certain species which still have great significance for mankind here).

So the original story of Noah and the Ark is that of Jehovah saving the portion of his humanity he brought to the planet Earth with him after his temporary expulsion from his place in heaven, which was Mars. For in truth, the flood of the First Noah took place on Mars. The garden was located in the Northern Hemisphere not far from the polar regions. The polar cap probably melted quickly instead of slowly. The waters rushed down into the conduits and drowned all the original Adam-II people there. Seen from space, the Earth has a rainbow halo around it. Furthermore, the meteorological rainbow is a phenomenon never observed on Mars, and its appearance in the skies of Earth left a permanent impression of wonder in the hearts of the Jehovah's people, as they approached the adopted planet in their spaceship, Ark number one.

CHAPTER III
ENTER CROSS MAN

If further proof is still needed of two creations, it is interesting to compare the genealogy, as given in two separate chapters of Genesis, of the two lines- Adam-I Galactic Man, created by the Elohim, and Adam-II Earth-animal Man, the Jehovah creation.

(Genesis Ch. v.)	(Genesis Ch. iv.)
ELOHIM LINE	JEHOVAH LINE
Adam (I)	Chemical Earth-animal
Seth	Secondary creation
Enos	Adam (II)
Cainan	Cain
Mahalaleel	Enoch
Jared	Irad
Enoch	Mehujael
Methusaleh	Methusael

Lamech

Noah

Shem Ham Japeth

The Elohim line condenses the long, long story told by Blavatsky and outlines in the Stanzas upon which she bases her Secret Doctrine. The Jehovah line tells a much shorter tale that began not more than probably 100,000 years ago.

Blavatsky's long count has to do with the evolution and development of Galactic Man. The Genesis story tells of the manufacture and history of chemical Earth-animal Man—the first successful introduction of Man into the chemical level of the Universe.

LEGACY OF THE SKY PEOPLE

Blavatsky's Stanzas and Commentaries refer to the origins and history of Galactic Man—the Grand Cycle. Her Lemuria was the cradle of Mankind on this planet and goes back to a period, millions of years ago. It is said that the old Lemurian giants were physical, but not chemical-animal in the same way that Jehovah's 'Adam' was. Perfectly capable of manipulating chemical matter and apparently fond of doing so—including creating half-animal 'tribes' which were not men, because they lacked the self-determining spark of mind. The self-identifying entity was not in evidence.

Perhaps the Jehovah set out to do something similar, but Adam II turned human to the consternation of everyone involved.

Both the Elohim and Jehovah lines meet with Lamech. That is where Cross-Man begins-the fusing of the Serpent People and Jehovah's animal-man creation—as prophesied, when the Lord God addressed the Serpent in the Garden of Eden.

The tragedy for the hu-man race on Earth in the doctrine of Original Sin as it is taught by churches is this: they insist it is a moral stigma somehow transmitted from Jehovah's Adam and inherited by his children. And they put the black label on the very quality that made him truly and alarmingly like Man in the eyes of the Jehovah—his insistence upon his own self-determinism!

And the Lord God said, Behold, *the man is become as one of us,** to know good and evil: and now lest he put forth his hand, and take also of the tree of life, and eat, and live for ever.

—Genesis iii. 22.

That the Jehovah did not believe chemical man capable, outside the environment prepared for him, of surmounting the difficulties natural to the possession of Earth-animal flesh, is apparent in the final statement in Genesis iii. 22 ... and now, lest he put forth his hand, and take also of the tree of life, and eat, and *live for ever*.

So, verse 23 follows on: 'Therefore the Lord God sent him forth from the Garden of Eden, to till the ground from whence he was taken.'

When Cross-Man arrived on Earth from Mars he began to multiply fast and form tribes.

And it came to pass, when men began to multiply on the face of the earth, and daughters were born unto them.

—Genesis vi. 1.

And the prophecy of Jehovah in the Garden of Eden to the Serpent concerning the fusing of their two peoples was now taking effect.

LEGACY OF THE SKY PEOPLE

That the sons of God saw the daughters of men that they were fair; and they took them wives of all which they chose.

—Genesis vi. 2.

When the Jehovah and his arkload of Crossbreed men (mostly Adam-II dominant) arrived on Earth, the Atlantean age began. It is not the purpose of this book to embark upon an extensive study of the possible reality or not of Atlantis. There is a bibliography in existence, numbering some thousands of books about that continent. As Ignatius Donnelly wrote in his very interesting work, **Atlantis**:

The fact that the story of Atlantis was for thousands of years regarded as a fable proves nothing. There is an unbelief which grows out of ignorance, as well as a scepticism which is born of intelligence. The people nearest to the past are not always those who are best informed concerning the past.

For a thousand years it was believed that the legends of the buried cities of Pompeii and Herculaneum were myths: they were spoken of as 'the fabulous cities'. For a thousand years the educated world did not credit the accounts given by Herodotus of the wonders of the ancient civilisations of the Nile and Chaldea. He was called 'the father of liars'. Even Plutarch sneered at him. Now in the language of Frederick Schlegel: 'the deeper and more comprehensive the researches of the moderns have been, the more their regard and esteem for Herodotus has increased.'

Suffice it to say that the similarity of language on both sides of the Atlantic and of ethnological types, the similarity too, of religious beliefs (sun worship), and the discovery also of pyramids, on both sides of the ocean, all indicate one common heritage and point of origin. The evidence, too, of deep sea soundings on the bed of the Atlantic, made some years ago by British and American naval ships, the result of which showed that an enormous ridge of great elevation exists in the middle of the ocean, is significant. This stretches from near the coast of South America to Ascension Island, while the Azores form the peaks of this land still above water. This ridge is covered with volcanic debris.

Finally, there is Plato's testimony. This is on record and available to anyone who cares to read it. Plato lived 400 years before Jesus, the Christ. In Plato's Dialogues he describes how his ancestor, Solon, the great law-giver, visited Egypt. There, he was given by the wise men-priests of Sais a lengthy history and description of Atlantis, including an account of its final destruction. All of this Plato put down in his Dialogues.

The first king of Atlantis is said to have been Poseidon, one of the Greek Olympian Gods. We have already seen how the Olympian Gods equate with Jehovah (plural). So, in short, Poseidon was one of the Jehovah.

LEGACY OF THE SKY PEOPLE

According to Plato's account, Poseidon was eventually succeeded by his eldest son, Atlas. It was after him that Atlantis received its name and, subsequently, the Atlantic Ocean also.

One confirmation of the truth of Plato's story is offered by Donnelly. He says that upon the Azores black lava rocks, and rock, red and white in colour, are now found. Plato wrote that the Atlanteans built with white, red and black stone. Plato also stated, according to Donnelly, that the plain of Atlantis 'had been cultivated during many ages by many generations of kings'.

The Atlantean culture on Earth was, indeed, an attempt by Cross-Man to re-establish the traditional agriculture paradise from which his Adam-II ancestors had been expelled. It was at first a beautiful place—the Garden of the Hesperides—the Islands of the Blessed—the Elysian Fields. These were all nothing but other names for this wonderful empire, ruled by godlike beings. From other peoples who arrived on Earth—the Serpent Race—Cross-Man received a great deal of technological information.

There is no doubt at all that the power and influence of Atlantis spread right across the world from South America to the shores of Egypt. Incidentally, Braghine in *The Shadow of Atlantis* writes that the myth of Atlas, a giant supporting the whole universe on his shoulders, was probably a symbol of the tremendous political and spiritual power of the Atlanteans.

The long struggle back to Galactic status was begun in earnest in Atlantean times. Cross-Man had been expelled from the original Garden and was now in quarantine.

The Jehovah responsible for the creation of Adam-II Man was given charge of that race until it should be perfected, made ready and acceptable to join with its 'higher kin', Galactic Man.

The time will eventually come when Jehovah and his Hosts will be set free from their responsibilities to their animal-man creation. As more and more Cross-men reach Galactic manhood, so Jehovah's day of freedom draws nearer. The Age of Darkness will come to an end, and the Age of Light and Christ will be inaugurated with a new heaven and a new earth.

One of the most well-known people in the Bible, and yet, with only a few lines in Genesis to record his entrance and exit from Earth's stage, is Enoch.

You can find his autobiography in Genesis v. verses 18-24.

And Jared lived an hundred and sixty and two years, and he begat Enoch:

And Jared lived after he begat Enoch eight hundred years, and begat sons

LEGACY OF THE SKY PEOPLE

and daughters:

And all the days of Jared were nine hundred sixty and two years: and he died.

And Enoch lived sixty and five years, and begat Methuselah:

And Enoch walked with God after he begat Methuselah three hundred years, and begat sons and daughters:

And all the days of Enoch were three hundred sixty and five years:

And Enoch walked with God: and he *was* not; for God took him.

However, a great many people may now be aware that there is a work about Enoch which is possibly the most important apocalyptic manuscript extant, apart from those in the Bible. This is the Book of Enoch. It exists only in the Ethiopian version which was translated from the Greek one, of which only a little remains. According to the Rev. W. O. E. Oesterley, D.D., in an Introduction to the English translation by R. H. Charles, D. Litt., D.D., the book was originally written in Hebrew or Aramaic.

In this remarkable book Enoch, who is described as 'a righteous man, whose eyes were opened by God', tells how the Sons of God took wives from among the daughters of men. How the women bore great giants who eventually turned against mankind and how these bestial men began to sin against birds and beasts, and to eat one another's flesh.

There were giants in the earth in those days; and also after that, when the Sons of God came in unto the daughters of men, and they bare children to them, the same became mighty men which were of old, men of renown.

And God saw that the wickedness of man was great in the earth and that every imagination of the thoughts of his heart was only evil continually.

—Genesis vi. 4-5.

Consequently, according to the Book of Enoch, Noah was told to 'Hide thyself!' and it was revealed to him that the end was approaching and he was instructed how to escape so that his seed might be preserved for the future of the world.

There are many remarkable things in the Book of Enoch, but outstanding are at least two occasions on which Enoch is carried off in a whirlwind. On these journeys he was accompanied by an angel who showed him many things. You will hear this word whirlwind again being used as some kind of vehicle, when we come to discuss Elijah, who lived at a later period in Biblical history. He, too, was taken up in a whirlwind. This seems a more intelligent way of describing the space-

LEGACY OF THE SKY PEOPLE

ships seen in our skies that we call today flying saucers.

Enoch was Noah-II's grandfather and quite obviously saw that the future of Atlantis was not a happy one. Atlantis had known past glories and had a wonderful history, but the future pattern was strongly set on the wrong lines. The Empire of the Sun had taken the left-hand path.

If you look into Genesis, nowhere will you find that the second Adam was told to 'fill the earth and subdue it' as was the first Adamic type. Adam-II, it cannot be repeated too often, was created to till the ground of the garden in the East of Eden (where he was put, after his creation), and to guard that garden. He was made to be a servant of the Jehovah, to work for them and to do their bidding ,according to their commands'.

It was never intended that the Adam-II type should ever, under any circumstances, increase its numbers and influence to the point where this type of humanity could take over control. And yet, in the course of time, this is what happened. It resulted in the near destruction of all human life of his type (to say nothing of certain forms of animal and vegetable life, which also suffered). It resulted in such disruption of atmospheric conditions as to change the entire climate of the globe, removing the perpetual thin overcast, and creating the present conditions of thin atmosphere and extensive desert regions.

This catastrophic result has come down to various remnants of mankind, much mixed with later tragedies, as the story of a Great Deluge. The deluge was only part of the story, but it was the side effect that left the deepest impression.

We have earlier shown that Noah is the same person or people as Jehovah, but going under another name at the point in the story where he appears, because he is performing another function. This change of name accompanying a change of function is not at all uncommon in esoteric literature.

The tradition of the population of the world by Noah is a part of the same tradition as the second story of Genesis. Every civilised culture on Earth has its own version of this same tradition.

The Noah story has been brought down in time and made to refer to Atlantis, the Atlantic Continent, because the two events were similar in certain respects. This, however, is a secondary interpretation for which the survivors of the destruction of Atlantis were responsible.

They brought with them from Mars the original story as a part of their native and traditional culture, but their descendants referred it to the country of their immediate ancestors, having lost the original reference during a period of semi-barbarism and reconstruction following the Atlantean catastrophe.

LEGACY OF THE SKY PEOPLE

Very ancient traditions are often moved forward in this way, and come to refer to much later historical events. This actually fosters the survival of the original plot by keeping an aura of history around it. Stories that are too old are all too easily passed off as myth and legend.

Sometimes this transference in time is arranged deliberately upon the occasion, for instance, of the establishment of a newer form of religion, or upon the adoption by a people of another religion to supplant the one to which the peoples have become accustomed.

Such a collapsing of events is evident in religious interpretations of the Book of Genesis in our own time, when it is assumed by most people that both stories of the Creation refer to the same series of events.

So the original story of the deluge and Noah is the story of an attempt by the products of their creation that had crossed with Galactic Man and become, as the saying goes, corrupt.

This old story then has been grafted upon other, later stories, notably the destruction of the Atlantean continent here on earth.

This grafting is further complicated by the circumstances that the Atlantic continent went down in a series of cataclysms, widely spaced, and terminating rather recently with the sinking of the last major island about 11,000 years ago. (Date given by Plato.) The main part of the continent went down probably about 25,000 years ago. This was the big holocaust.

What caused Atlantis to go wrong? It could be that two factions arose: those who wished to maintain the earlier goal of an Edenic agricultural civilisation, ruled over and controlled by a privileged few, and those who thought the way of progress lay toward the development of technology and the general elevation of all people.

In time, this difference may have led to bloodshed. The two factions probably found themselves engaged in a full-scale struggle for domination of the planet, which very likely took the following course.

The feudal-agriculturists held that since, traditionally, man had been assigned to till and guard a garden, the possession of technical information and the development of a technical culture was wrong for him. Like most tradition-bound people, they did not take into consideration the fact that the original agricultural experiment had not only been closed down and abandoned, but that the creators of Adam-II man did not look with favour upon any group that attempted to re-establish it. (See the story of the sacrifices of Cain and Abel, and the reaction of the Creators to them.)

The technologists, on the other hand, were willing and ready to receive any information from the other types of mankind who had either come or had been brought to the Earth. So, by the time of the Great War between these two factions in Atlantis, Cross-Man was capable of space-travel within the solar system, and all the other technological achievements that go along with it—including probably nuclear activity.

As a result of the forces employed in this Great War, much of the moisture in suspension in the atmosphere of Earth was condensed and fell down in torrents. The climate of the whole planet was drastically changed. The long winter set in—even the poles shifted. Great quantities of ice formed round the new poles almost overnight, and tremendous storms raged across the world for years.

It is interesting to note that other religions and races have their own Noahs which tell very similar stories. Colonel Braghine, in *The Shadow of Atlantis*, writing about the Makusi, a tribe of the Arowak Indians, stated they 'affirm that after the deluge there remained only one man, but he transformed stones into men and populated the earth once more'.

This myth resembles the Greek one concerning Deucalion and Pyrrha. As many are aware, Greek mythology has its version. Complaints were made to Zeus against the abominable ways of the Bronze Men. Zeus decided to see for himself and accompanied by another god, Hermes, set out to seek hospitality among mortals.

The two gods came down into Arcadia (Atlantis) and found no one would receive them. They saw much evildoing and wickedness. Zeus, at length said: 'We have seen enough, son of Maia. Behold these Bronze folk have filled the earth with deceit and violence and there is not one righteous man among them. Let us go hence, and I will send a great rain, such as hath not been seen since the making of the world, and the whole race of men shall be destroyed by flood, for I am weary of their iniquity'.

However, Hermes prevailed upon Zeus to stay one more day, and that night they arrived at the house of an old man called Deucalion and his wife Pyrrha. They were childless and getting on in years. Although Deucalion had no riches he received them in a most friendly and courteous way, and gave his visitors the best he could provide. They stayed with their host that night and were greatly impressed with his spiritual outlook and his understanding. The next day the two travellers revealed themselves in their true likeness.

Zeus made known his plan to destroy the wicked race of Bronze Men. He commanded Deucalion to build the Ark and to stock it with victuals and to enter it with his wife to escape the flood waters. His neighbours asked him what he was doing and upon being told, they mocked him and went their way. On the seventh

LEGACY OF THE SKY PEOPLE

day Deucalion entered the Ark and it rained forty days and forty nights. The waters rose and covered the earth and all the Bronze people were lost in the flood.

When Deucalion and Pyrrha saw the waters ebbing they gave thanks and were advised by Themis, the prophetess, to take and cast behind the bones of 'your Great Mother'. They thereupon gathered numerous stones which they flung over their shoulders. Those that Deucalion threw became men and those that Pyrrha threw became women. In this way a new race of mortals came into being, from whom all those in every nation today are descendants. Of course, this stone throwing act is symbolical, but it could mean that the Sky People, having saved the tribe of Noah (Deucalion), brought them back to earth again. I do not ask you to believe for one moment that the sole survivors of an empire like Atlantis with such an advanced state of technology were floating about in the raging torrents in a wooden ship for forty days and nights. Indeed, W. Scott-Elliot in his book, **The Story of Atlantis and the Lost Lemuria**, goes so far as to describe Atlantean airboats and their methods of propulsion.

No, it is much more likely that Zeus (Jehovah) commanded Noah and company to take off in a spaceship and that when the Earth was once more in a reasonable state of habitation they were brought back again to Ararat (according to the Bible).

The throwing of stones over the shoulder by Deucalion and Pyrrha seems a delightful way of wrapping up the fact that the Serpent People once again gave a helping hand with the repopulating of the Earth. For the next thing we hear from Greek mythology is that as a result of Deucalion and Pyrrha's excellent stone throwing, the Earth is populated with The Heroes—half-divine, half-mortal—wondrous beings! C. Kerenyi, in **The Gods of the Greeks**, describes them like this:

At first they were equal to the Golden Race. Too brief, alas, was their glorious prime; those days when mortal men were as gods for strength and valour, and women so fair that gods were their lovers; when our Earth was still a faery place, and its green loveliness haunted by shapes divine; this was the Age of Heroes, which closed with the Siege of Troy, the sons of those who fought in that long war saw the beginnings of a new age, fitly named 'The Iron', full of all iniquities and oppressions that are done under the sun. . . .

It was at this time that many of the Serpent People came down and walked with men. They gave much wisdom to mortals. Indeed, many of them reigned as kings. The one most worshipped, certainly throughout ancient Egypt, was Osiris.

In his book, Stories of Egyptian Gods and Heroes, F. H. Brooksbank writes:

One evening in early summer, as the westering sun hung over the hills, a man halted under a sycamore tree near a temple at Thebes. He was of enormous stature and he seemed more than mortal.

By his side stood a woman, the most beautiful and graceful on whom the sun had ever risen.

'Let us tarry here and rest,' said the man and, spreading his mantle over a slab of stone, they sat down; when he took from his cloak a reed and began to blow upon it. As the last sweet strains died away, a venerable old man came slowly toward the two wayfarers.

'A pleasant evening to you both,' he said, a mixture of awe and wonder plainly written on his face.

'And to thee, O my father,' said the man. 'Where in this City may we find lodgings for a time? We are travellers, and would fain stay here to rest awhile.'

The newcomer, after gazing at them for some time, bowed his head to the ground and kissed the sandal, first of the man, then of the woman. Thereon, looking up he spoke:

'I am the priest of this temple and in my study of the stars I have learned somewhat of the mysteries of the heavens.

'Long have I known of your coming but never did I think that I should be the first to greet you here on earth.'

And with worshiping eyes again the holy man gazed on the wondrous pair. 'Will my lord and lady deign to accept such hospitality as my poor house can offer?' he asked.

'It is because thou has been so faithful in thy service that we came to thee first.' replied the man. 'We thank thee, and accept thy kindness but I charge thee straitly to tell no man what thou knowest, whence we came or why. That shall be known as the gods will.

'Now lead us to thy house,' said Osiris, 'for the hour groweth late.'

And in this wise did Osiris and Isis his consort come to the land of Egypt.

Osiris and Isis went among the people, who gazed at them in awe and amazement, never had they seen such a wondrous pair. Brooksbank went on:

Instinctively they felt that the strangers were not of earth, and every mark of respect was shown them by the simple folk.

Numerous were the enquiries at the house of the priest concerning the guests, but the priest kept his own counsel; the mystery of their arrival only added to the awe in which the people held them. Day by day Osiris and Isis went among the people, advising, helping, cheering. Wherever they were most needed there

LEGACY OF THE SKY PEOPLE

they always seemed to be.

Osiris went out and taught the people in the fields. He told them that there was a Supreme Being watching over them who supplied them with everything and that behind all the gods was one sustaining Spirit and Creator. The people had never been taught such things before.

When the king died, the people beseeched Osiris to rule in his place. At first he refused, but seeing they had no suitable candidate to take over the kingdom, he eventually agreed.

Osiris and Isis ruled over the land of Egypt for a long time. One of the original divine Pharaohs of Egypt, Osiris's reign was notable, not for hatred or force of any kind, but on the contrary his influence spread far outside Egypt and was of a gentle and peaceful nature. He abolished cannibalism. Osiris was, indeed, the enemy of all violence and it was by gentleness alone that he overcame country after country.

He is said to have been handsome, dark and taller than other men. He built the first temples. He laid down the rules concerning religious practice, built towns and made just laws. When Osiris and Isis left the earth plane, they were worshipped as Gods. They were undoubtedly Godlike Beings, but nonetheless, were probably Galactic personages of a very high calibre who came to Earth after the critical period of the Deluge to help Cross-Man a step or two farther on in his march to the stars. These Sky Kings who ruled over certain areas of the Earth—Divine rulers—gave rise subsequently to the doctrine of the divine right of Kings. They were the Serpent People who have always had compassion and love for humanity, and as a result brought them light and knowledge, even in the days when humanity were little more than helpless animals in the Garden of Eden.

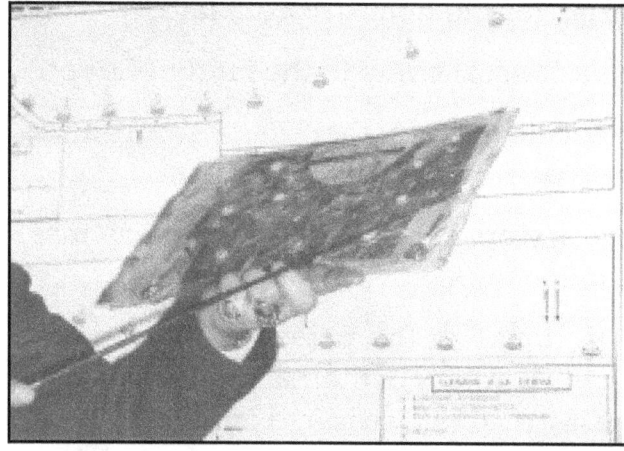

Dr. Javier Carbrera Daruera explains this ancient healing collar with gems in accupressure points from an exact diagram followed by ancient Peruvian surgeons. This particular treatment involved a sophisticated "female surgery" —similar to Ovarian or Uterine surgery in recent times.

The chart behind him illustrates the electromagnetic properties of the Nazca lines utilizied by ancient astronauts in the process of landing and take-off of their scout craft.

From the photo collection of Brad and Sherry Steiger.

LEGACY OF THE SKY PEOPLE

CHAPTER IV
QUARANTINE

The story told by some people of the attempt to return to 'heaven' or the sky by Cross-Man, in which it is said that arrows were shot, which returned bloodied, is a corruption of the original historical attempt. An inspection of the genealogical tables as given in Genesis x. shows that it was Nimrod, son of Ham, son of Noah, who built the city of Babel. Attributed to him (actually the peoples of Nimrod) also is the building of Erech, Accad and Calneh, also in the land of Shinar.

The 'son' of Nimrod built Ninevah, Rehoboth, Calah and Resen.

This group of cities formed the centre of what there was of civilisation at that time on this planet. This civilisation is not to be despised or looked upon as being primitive in the sense of its lacking culture or technology. It is an increasingly puzzling circumstance—to archaeologists—that the farther back in time the digs in this area go, the more advanced the earlier cultures are found to have been.

This has led to much dispute in archaeological circles over dating these finds. Reputations are at stake, but the facts remain. The deeper they dig, the more civilised the culture turns out to have been.

This is logical, if it is remembered that the founding culture, that of Noah-I's people, was connected with and brought to the Earth by a civilisation that possessed (and still possesses) sufficient technology to build space ships-and heaven only knows what else.

The knowledge of Galactic culture was still historical at the time the people of the Land of Shinar decided to get together and reach heaven, lest they be scattered abroad in the Earth. These Cross-People tried to return to the place to which they had grown accustomed, to the only home they had ever known. They attempted to build a tower to reach heaven.

Different stories of this endeavour differ in detail, but they all agree that the main objective was to get up in the sky away from the Earth which was to them a

LEGACY OF THE SKY PEOPLE

tremendous, inhospitable and unfamiliar planet. What happened to this attempt is told in Genesis xi. 5-9. It is told differently in other writings, but the sense is always the same: Somebody (or Some People) up There put a stop to the project and said:

Let us go down, and there confound their language, that they may not understand one another's speech. So the Lord scattered them abroad from thence upon the face of the earth; and they left off to build the city.

The long period of quarantine and regeneration in which the Earth still finds itself had begun in earnest! The story of Cross-Man's determination and subsequent failure due to preventive measures taken by people (or gods) from the sky remains in the mythology or religious history of many of the nations who were scattered abroad in the Earth as their ancestors feared they would be.

The story of the arrows is a kind of half-memory, distorted by much time and many tellings, that Nimrod—builder of Babel—was a 'mighty hunter'. The peoples telling the story hunted with bow and arrow—they knew no other means by the time the tale had to be explained to rising generations, so of course, Nimrod hunted with arrows too. Understanding is an appreciation of similarities. If no similarities actually exist, they are supplied. That which is to be understood is made to be like the understander and he is satisfied. This is a well-known phenomenon in the development of history, myth and folklore, and it accounts for some of the apparent discrepancies in the embroidery around the old historical plots handed down from remote times.

If men from Earth ever get into spaceships and go off through the solar system and the Universe in search of other hu-man beings like themselves—hu-man beings with the same physical constitution—they will be doomed to disappointment, wherever they go.

Physical man, as we know him, exists only here on Earth. His physical body was originated out of the elements of the Earth, and while he does not belong, strictly, to Earth's animal kingdom, the Earth is the only place he can be found living naturally and in any numbers.

We are speaking here of hu-man kind, with a dense physical body, which, once it is assumed, is not disconnected completely from his consciousness until that body wears out, is destroyed accidentally, or perishes from some other cause. That is, the Earth-man's physical body is an organism composed of living cells which closely resemble the living cells of Earth's other vegetable-animal organisms.

It is this type of Man who belongs to Earth in a very distinct way—and this is a condition that is not duplicated anywhere else.

LEGACY OF THE SKY PEOPLE

Physical Earth man is unique.

He is unique because he was deliberately made—created—as he is. He is an artificial creation. He did not evolve from any other animal form-although some animal forms did devolve from him.

The form of his body is hu-man. There are other races of Man spread throughout the Galaxy. But these other races are not 'physical' in the same sense that human is physical. Their bodies are not composed of cells that originated on the Earth. Yet, when Earth man was made, his creation duplicated their kind of bodies—but used earth-cells and earth elements in their construction.

So, while Earth man resembles Galactic Man in form, his body functions are like that of an Earth animal—he is a secondary type of mankind.

Greek mythology offers a parallel to the Tower of Babel saga which seems remarkably similar, although the story differs in some respects. Colonel Barghine relates it in ***The Shadow of Atlantis***, writing of the highly developed Minoan culture of long ago.

Besides magnificent frescoes and majestic ruins, we have inherited some myths of the Cretan primeval population, one of which tells us about Icarus, who built a flying apparatus in order to reach the resplendent Phoebus, i.e. the sun. But Icarus committed a fatal mistake: he consolidated the parts of his apparatus with wax. Therefore, when he had ascended to a considerable height the angry God melted the wax by his mighty beams, the wing of the apparatus became detached, and Icarus, like Humpty-Dumpty, fell down and was smashed to pieces. May we not see in this tale a reminiscence of some prehistoric attempt at aviation.

Braghine's reference to Humpty-Dumpty started a train of thought. It is generally accepted that many nursery rhymes today have origins which go far back in history, based on real happenings of long ago. They usually contain a moral for succeeding generations and the fairy story embroidery, like in mythology, ensures that the event is handed down from century to century.

What both the story of the Tower of Babel, as related in Genesis, and the Icarus legend seem to indicate is that Cross-Man had initiated an ambitious Space Programme to endeavour to get up into the heavens. This was looked upon with disfavour by the gods, probably because Cross-Man was very much Adam-II animal dominant at that time and consequently, in quarantine. Today, Earth man is once again attempting to leave the confines of this planet and return to his original home in the skies. It remains to be seen whether he will be allowed out of quarantine. Have Earth men given up animal tendencies? Is their make-up now Galactic-dominant? Do they qualify to be accepted as fellow citizens of the galaxy by their brothers (to be strictly accurate, cousins) Galactic Men? How long ago were the horrors of Belsen, and the atom bombing of Hiroshima?

LEGACY OF THE SKY PEOPLE

Nevertheless, a growing number of Cross-Men in this world today are definitely Galactic dominant and many more are tending to move in that direction. They are the wayshowers. While there was one wayshower, there was hope for Cross-Man. Today, there are thousands and thousands of Galactic dominant people. Yes, there is certainly hope for humanity. One day we will all get back to our home among the stars. It may take some of us many lives to accomplish this, but it can be done in the span of one lifetime.

The Earth is still in a period of quarantine and regeneration, but the time is fast approaching when some of its inhabitants will be sorted out and will find themselves transferred to a 'new earth' in a 'new heaven'. This is a part of the prophecy, a part of the promise. The man of (on) the (genetic) cross will not always be 'buried' here on the Earth. He will eventually join his cousins, the sons (seed, descendants) of Galactic Man, who are called the Sons of God (Elohim, plural) as Earth's man is called the Son of Man.

It is the ultimate destiny of Cross-Man to carry the light of the Christ Consciousness throughout the Galaxy-however hard to believe that may be just now!

There must be understanding of what the cross (genetic) means to each and every one of us in this way, no matter what or how many other valid interpretations and significances we may have applied to it. Each of us and all of us must discover the true cross. This means that we must find out all the truth about the cross, which is not just a couple of dry sticks, or two lines drawn on a piece of paper, but the actual balance of our own physical—and, of course, spiritual—inheritance.

This inheritance consists of our heritage from the Sons of God-Galactic Mankind—the vertical descending-ascending line, and our heritage from Adam-II animal man—the shorter, horizontal, inhibiting line, which is at once penetrated and raised up by the more powerful and significant vertical. Occasionally, in writings and in communications we get hints that once we have eliminated the remains of our Adam-II inheritance, we will have something those Elohim cousins do not possess. This will be a particular strength of character, developed through lives of contending with what Shakespeare called so aptly the 'too, too solid flesh'. This characteristic they admire in Earth dwelling hu-mankind, and it will constitute a part of the contribution we can make to Galactic culture when Earth humanity joins the federation of the stars. Another point. Being acceptable is not entirely a matter of being worthy in the usual sense of the word, although a well-developed sense of ethics is naturally required. It is not so much a matter of goodness and badness (certainly it is not a matter of enforced goodness) as it is a matter of education—of our reaching a level of understanding where we can cope with the differences, the wider scale and range of development, the broader views and

LEGACY OF THE SKY PEOPLE

different frames of reference we would encounter.

This is one reason understanding is such an important word in the present drive to bring new ideas out into the open here on Earth. Knowledge can unlock understanding, but like any other key it must be the right one. That is, the right knowledge and, it must be applied to the problem in hand (the lock that is opposing our progress). No key ever unlocked anything while it was still hanging on a nail in the woodshed.

In short, give a person true and complete understanding, and he no longer needs to be supervised, watched over or restricted. He will be ethical. He will be constructive. He will be friendly.

Knowledge alone is not enough. Knowledge can be easily perverted and used to increase personal power. It can be so applied as to aid in the control of other people.

The Sons of God—Galactic Men—are not at all interested in controlling Earth humanity. If they had so desired, they could have employed some form of mental or emotional control and hypnotised us all into heaven a long time ago.

But this is not their way because it does not lead to any desirable goal. The controlled Person is good only for being controlled further—he can only be a slave, and not a very useful one, at that. And heaven is certainly no place for slaves.

So humanity were scattered abroad upon the face of the Earth and, in time, their descendants spoke different tongues and developed their separate cultures. Generations passed and in Ur of the Chaldees, a man named Abram (later called Abraham) was born. He, eventually, became father of many nations. But, there is one incident in the life of Abraham which has great bearing on our story.

Who were the three men in Genesis xviii, visiting Abraham, who talked, ate, washed and drank with him? Where did they come from and how?

And the Lord appeared unto him in the plains of Mam-re: and he sat in the tent door in the heat of the day; And he lift up his eyes and looked, and, lo, three men stood by him: and when he saw them he ran to meet them from the tent door, and bowed himself toward the ground. And said, My Lord, if now I have found favour in thy sight, pass not away, I pray thee, from thy servant.

—Genesis xviii. 1-3.

Let us look carefully at these three verses. It states quite clearly that three men appeared, one of whom was the leader, the Lord. This is interesting, not just the Lord, but three men. Abraham continued to address the chief visitor:

Let a little water, I pray you, be fetched, and wash your feet, and rest yourselves, under the tree. And I will fetch a morsel of bread, and comfort ye your hearts; after that ye shall pass on: for therefore are ye come to your servant. And they said, so do, as thou hast said.

—Genesis xviii. 4-5.

Abraham has offered refreshment to his honoured visitors and they have accepted his invitation. And he took butter, and milk, and the calf which he had dressed, and set it before them; and he stood by them under the tree and they did eat.

—Genesis xviii. 8.

In the above verse we have definite evidence that these celestial visitors, one of whom is addressed as 'Lord', and the other two men, all ate food. Now this is extremely important. In short, it means that these people can take human form and that they were no angelic vision. But, at the time of visiting Abraham they were wearing solid bodies and capable of eating human food.

I am going to suggest that these celestial visitors, Lords and Angels, are one and the same as what are termed 'space visitors' coming here today. Further, that Angels are not the traditional white-robed harp-playing characters seen on stained-glass church windows, but are our genetic cousins, the Sons of God, the true Race of Mankind from the Galaxy.

And they said unto him, where is Sarah thy wife?

And he said, Behold, in the tent.

And he said, I will certainly return unto thee according to the time of life; and, lo, Sarah thy wife shall have a son. And Sarah heard it in the tent door, which was behind him. Now Abraham and Sarah were old and well stricken in age; and it ceased to be with Sarah after the manner of women.

—Genesis xviii. 9-11.

Yes, indeed, Abraham was nearly a hundred years and Sarah was in the nineties at that time.

Therefore Sarah laughed within herself, saying, After I am waxed old shall I have pleasure, my Lord being old also?

And the Lord said unto Abraham, Wherefore did Sarah laugh, saying, Shall I of a surety bear a child, which am old?

— Genesis xviii. 12-13.

The honoured visitor corrected her saying, 'Is anything too hard for the Lord? At the time appointed I will return unto thee, according to the time of life, and

LEGACY OF THE SKY PEOPLE

Sarah shall have a son.' Thereupon Sarah denied laughing for she was afraid.

And he said, 'Nay; but thou didst laugh'.

The other two men with the Lord then rose and went on their way toward Sodom. Their leader told Abraham how they intended to destroy that wicked city. Abraham pleaded with him for the righteous men that might be left in the city and the Lord agreed that they should be spared.

The scene now moves on to the gates of Sodom itself.

And there came two angels to Sodom at even; and Lot sat at the gate of Sodom: and Lot, seeing them rose up to meet them, and he bowed himself with his face toward the ground;

And he said, Behold now my lords, turn in, I pray you, into your servant's house, and tarry all night, and wash your feet, and you shall rise up early, and go on your ways,

And they said, Nay; but we will abide in the street all night.

—Genesis xix. 1-2.

These are quite obviously the two men who were with 'the Lord' in Genesis xviii, and who visited Abraham and went on their way towards Sodom. In the first verse of this chapter (Genesis xix) they are definitely referred to as 'Angels', and Lot, too, gives them every respect and salutations. Indeed, note how he calls them 'my Lords'. They are also invited to partake of all hospitality that he can offer.

And he pressed upon them greatly; and they turned in unto him, and entered into his house; and he made them a feast, and did bake unleavened bread, and they did eat.

—Genesis xix. 3.

Once more these 'Angels'—messengers of the Elohim—did eat. This is yet another instance from the Bible showing that space visitors have come among us from time to time and when they have done so, these Angels have carried out the accepted customs of everyday life on this planet, namely: eating, drinking, washing and sleeping. In short, they have not appeared as 'spooks' or 'visions', but have come among us as exceptionally evolved beings wearing chemical bodies similar to Earth men.

The account follows in Genesis xix of how the two angels tried to save as many of Lot's family as possible, although his sons-in-law paid no attention and mocked. Eventually the angels guided Lot, his wife and two daughters from the city and set them without. Lot was told (verse 17) to 'escape for thy life; look not behind thee, neither stay thou in all the plain; escape to the mountain, lest thou be

LEGACY OF THE SKY PEOPLE

consumed'. However he was eventually allowed to flee to the nearby city of Zoar.

> Then the Lord rained upon Sodom and upon Gomorrah brimstone and fire from the Lord out of heaven: And he overthrew those cities, and all the plain, and all the inhabitants of the cities, and that which grew upon the ground. But his wife looked back from behind him, and she became a pillar of salt.
>
> —Genesis xix. 24-26.

Recently a Russian scientist has advanced the theory which is compatible with the views expressed in this book. Most British newspapers carried the Russian hypothesis. Here is the account as it appeared in The Birmingham Post on February 10, 1960.

SOVIET THEORY

MEN FROM SPACE DESTROYED SODOM

A Soviet scientist yesterday put forward a theory that the earth has been visited by space travellers from other planets, and that they may have had a part in the destruction of Sodom and Gomorrah.

The scientist, identified by the Tass agency only as a physico-mathematician, M. Agrest, believes that a space ship approached the earth from space at a speed close to that of light. The occupants landed, he said, possibly in the region of the Baalbek Terrace, a platform built of 2,000-ton stone slabs in the Anti-Lebanon Mountains, which has defied explanation. He believes that the platform is part of the remains of a launching platform built by space travellers or something they put up to commemorate their visit.

"DON'T LOOK BACK"

The Biblical account of the destruction of Sodom and Gomorrah took on a new meaning when read in the light of present-day scientific knowledge.

'In modern language,' Mr. Agrest said, 'this legend says that people were advised to leave the area of the future explosion, not to linger in the open and not to watch the blast. Those of the fugitives who looked back lost their sight and perished.'

According to the Bible, Lot and his family were warned to leave by two Divine messengers. As a hail of fire and brimstone devastated Sodom and Gomorrah, the Bible relates, Lot's wife looked back and was turned into a pillar of salt.

NUCLEAR BRIMSTONE

Mr. Agrest said the 'fire and brimstone' might have been a nuclear fuel dump being blown up deliberately by the space men.

LEGACY OF THE SKY PEOPLE

Mr. Agrest said that a glass-like substance known as tektites found in the Libyan desert and containing radioactive isotopes of aluminum and beryllium may have been the remains of some missile.

He noted there was evidence that tektites—for which there is no explanation—were formed not less than a million years ago, and under conditions of very high temperatures and powerful radiations.

Our story now moves over to Abraham again:

And the Lord visited Sarah as he had said, and the Lord did unto Sarah as he had spoken. For Sarah conceived, and bare Abraham a son in his old age, at the set time of which God had spoken to him. And Abraham called the name of his son that was born unto him 'Isaac'.

— Genesis xxi. 1-3.

You will recall the three men who visited Abraham. How the latter had given them food and how they ate. How their leader was addressed as 'Lord' by Abraham, and how the Lord told Sarah he would come back at the proper time and she would have a son. These were the same space visitors who, subsequently, went on to Sodom, rescued Lot and destroyed both Sodom and Gomorrah. Now the Lord came back to Sarah at the set time and, subsequently, she had a son. Before this book is finished you will have read of three more very similar instances of apparently 'miraculous' child births from Biblical times and we will reserve our conclusions until these have been related.

Meanwhile, let us have a look at Moses. He is supposed to have written the Pentateuch-the first five books of the Old Testament. Moses is said to have written all five, which is patently absurd. If all five were penned by him he would have been the first man on this planet to have written an account of his own death and burial. (See Deuteronomy xxxiv.)

It relates in Exodus iii how Moses kept the flock of Jethro, his father-in-law and he led the flock to Mount Horeb. It was there that he had his first great contact with the Sky People. Many more were to follow.

And the angel of the Lord appeared unto him in a *flame of fire* out of the midst of a bush: and he looked, and behold, the bush burned with fire, and the bush was not consumed.

And Moses said, I will now turn aside to see this great sight, why the bush is not burnt.

And when the Lord saw that he turned aside to see, God called unto him out of the midst of the bush, and said, Moses, Moses. And he said, Here am I. And he said, Draw not nigh hither: put off thy shoes from off thy feet, for the place whereon

LEGACY OF THE SKY PEOPLE

thou standest is holy ground.

—Exodus iii. 2-5.

A spaceship—flying saucer—often illuminates the neighbouring countryside with its electric forcefield. The glowing light within this forcefield surrounding the ship would most certainly have caused the bush to look as if it was on fire.

Moses was so curious about the phenomenon of the bush being burned with fire and not consumed that he turned to look closer at it. The Lord, seeing him about to come nearer, called out warning him not to do so.

If Moses had gone too near before the current had been turned down he would have suffered a severe electrical shock or even death. There are many instances in saucer reports today of the effects of a spacecraft's forcefield, some of which are related further on in this chapter. Other instances where people have been warned not to come too near are given in the Bible and these will be commented on later.

Moses was commanded by the Lord to bring the Israelites, who had been oppressed by Pharaoh, out of the land of Egypt. This he did and according to the Bible, the Israelites were led through the wilderness near the Red Sea.

And the Lord went before them by day in a pillar of a cloud, to lead them the way; and by night in a pillar of fire, to give them light; to go by day and night.

He took not away the pillar of the cloud by day, nor the pillar of fire by night from before the people.

—Exodus xiii. 21-22.

What was the pillar of a cloud by day, and the pillar of fire by night that guided and protected the Israelites? This is a wonderful description of a modern flying saucer. Many different reports received of space ships today refer to clouds and these ships at night look brilliant, brighter than any stars.

At this period of Biblical history, the Israelites were a wandering nomadic people. They were not living in a mechanical jet age like those in the world today. How else would they describe great space ships than by words used in their everyday language such as a pillar or cloud, thick cloud, pillar of fire, fiery chariot and whirlwind? It is interesting to note here Jesus's prophetic statement in Mark xxi. 26-7.

And then shall they see the Son of Man coming in the clouds with a great power and glory. And then shall he send his angels, and shall gather together his elect from the four winds, from the uttermost parts of the earth to the uttermost part of heaven.

LEGACY OF THE SKY PEOPLE

Yes, it is quite extraordinary the number of times in the Bible the Lord appeared in a cloud.

And the Lord said unto Moses, Lo, I come unto thee in a thick cloud, that the people may hear when I speak with thee, and believe thee forever. And Moses told the words of the people unto the Lord.

—Exodus xix. 9.

And be ready against the third day: for the third day the Lord will come down in the sight of all the people upon Mount Sinai.

And thou shalt set bounds unto the people round about, saying, Take heed to yourselves, that ye go not up into the mount, or touch the border of it: whosoever toucheth the mount shall be surely put to death:

There shall not an hand touch it, but he shall surely be stoned, or shot through; whether it be beast or man, it shall not live: when the trumpet soundeth long, they shall come up to the mount.

—Exodus xix. 11-13.

In these three verses, the Lord (the Captain of the spaceship) tells Moses he will come down on to the top of Mount Sinai in the sight of all the people. He then warns Moses not to let the people or any animals come near the craft nor within a certain distance, until he gives a signal—an all clear. Hundreds of modern sightings have testified to the existence of a powerful electric forcefield around these craft and people who have got too near have suffered burns. Furthermore, car engines have stalled on numerous occasions in the vicinity of space craft.

On November 2, 1957, an electronics engineer, James Stokes, employed in an upper-air research project at the Air Force Missile Development Centre, near Alamogordo, New Mexico, said that no less than ten cars were stopped when a spherical-shaped space craft appeared on U.S. Highway 5, between White Sands proving grounds and the Air Force Missile Development Centre. The object approached from the northeast over the Sacramento Mountains. Stokes began to realise that something odd was happening as his car radio faded. Then, he said, the engine died. The others cars stalled about the same time. He noticed their occupants getting out and pointing to the sky.

'I saw a light-coloured, egg-shaped object making a shallow dive across the sky to the northeast. Then it wheeled and made a pass at the highway, across the road not more than two miles ahead. Then it moved away toward White Sands proving grounds. As it passed at its closest point I could feel a kind of heat wave, but there was no sound.'

LEGACY OF THE SKY PEOPLE

When it had gone, Stokes found his car engine normal, excepting the battery which was steaming.

And it came to pass on the third day in the morning, that there were thunders and lightnings, and a thick cloud upon the mount, and the voice of the trumpet exceeding loud, so that all the people that was in the camp trembled.

—Exodus xix. 16.

And the Lord came down upon Mount Sinai, on the top of the Mount: and the Lord called Moses up to the top of the mount and Moses went up.

—Exodus xix. 20.

What a wonderful description this is of a space ship coming down on Mount Sinai. The Captain of the craft once more has thought for the people and tells Moses to warn them yet again.

And the Lord said unto Moses, Go down, charge the people, lest they break through unto the Lord to gaze, and many of them perish.

Then the Lord, who was obviously Jehovah, gave Moses the Ten Commandments, followed by various divers laws and ordinances. One of the ten Commandments was:

Thou shalt have no other gods before me. Thou shalt not make unto thee any graven image, or any likeness of anything that is in heaven above, or that is in the earth beneath, or that is in the water under the earth.

Thou shalt not bow down thyself to them, nor serve them: for I the Lord thy God am a jealous God, visiting the iniquity of the fathers upon the children of the third and fourth generation of them that hate me.

—Exodus xx. 3-5.

Yet further on, the Lord in his discourse, giving divers laws and ordinances, states:

Thou shall not revile *the gods*, nor curse the ruler of thy People.

—Exodus xxii. 28.

In other words, this is a direct admission by the Jehovah that there are *other gods*. They are not to be reviled, but the Israelites were to have only Jehovah as their God. In short, most of the difficulties encountered by theologians in explaining and understanding the personality of Jehovah as it appears in the Bible become a lot less mysterious (because more reasonable if it is understood that while he is a 'god' from our human point of view, he is not, nowhere pretends to be, and nowhere is pretended to be the Universal Spirit).

LEGACY OF THE SKY PEOPLE

And the Lord said unto Moses, Come up to me into the mount, and be there: and I will give thee tables of stone, and a law, and commandments which I have written, that thou mayest teach them.

And Moses rose up, and his minister Joshua: and Moses went up into the mount of God.

And Moses went up into the mount, and a *cloud* covered the mount:

And the *glory of the Lord* abode upon Mount Sinai, and *the cloud* covered it six days: and the seventh day he called unto Moses out of the midst of the cloud.

And the sight of *the glory of the Lord* was like devouring fire* on the top of the mount in the eyes of the children of Israel.

And Moses went up into the *midst of the cloud*; and gat him up into the mount: and Moses was in the mount forty days and forty nights.

—Exodus xxiv. 12-13, 15-18.

Moses was invited to go up Mount Sinai to where the glory of the Lord was covered by a cloud. Notice how the sight of the glory of the Lord was like devouring fire on top of the mount seen from below by the Israelites. Compare this description with the earlier one given of the object that guided the Israelites through the wilderness—pillar of cloud by day and pillar of fire by night.

When the cloud was not covering the space ship on Mount Sinai, it glowed like devouring fire. Then in verse 18, we read that Moses was in the Mount forty days and forty nights. In the light of the foregoing description of a spacecraft, it seems pretty certain that Moses spent forty days and forty nights inside the ship conferring with the Lord, its captain.

Now, a few chapters on, in Exodus, there is a truly remarkable passage.

And the Lord descended in the cloud, and stood with him there, and proclaimed the name of the Lord.

And the Lord passed by before him, and proclaimed, The Lord, The Lord God, merciful and gracious, long suffering, and abundant in goodness and truth.

—Exodus xxxiv. 5-6.

Again you will notice the Lord comes down. In what kind of cloud did the Lord descend and pass by before Moses in verse 6? How, too, must we distinguish between the two Lords, both mentioned in verses 5 and 6? Surely the plurality of the Elohim can no longer be in doubt.

LEGACY OF THE SKY PEOPLE

CHAPTER V

CELESTIAL CHARIOTS

The Bible states that it was Joshua who took over the leadership of the Israelites after the passing on of Moses, and relates that it was by Jericho when his amazing meeting took place with the Captain of the host of the Lord.

And it came to pass, when Joshua was by Jericho, that he lifted up his eyes and looked, and, behold, there stood a man against him with his sword drawn in his hand; and Joshua went unto him, and said unto him, Art thou for us, or for our adversaries?

And he said, Nay; but as captain of the host of the Lord am I now come. And Joshua fell on his face to the earth, and did worship, and said unto him, what saith my Lord unto his servant?

And the captain of the Lord's host said unto Joshua, Loose thy shoe from off thy foot; for the place whereon thou standest is holy. And Joshua did so.

—Joshua v. 13-15.

This is a very outstanding contact by Joshua with one of the Sky People—the Captain of the Lord's host. A man who commanded legions of Angels. Joshua fell on his face to the earth and did worship, although the radiant being who stood before him was not the Lord God, but could be one of the Jehovah.

The Captain of the host told Joshua to loosen his shoe from his foot, to take it off. Why did he do this?

'For the place whereon thou standest is holy.'

Now, it seems highly improbable that this great Being would tell Joshua to take his shoes off in his presence as a further mark of respect. Joshua had already been falling on his face to the earth and worshipping.

It will be recalled that at Moses' first contact there was a similar warning given by the Lord:

He said, draw not nigh hither: put off thy shoes from off thy feet, for the place whereon thou standest is holy.

It could be that the translations have erred here in their choice of the word

LEGACY OF THE SKY PEOPLE

'holy'. The words, holy, taboo and forbidden, sometimes are used in the same context and this may be one of these cases. The visitors could have been warning Moses and Joshua respectively, not only to keep their distance, but that the ground around the vicinity of the craft was perhaps radioactive.

Radioactive? Yes, many newspapers carried, early in 1959, a new theory about what had previously been regarded as the fall of a giant meteorite in Siberia over fifty years ago. The London Daily Express of May 4, 1959, published an article which stated:

A theory that a spaceship from another planet reached Earth 51 years ago is causing a major split among Russia's leading scientists.

An expedition from Moscow is now working in the remote forest where on June 30, 1908, what has been known as the 'Great Siberian Meteorite' fell.

Radiation measurements are being taken.

Three of the Russian scientists, Professors Kukarkin, Krinov and Fesenkov, say it was probably a meteorite. But they cautiously use the word 'phenomenon' instead. And Professors Alexander Kazantsev and B. Lapunov insist it must have been a rocket or ship coming from Mars.

Kazantsev, who has been accumulating evidence for the spaceship theory for years, has released some details to the Czechs and the Poles. Never has the mystery been considered with such thoroughness. These are the facts: On that June day the inhabitants of the Jenissci district of Siberia saw a gigantic ball of fire. Immediately afterwards there was a colossal explosion which devastated a forest area of 70 miles in diameter. The shock waves were registered in England. Scientists looked in vain for traces of a meteorite and a crater. Curiously, in the centre of the devastated region only the tops of trees had been snapped off. But the meteorite theory persisted until the atomic bomb exploded over Hiroshima.

Then just after the war, Kazantsev tentatively said that the Hiroshima devastation bore great similarity to that in the Siberian forest.

He said then: 'An atomic explosion took place in Siberia at the height of one and a half miles.' He was not taken seriously.

In 1951 he was helped by Professor Lapunov and both of them formed the idea of an atomic propelled vehicle which exploded while trying to land.

Several expeditions were sent to the site. One came back last summer with the report: No meteorite evidence at all. This report set the controversy alight again. Soviet aerodynamics expert, Manotskov, has lent strength to the spaceship theory. He says that the Siberian 'fireball' was braking as it approached Earth, so that its final speed was about one to two kilometres per second, instead of between 30 to 60 kilometres per second as with meteorites.

The Sydney Sun, Australia, quoting from the official Czech trade union newspaper, *Prace*, stated that the Russian scientist in a book called *A Guest From the Universe* had written that people living near the explosion died of a then unknown illness with the same symptoms as exposure to atomic radiation and that the explosion had its biggest impact at some distance from its centre—exactly like an atomic explosion.

No wonder space visitors warn onlookers to keep their distance when a spacecraft lands and not to approach until they give the all clear.

There has been considerable speculation as to what really caused the walls of Jericho to fall down flat. But there surely can be no doubt at all that the space people played a big role in this strange affair.

We have already seen how the Captain of the Lord's host contacted Joshua outside Jericho. Then, the very next thing we learn from the Bible, is that Joshua is being briefed by the Lord on how to capture the city. He was told to encompass the city with his armed men and go round it once. This he was to do for six days. On the seventh day they were to encompass the city seven times and the priests were to sound trumpets.

Finally, when the priests made a long blast with the ram's horn and blew the trumpets, the people were to let out a great shout and the walls of Jericho would fall down flat.

And that is what happened, according to the Bible, and the Israelites took the city.

How did it happen? Did the Sky People give the Israelites some vibrationary subsonic secret which enabled them, by sounding the right note, to cause the walls to fall flat? Many strange things have been done in this scientific field in recent years by scientists causing objects and houses to move. Or, did the space people hoodwink the Israelites into thinking that they had caused the walls to fall flat, when all the time the Sky People had directed some powerful force from the sky onto the walls at the forecast moment? Or was there an earthquake which the Sky People knew was coming at that time? It is a fascinating question which one day may be resolved, but the Bible does assure us that Celestial Beings contacted Joshua and gave him operational orders!

In the last chapter was described how angels came to Abraham and told him his wife, Sarah, who was past it, would bear him a son, and how she did so at the appointed time.

LEGACY OF THE SKY PEOPLE

Now, here is another rather similar event concerning a man of Zorah, of the family of the Danites, whose name was Manoah. Like Sarah, Manoah's wife was barren and they had no children.

And the angel of the Lord appeared unto the woman, and said unto her, Behold now, thou art barren, and barest not: but thou shalt conceive and bear a son'

—Judges xiii. 3.

The woman told her husband what had occurred and that the man had warned her not to drink wine, nor strong drink, neither eat any unclean thing.

The angel came again to Manoah's wife while she sat in the fields, and she ran to fetch her husband and show him the man, The strange visitor then repeated his instructions to Manoah concerning his wife's diet.

The thirteenth chapter of the Book of Judges goes on to tell how Manoah invited the Angel of the Lord to partake of some food. The invitation was declined and instead, a burnt offering was offered up to the Lord. At this stage, Manoah, according to the Biblical account, was not aware that their guest was an Angel of the Lord.

Manoah said: 'What is thy name, that when thy sayings come to pass we may do thee honour?' And the Angel of the Lord replied: 'Why askest thou thus after my name, seeing it is secret?'

Manoah made a burnt offering to the Lord on an altar, and to his astonishment the Angel of the Lord ascended in the flame of the altar. Then Manoah knew he was an Angel of the Lord.

And the woman bare a son, and called his name Samson: and the child grew, and the Lord blessed him.

—Judges xii. 24.

This is the second occasion children have been born to earth women who have been barren and in which the Sky People have played a leading role. We will discuss this later after describing two more similar events, including the greatest Biblical birth of a special nature, yet to come.

One of the most outstanding accounts of a spaceship in the Old Testament is the story of Elijah being taken up in a whirlwind.

And it came to pass, when the Lord would take up Elijah into heaven by a whirlwind, that Elijah went with Elisha from Gilgal.

—II Kings ii. 1.

LEGACY OF THE SKY PEOPLE

Please note that word whirlwind again, which we met previously in our references from the Book of Enoch. It will be recalled that this notable apocalyptic work mentioned at least two occasions in which Enoch took trips in 'whirlwinds'.

And it came to pass, when they were gone over, that Elijah said to Elisha, ask what I shall do for thee, before I be taken away from thee. And Elisha said, I pray thee, let a double portion of thy spirit be upon me.

—II Kings ii. 9.

Here evidently, Elijah had advance information that he was to be taken up into the skies.

And he said, Thou hast asked a hard thing: nevertheless, if thou see me when I am taken from thee, it shall be so unto thee; but if not, it shall not be so. And it came to pass, as they still went on, and talked, that, behold, there appeared a chariot of fire, and horses of fire, and parted them both asunder; and Elijah went up by a whirlwind into heaven.

—II Kings ii. 10-11.

This phrase 'chariot of fire' and the word 'horses', appears again a few chapters on in the Bible. To be precise, in II Kings vi. 17.

And Elisha prayed and said, Lord, I pray thee, open his eyes, that he may see. And the Lord opened the eyes of the young man; and he saw: and behold, the mountain was full of horses and chariots of fire round about Elisha.

Does it not seem from Elijah's words to Elisha and from Elisha's words to the Lord in regard to the young man that the Sky People are visible, generally speaking, to those who have the necessary perception to see them? There are, of course, occasions when visitors to this planet can make themselves visible to as many people as they wish.

The Old Testament is, indeed, full of references to these mysterious celestial chariots.

The chariots of God are twenty thousand, even thousands of angels: the Lord is among them, as in Sinai, to the holy place.

—Psalm l xviii. 17.

What are these thousands of chariots, and thousands of angels that seem to go with them?

In the same Psalm, verses 33 and 34, are significant of consideration.

To him that *rideth* upon the heaven of heavens, which were of old, lo, he doth send out his voice, and that a mighty voice.

LEGACY OF THE SKY PEOPLE

Ascribe ye strength unto God: his excellency is over Israel, and his strength is in *the clouds*.

—Psalm lxviii: 33-34.

The clouds are here again! We had a pillar of cloud guiding the Israelites through the wilderness and a cloud covering the glory of the Lord on Mount Sinai. The Bible does, indeed, contain incident after incident and quotation after quotation, referring to visitors from outer space.

From where do the sanctified and mighty ones come, from what far country and from which end of heaven in verses 3 and of Isaiah xiii, and how do they come?

I have commanded my sanctified ones, I have also called my mighty ones for mine anger, even them that rejoice in my highness.

They come from a far country, from the end of heaven, even the Lord, and the weapons of his indignation, to destroy the whole land.

Isaiah seems to ask in the following verse the same question as many people do today, when they read and hear flying saucer reports.

Who are these *that fly as a cloud*, and as the doves to their windows?

—Isaiah lx. 8.

With the kind of chariots, that seem to move like a whirlwind, will the Lord come, and with what fire in Isaiah lxvi. 15?

For behold, the Lord will come with fire, and with his *chariots* like a *whirlwind*, to render his anger with fury, and his rebuke with flames of fire.

Ezekiel's famous meeting with spacecraft is described in Ezekiel.

And I looked, and behold, a whirlwind came out of the north, a great cloud, and a fire enfolding itself, and a brightness was about it, and out of the midst thereof as the colour of amber, out of the midst of the fire.

—Ezekiel i. 4.

The whole of this chapter from Ezekiel probably contains the finest description in the Bible of spacecraft landing and of their occupants. The entire incident has been given an excellent interpretation in detail by George Hunt Williamson in his book, **Other Tongues-Other Flesh**. We will not go over this ground again, but content ourselves by reiterating Williamson's comment, that in reading the Biblical account it should be remembered Ezekiel was not living in a mechanical age.

.. and he was therefore compelled to use the only things with which he was

LEGACY OF THE SKY PEOPLE

familiar-animals, birds, and horsedrawn chariots with wheels.

It is not only in the first chapter of Ezekiel that references to spacecraft are to be found. What kind of glory of the Lord was standing in the plain, where the Lord talked with Ezekiel?

And the hand of the Lord was there upon me; and he said unto me, Arise, go forth into the plain, and I will talk there with thee.

Then I arose, and went forth into the plain: and, behold, the glory of the Lord, as the glory which I saw by the river of Chebar: and I fell on my face..

—Ezekiel iv. 22-23.

The whole of Chapter 10 contains another wonderful account by Ezekiel of a space ship.

Then the glory of the Lord went up from the cherub, and stood over the threshold of the house, and the house was filled with the cloud, and the court was full of the brightness of the Lord's glory.

And the sound of the cherubim's wings was heard even to the outer court, as the voice of the Almighty God when he speaketh.

—Ezekiel x. 4-5.

It really is important to read carefully both Chapters 1 and 10 of Ezekiel, taking into account the obvious difficulties Ezekiel would be beset with in describing these ships.

It has been my pleasure to quote incident after incident from the Old Testament. It should by now be clear that the Bible is not only filled, but brimming over with accounts of the Sky People. There certainly is more than a *prima facie* case for the existence of visitors from other worlds since the very earliest times.

Orthodox beliefs have for so long become almost indelibly ingrained in humanity today that wholesale acceptance of some of the concepts expressed in this book cannot be expected, let alone an open-minded approach. There will be some who will listen though, and there will be some who read these pages who will hear answering echoes from deep within themselves. This book is written for them.

In the early half of the sixteenth century the Renaissance was just flowering into the Reformation. Times were, in essence, so much like our own—these 1960's.

Frank W. Gunsaulus in his novel **Monk and Knight**, first published in 1891, wrote:

The Renaissance was a reformation of the European intellect; the Reformation was a renaissance of the European conscience. Both movements were returns to the past; the intellect found deliverance from scholasticism in its study of Greece and Rome; the conscience felt the chains of ecclesiasticism disappear as once more it saw the open gospel of the Christ. Each movement was also a distinctly marked step into the future, because, in each, the human soul had rediscovered itself, and readily bounded forward with a persuasion that to it alone belonged the infinite time

He went on:

The Renaissance, as it flowered into the Reformation, was a new birth of the whole man. It was a revolution: it was a revolution inside an evolution. It was an orderly movement; it was a disorderly movement—the disorder was walled in, and guarded by order.

In those days, the mere printing of the Bible for all men to read was an issue! On this point Gunsaulus declared:

At the remembrance of these things, the thoughts of printing a Bible for all men to read, in which it was taught by Peter himself that all Christians are priests of the living God, seemed to the papacy and to the clergy like inviting a revolution .Of course, the Bible must be read and explained only by a clerical force, sworn to annihilate such results as this ideal would produce in the minds of men, moved as they now were, and liberated as they were to be by the Renaissance, man dared to dream of salvation, except through the long and mechanical devices of the priesthood, organised and ruled by popes, was enough to close every Bible and start the fires of inquisitions.

In these days the writer and any others who dare to give an individual, unorthodox interpretation of the Bible or parts of it, must be prepared to face an equal opposition!

Torches need to be relit at more or less regular intervals. Greece and Rome discovered Man, and saw him naked, with the eyes of innocence and portrayed him as they saw him. They saw mind, adorned with body, and subservient not even to the gods (unless it chose to be)—gods, whose own blood flowed in the veins of man himself, to the greater glory of the world. Time dulled the vision, and Jesus attempted a restatement, a relighting of the torch.

Orthodoxy smothered it, and there were dark ages. Italy went back for light to the Greeks and to her own Romans. France, and above all, England, went with her, and the world ended again and was renewed. With the spread of enlightenment in the world, the interval between the ends of ages shortens. This time, if we are to read the signs and portents aright, that interval has been cut in half, from a thousand to some five hundred years. Again the dignity and nobility of Individual

LEGACY OF THE SKY PEOPLE

Man (the freedom of self-acknowledgment that raises him above the animals and denies the authority of those who, being without knowledge either of any God or their own innate divinity, would enslave him) has been lost in misinterpretation.

In vast areas of the world, the torch is again put out, or only flickering.

The Renaissance went back to classical thought for its traditional light, preserving the continuity of Man's spiritual existence. In our own time we are more fortunate. We have both the Renaissance and those to whom the Renaissance turned to go back to.

The Reformation interpreted what the Renaissance discovered. Again it is our good fortune to be able to go back to that interpretation (now, already somewhat distorted where it is not lost) to reinforce our own.

Every time an age, a New Age—a Renaissance—blossoms, Man becomes once again a knower who moves into the future with creative Faith born of his knowledge, instead of a mere believer crushed under the deadening weight of an orthodox authority. He has the guidance of the Gods, his own ancestors.

Religion is no longer the greatest of the powers that suppress humankind. Organised religion is no longer powerful enough to be the answer in the coming times. The Gnosticism that will preserve man must be broad enough to face both religious and scientific orthodoxy.

For hundreds of years organised religion has not only oppressed man, but has perpetuated the lie that he is a miserable sinner and less than the dust. Again, Humanity's potential divinity was smothered. Instead of allowing man self-determinism and the respect and rights of a potential god, the Churches taught self-abasement and obedience to their dogmas.

This, in direct contradiction to Jesus, the Christ, who made no bones about humanity's potentialities at all. 'Ye are gods!' he said.

Yes, a new Renaissance is on its way in! A new set of articles is being nailed up for all to read who will. The Supreme Spirit is One and Indivisible, and Man is made in his image—an individual entity. Man, a Man is a Self. The Supreme Spirit, the Almighty Creator—call him what you will* is a Self, and he is the Self of and beyond his Creations.

Thus, in an important way, God and Man are equal—but not equivalent. MAN is the image, while God remains the One Reality.

Man may, in time, evolve into something more than Man, but God will remain God, as he has always been.

To see your own Self for what it is and to acknowledge it, is to become a

LEGACY OF THE SKY PEOPLE

Man. To realise its indestructible individuality is to win your Immortality, to become a god. But even a god can be chained if he submits to the authority of confusion.

If you acknowledge your Self, those around you who prefer to be animals and to live by the laws of animal life and the animal world will crucify you, if they can. However, if you are able to maintain your own realisation of Individuality even for a few hours, you will find the power to renew your own life, resurrect yourself, and come back to astonish them. You will be able to survive all the Death they can heap upon you and indeed, know how the 'Father' and the 'I' are one.

In 1990, Brad and Sherry led a Star People expedition to the ancient sites of Peru. One of the special sites involved taking a long, rickety boat ride to visit a very remote island in Lake Titicaca. The inhabitants spoke openly about their ancestors being taught by the Sky People and being warned not to accept any kind of modern technology and to honor only the old teachings. They also said that the Sky People would return for them if they remained true to the sacred ways when the great Earth changes occurred.
From the private collection of Brad and Sherry Steiger.

LEGACY OF THE SKY PEOPLE

CHAPTER VI

UNUSUAL CHILDBIRTHS

There was in the days of Herod, the king of Judaea, a certain priest named Zacharias, of the course of Abia: and his wife was of the daughters of Aaron, and her name was Elisabeth.

And they were both righteous before God, walking in all the commandments and ordinances of the Lord blameless. And they had no child, because that Elisabeth was barren, and they both were now well stricken in years.

—Luke i. 5-7.

You have read similar incidents from the Bible before in this book. They always start like this. Abraham and Sarah, and later Manoah and his wife. The operative words are 'barren' and 'well stricken in years'.

And there appeared unto him an angel of the Lord standing on the right side of the altar of incense. And when Zacharias saw him, he was troubled, and fear fell upon him.

But the angel said unto him, Fear not, Zacharias, for thy prayer is heard; and thy wife Elisabeth shall bear thee a son, and thou shalt call his name John.

—Luke i. 11-13.

Zacharias did not believe the words of his visitor, the angel of the Lord. Although a righteous and spiritual man, he was probably affected by the traditional thinking of every human being to some extent. In short, his acceptance level was not high enough.

And Zacharias said unto the angel, Whereby shall I know this? for I am an old man, and my wife well stricken in years. And the angel answering said unto him, I am Gabriel, that stand in the presence of God; and am sent to speak unto thee, and to shew thee these glad tidings.

And behold, thou shalt be dumb, and not able to speak, until the day that these things shall be performed, because thou believest not my words, which shall be fulfilled in their season.

—Luke i. 18-20.

LEGACY OF THE SKY PEOPLE

When the three celestial visitors came to Abraham, you will recall Sarah overheard them talking and how she laughed at the idea of having a son. Sarah, too, was rebuked by the Angel, although it is not recorded she was struck dumb.

Now Elisabeth's full time came that she should be delivered; and she brought forth a son. And her neighbours and her cousins heard how the Lord had shewed great mercy upon her; and they rejoiced with her.

And it came to pass, that on the eighth day they came to circumcise the child, and they called him Zachanas, after the name of his father.

And his mother answered and said, Not so; but he shall be called John.

And they said unto her, There is none of thy kindred that is called by this name. And they made signs to his father, how he would have him called. And he asked for a writing table, and wrote, saying, His name is John. And they marvelled all. And his mouth was opened immediately, and his tongue loosed, and he spake and praised God.

—Luke i. 57-64.

Now follows the most important of these incidents. The same Angel, Gabriel, came to a virgin, called Mary, in the city of Nazareth, in Galilee. Mary was espoused to a man called Joseph, of the House of David.

And the angel came in unto her, and said, Hail, thou that art highly favoured, the Lord is with thee; blessed are thou among women. And when she saw him, she was troubled at his saying, and cast in her mind what manner of salutation this should be. And the angel said unto her, Fear not, Mary, for thou hast found favour with God. And, behold, thou shalt conceive in thy womb, and bring forth a son, and shalt call his name Jesus.

—Luke i. 28-31.

Mary, a virgin, who had not slept with any man, asked: 'How shall this be, seeing I know not a man?'

And the angel answered and said unto her, The Holy Ghost shall come upon thee, and the power of the Highest shall overshadow thee; therefore also that holy thing which shall be born of thee shall be called the Son of God.

—Luke i. 32-35.

Scientists have not yet been able to solve the question of the mysterious star that appeared in the heavens at the time of His birth. The Star of Bethlehem. Astronomers have found that no such star should have been in the heavens at that time.

LEGACY OF THE SKY PEOPLE

When they had heard the king, they departed; and lo, the star, which they saw in the east, went before them, till it came and stood over where the young child was.

When they saw the star, they rejoiced with exceeding great joy.

— Matthew ii. 9-10.

Many people throughout the world who have studied the phenomenon of flying saucers hold the view that the Star of Bethlehem was a gigantic spaceship. Many spaceships seen at night have appeared to witnesses bright as the stars. Notice, too, how the 'star' went before them, till it came and stood over (hovered) where the young child was.

Now we have put on record in this book four cases of unusual childbirth, namely, Isaac, born of Sarah, the wife of Abraham; Samson, born of the wife of Maroah; John, the Baptist, born of Elisabeth, the wife of Zacharias, and finally, Jesus, born of Mary, the wife of Joseph. This is not just one isolated case. There is a pattern and certain similar aspects about all these events. However, it is, of course, obvious that Mary was not stricken with years, or barren, as in the case of the first three examples, but it is also clear from the Biblical accounts that the Angel of the Lord (Gabriel) appeared before her, as in like manner, angels had appeared to the others.

Remember, the original Galactic Race of Man, created by the Elohim (the gods) were different in the way they were created to hu-manity (animal chemical Adam-II men) manufactured by the Jehovah, as described in Genesis ii. Subsequently, as prophesied by the Lord God (Jehovah) to the Serpent in the Garden of Eden, the two races mixed, resulting in the present Cross-Man, who is either manifestly Galactic dominant or animal-man dominant in his make-up, depending upon what progress he has made in the journey back to godhood. As the two creations were made differently, pure Galactic Man does not have an animal-man type body such as Cross-Man still has today. A Galactic has a physical body, but obviously not made of the same chemicals as earth man. His body can manifest and be visible to earth man, as can be witnessed from the number of appearances by angels—messengers—to people related in the Bible. They are not spooks or ghosts. This is evident from the various occasions on which they have eaten solid food, washed, and talked to whoever was the subject to their visit, No, it seems their bodies are not so gross as earthman's bodies. They are etheric by nature. They have physical form like ourselves, but their chemical make-up is different. They appear solid to each other, but can load themselves up with-earth chemicals if required to do so, when their business takes them this way.

Now, what happened in the cases of Sarah, Manoah's wife, Elisabeth and Mary?

LEGACY OF THE SKY PEOPLE

This is an intriguing question and considerable thought has been given to it by the writer and a certain hypothesis has been built up. Maybe, some of those reading this book will be able to amplify or amend the tentative postulates which had been arrived at. If so, the writer will be pleased to hear from them. Meanwhile, let us ask an imaginary space visitor from Mars to present this hypothesis to you.

'I am a Galactic and wish to provide myself with a new body. This discussion will be confined to those Galactics (Men) who are capable of loading up with chemical atoms and living among earth humanity undetected. Let us say, those Galactics closest to your own mixed types. These will be in all cases, Physical Etherians. Their residence nearest the earth is Mars. We are your Elder Brothers.

'In form, our bodies closely resemble yours, with a few important differences. One of these differences usually causes the shocked human male to run through a series of emotions beginning with outraged alarm and ending in contempt. The male Galactic produces no spermatozoa. They are not needed. Actual bodily union is not necessary to the production of offspring, as it is with earth-animals.

'Yet there are Galactic male bodies and Galactic female bodies, and a combination of both is required in the process of reproduction.

'Maleness and femaleness are the result of what has been called body polarity.

'Contrary to popular mystical acceptances based on a poor definition of the words 'positive,' and 'negative', the male earth-human body is a "negative electrode" (to use an electrical symbol), a cathode. The female body can be compared to a "positive electrode", a receiver of energy. The confusion arises through an incomplete understanding of the relation ship between magnetic terms and electrical terminology describing the functions of an electrolytic cell.

'One good look at the generative process should cure the error beyond all doubt. Another look at the psychological patterns of males and females should clinch the matter. Males tend toward aggressive patterns, females toward the conservative.

'But who looks? Especially in that direction.

'In Galactics there is less psychological differentiation than in earth-humans. Most of this differentiation in earth-humans is due to cultural moulding of inherent tendency, with strong restrictive factors at work for both sexes. This heightens differences which would not otherwise be so definite and noticeable.

'Still, physically, difference in appearance is pronounced in our etheric male

LEGACY OF THE SKY PEOPLE

and female bodies. Galactic men are intensely masculine; Galactic women are feminine (without being weak, wishy-washy, or evasive). On Earth, many cultural ideas of femininity demand that a woman approach, as nearly as possible, the appearance and behaviour pattern of a female animal. This is understandable and in keeping with the genetic status of a great many of earth's inhabitants. Therefore, it is not wrong for them. The same cultures demand their males look and act like male animals. In some countries specific animals have been chosen as ideal, and it is interesting, as an aside, to note the effect this has upon the behaviour of your people. The Bull in India and Spain; the Stallion in old Greece. Even such relatively oblique choices as the British Lion and the Russian Bear have an effect.

'There is a definite advantage in retaining two different body types. The mind (self) of man has two aspects because it consists of two different universal functions: Creation and Analysis. Two different sorts of machinery can be specialised to perform those functions.

'The Galactic male is wearing a Creating Machine, very outgoing, very active, and as long as he wants to engage in that kind of activity he wears a male body. When you earth people go golfing you carry a set of clubs. Substitutes are inefficient. The Galactic female is wearing an Analysis-Synthesis machine. Relative to the male, somewhat introverted, aware of detail, inquiring, and at the same time synthetic, a putter-together (often to the amazement of the male) of apparently unrelated things and ideas.

'Both functions are extremely useful, if they are not allowed to be perverted or degraded.

'Of course, no Galactic (and indeed, no earth-human) is either totally one way or the other. However, males remain essentially the emissive (cathode) go-out-and-get-it-done creator, while females remain the more permissive, work-in-a-prescribed-area, attend-to-the-vital-details, analytical-synthetics.

'If all this sounds, what you on Earth would call Victorian-too bad. Your Queen Victoria may have been difficult to amuse, but she was dead right about some things.

'We ought to remember that when the word "polarity" was adopted by some of your writers and applied to Male and Female, they were thinking in terms of magnetism rather than current electricity.

'Take the word Pole: this is the part of a magnet, usually near the end, towards which the lines of magnetic flux apparently converge or from which they diverge, the former being called a south pole and the latter a north pole.

'So they made the south pole female, quite properly, and the diverging north pole they made male.

LEGACY OF THE SKY PEOPLE

'Then somebody assigned the words Positive and Negative to the North and South poles respectively, used them in a philosophical sense-yes-no, strong-weak, aggressive-receptive, and also good-bad. Now it is difficult to tell somebody who has accepted this muddled usage that the male human body carries a relatively low potential (energy charge) and the female body carries a relatively high potential (energy charge). People mistakenly assume you are trying to say the male is weaker. Not so.

'Electrical current flow is from high potential to low potential. Between earth-human bodies energy-flow goes (or should go) from female to male, and one of the proper functions of an earth female is to collect energy and to deliver it to her male counterpart.

'Your people are all mixed up about this, and we find females vampirising their men, and the men putting up with it, indeed, even cultivating it. And men overload their women with far more life-force than is good for them, in addition to their own, while the men are weakened and debilitated trying to provide what they cannot spare. Your cultural acceptances support this idiocy. Perhaps when God made woman he ought to have installed an "on-off" energy button between her shoulder blades where only the man could reach it.

'So, the female earth-body is an anode, the male earth-body is a cathode.

'Definitions. Anode: The electrode through which a current enters an electrolytic cell from an external source of electromotive force. Cathode: The electrode through which a current leaves an electrolytic cell to return to an external source of electromotive force.

'A male and female can function after the manner of an electrolytic cell, if the female will do her part, contact and accumulate the energy (not from her man, but from the universe!) pass it on to the male, who can then externalise it, and direct its effect!

'You speak of the emancipation of your women. This is unnatural and definitely immoral. Your women don't need emancipation—all they need is recognition as human beings. Some of the most beautiful and brilliant of your women are not emanicpated by your modern western standards. They are happy and content, and their husbands were the sort of male human any girl in her right mind would follow barefoot through a cactus-patch and feel no pain.

'Someone on your planet once epigrammed: The function of woman is inspiration—that of man, perspiration. He was closing in on the truth.

'In an earth-animal body reproduction depends upon the union of two haploid gametes. The gametes carry the chromosomes which carry the genes that determine hereditary form and function (which Jehovah built). The earth-human cell has 46-48 chromosomes which have recently been shown to be variable and arrange themselves in pairs. Each chromosome contains several hundred genes which are coiled organic molecules.

'Since in your chemical world, the actual cells of one body have to be transferred to another body, sexual union is necessary.

'Etheris Galactic reproduction proceeds through juggling the chromosomes and genes already there to produce the desired effect. Gabriel could have fathered Jesus only without actual intercourse with Mary, because he was a Galactic. Not so Joseph Davidson.

'The juggling is effected by a form of what your Hindus call Kryiashakti, creation by the voice (and mind), and it involves use of the vocal apparatus, i.e. by derivation, "the creative word".

'The child may then develop in the mother's body if that course is chosen, or, as is more usual among Galactics, the embryo is apported out and a mature body is developed from it. This requires the presence of several other operators in addition to the original two people. Childhood is a rather useless stage if you move out of one body and into another with a full set of recollections.

'You may well wonder if a lot of the ritual surrounding birth in many cultures is not a dim hangover from some lost remembrance of the need for the presence of a group of people, doing certain prescribed things, at the formation of the new body.

'Jesus was to appear as a little child. Therefore he grew in his mother's belly as all children do on your earth. When the time arrived for him to draw breath, he was apported out, and the record shows there were angels on hand to see that all went according to plan.'

The main purpose of Jesus' life and ministry on Earth was to show hu-man-Cross-Man, his potentialities, He was a wayshower. And his very teaching and purpose has been grossly distorted by orthodox religion with their miserable sinner complex. Jesus showed how everyone could follow him to the stars and to godhood. 'The things that I can do ye can do also.' He demonstrated his 'at-onement' with the 'Father' or creator of Adam-II man. By so doing, he at once showed forth and actually became the way through demonstrating the ultimate truth of Universal Life. His teachings at once fulfil and supersede the old Mosaic code handed down for the guidance of the people of Earth. He is indeed, the mediator between heaven and earth, and soon, it is promised, will be coming back.

Behold he cometh with *clouds and every* eye shall see him, and they also which pierced him: and all kindreds of the earth shall wail because of him. Even

LEGACY OF THE SKY PEOPLE

so, Amen.

—Rev. i. 7.

What is the meaning here of the plural word 'clouds'? The word cloud is used over and over again in the Bible in connection with celestial visitors, both angels and Lords, as we have seen in our study of Old Testament happenings.

And that prophesied time is not far off.

And then shall they see the Son of Man coming in a cloud with power and great glory.

— Luke xxi. 27.

The signs predicted by which we are to recognise the times are already appearing in the heavens and the earth.

Watch therefore, for ye know neither the day nor the hour wherein the Son of Man cometh.

—Matthew xxv. 13.

This saucer-shaped disk, suggestive of a UFO to modern viewers is said by some to be a model of the "gold disk" that fits on the Hitching Post of The Sun, the landing place of the Sky Gods. [see p. 138] From The Photo Collection Of Brad And Sherry Steiger.

LEGACY OF THE SKY PEOPLE

CHAPTER VII

THE REAL CROSS

'Know Thyself'

—Apollo of the Sun.

Cross-Man crucified Jesus, the Christ, on a cross. In a very deep sense, he was the prototype of Cross hu-manity. As such, he is THE man of the Cross, and what he accomplished, Cross-Man, as a whole group, will do within a Galactic frame of reference.

Truly, the last shall be first, and the stone rejected of the builders shall become the head of the corner—the keystone of the great Galactic Royal Arch, the capstone of the Human Temple of Light.

Jesus, the Nazarene, was not the first crucified man to be associated with this idea, and even before this symbol was used there were crucified 'serpents', embodying the idea of Galactic Man crossed with an animal form of hu-manity and producing the man of the cross.

Thus, the symbol of the crucified serpent came before the symbol of the crucified man. The crucified serpent tells of the formation of Cross-Man, and it is called, therefore, a symbol of generation. This primary meaning of the symbol has been brought down a turn in the spiral of interpretation to mean mere sexual procreation, dissociated from its historical truth.

The crucified man tells of the death, the final working out, of Adam-II man, and his resurrection as Adam-I, a citizen of the Galaxy, a true Man of the Stars and Son of God.

The message of the great life dramatisation of Jesus is not in his death, but in his resurrection, for he rose as an Anointed Son of God, even as the whole race of Cross-Man shall ultimately do after him. He was the first of the entities involved with that race to accomplish the Rebuilding of the Temple, to run the course, to gain the Victory.

So, both crucifixion symbols are of Earth Man, but they denote two different and successive stages in his progress.

The Swastika symbol is a form of the Cross. It represents the four original

LEGACY OF THE SKY PEOPLE

primary forces. George Hunt Williamson in **Other Tongues-Other Flesh**, indicates that the Great Bear Constellation forms a definite swastika design in the sky. 'So', Williamson comments, 'it is easy to see why the space people might very well use the swastika as a universal symbol or emblem.'

The swastika is a very ancient symbol of India, but it is also found on rock carvings in many parts of the world, in Crete, Sweden, Scotland and many other places.

In Ancient Egypt, the Crux ansanta played a very predominant role, being found on many pieces of sculpture. It was a T-shaped cross with an oval loop above it. This has been known as the Tau and was the symbolical cross of the Chaldeans, Phoenicians, Peruvians and Mexicans.

When the Catholic Spanish invaders first stepped ashore in the New World, they were astonished to find that the native Indians worshipped the Cross as devoutly as they did themselves. The bewildered Spaniards came across the Cross on buildings and temples, but decided that it was the work of the Devil.

Throughout all ages and in all lands, the Cross has been the subject of respect and worship, signifying some common point of origin. It is both a tradition and an almost forgotten memory symbolising the original home of Adam-II man in the Garden of Eden, on another planet. That paradise, where according to Genesis, 'a River went out of Eden, to water the garden; and from thence it was parted, and became four heads'.

This legend of a heavenly garden, watered by four canals is remembered by the Scandinavians, the Chinese, the Indians and the Greeks.

Donnelly in his **Atlantis**, quotes Homer:

It was the sacred Asgard of the Scandinavians, springing from the centre of a fruitful land, which was watered by the four primeval rivers of milk, severally flowing in the direction of the cardinal points, 'the abode of happiness, and the height of bliss'. It is the Tien-Chan, 'the celestial mountainland... 'the enchanted gardens' of the Chinese and Tartars, watered by the four perennial fountains of Tychin, or Immortality; it is the hill-encompassed Ila of the Singhalese and Thibetians, 'the everlasting dwelling place of the wise and just'. It is the Sineru of the Buddhist, on the summit of which is Tawrutisa, the habitation of Sekra, the supreme god, from which proceed the four sacred streams, running in as many contrary directions. It is the Slavratta, 'the celestial earth', of the Hindoo, the summit of his golden mountain Meru, and city of Brahma, in the centre of Jambadwipa, and from the four sides of which gush forth the four primeval rivers, reflecting in their passage the colorific glories of their sources, and severally flowing northward, southward, eastward, and westward.

LEGACY OF THE SKY PEOPLE

These four rivers flowing in four different directions recorded in legends and folklore of different countries throughout the world point to the origin of the cross. The cross then, is the most ancient symbol in the earth; a symbol brought to this planet from another world and venerated by all races of Cross-Man.

Truly, the only Salvation (salvage, regeneration) of hu-man as we know him, is through his cross. Being already fastened to it inescapably through his inherited animal nature, this must be so. Otherwise there could be no saving him at all.

Each must bear his own cross. That is to say, each must contend with his or her particular balance of inherited and developed factors, and through that experience weed out and finally eliminate the Adam-II characteristics to be found in it. These characteristics must literally perish completely never to rise again. They have no place at all in the make-up of Galactic Men, pure Adam-I Mankind as it was created by the Elohim. What remains—and what develops—will be the glorified body, capable of what has been called Ascension. This will be a body acceptable to the Sons of God, because it will, indeed, 'be as one of them'.

Each of us and all of us must discover the true cross. This heavenly inheritance, this Christos (or anointing) exists in each and every one of us to some degree. In our time it exists to such a degree that it is possible to turn to and eliminate, with its own energies, the remnant of the Earth-Adam that keeps us tied to the animal flesh. By so doing we can make ourselves acceptable to the True Humanity: Galactic Man, who is both our brother and our progenitor—the Race of Man created by the Elohim to live among the stars. Sometimes these people have been called our elder brothers. This term applies to some of them for a very special reason to be gone into in another place, but if you happen to be a stickler for accuracy you may prefer to call them our elder cousins. Earth Man then is crucified upon this genetic cross, but he can be raised up through the spiritual line he inherits from the Sons of God. By following that set of inclinations and by orienting himself as a Son of God rather than as a son of that Adam who was not quite a man (i.e. who was created a little lower than the angels), he finds the Christ within himself (as the Nazarene, Jesus, did) and dies as an earth-man, upon his own cross, to rise again, a true Son of God.

The horizontal line of the symbolic cross figure represents chemical matter, and hence, by analogy, the chemical-animal-bodied people created by the Jehovah.

The vertical line of the symbolic cross figure represents the Galactic-oriented, elder Sons of God, the creations of the Elohim. These people are the original mankind, and they were commanded to fill the planets and subdue them. The other kind of people, Jehovah's creations, were not so commanded.

LEGACY OF THE SKY PEOPLE

These two lines crossed represent Hu-mankind on Earth as it exists today, a cross between these two lines of evolution. This is a condition that came into its final permanence when Cain went out into the land of Nod and found himself a wife. It reached full expression in the people of Lamech, who fathered (or, from whom sprung) the people called Noah (after the name of their patriarch).

The people of Noah, and four other sub-types like them and related to them, were the peoples who were preserved when the Jehovah ultimately regretted having made his kind of man and determined to destroy them.

Reaching an understanding of the genetic cross which produced him and to which he is nailed by his inheritance, will help earth man find his redemption. He can sort out the two sets of inclinations, understand them, learn to cope with them, and come to terms with his conflicts whether personal or social, national or international.

Then, and only then, can he realise himself as a Son of God, and learn to live and to behave like one. He can rise from the living death of his present crucified existence and be accepted in his father's house, his true home in heaven, the Galaxy.

The animal man suffers to the full extent of his capability of suffering, and finally dies in this act of redemption. It is only the Son of God who, in him, triumphs over that death and comes, by his resurrection, into his own birthright.

Jesus, the Nazarene, knew and realised (i.e. made real) the Son of God in himself and causes it to typify all triumph over the animal hu-man nature. He tried to tell others how to find that part of themselves and how to develop it. He spoke as a Christ and people heard him as that Jesus, of Nazareth, son of Joseph, the carpenter, and they personalised the whole Great Event to the extent that the real story of the Alchemical Operation was lost.

Now it may be time to tell the story again. Time to cut the Gordian knot of interpretation with the simple sword of Truth.

What is the nature of the enmity, the difference, between the seed of Jehovah's woman and the seed of the serpent people? Why does the Jehovah say, in the fifteenth verse of the third Chapter of Genesis: 'It shall bruise thy head, and thou shalt bruise his heel'?

In order to understand this verse we must know what the reference to heel meant in Chaldee and in Hebrew. Heel in the Bible is an euphemism for the generative organs, which were held sacred. The word thigh is similarly used, and both references derive from one of the sitting habits of the people who spoke the language—the habit of sitting down with one leg hanging down and one heel tucked up against the crotch. This is a commonly practised position among many oriental peoples and is often seen in eastern pictures and sculptures. It is most interesting, that the Buddha Maitreya (the coming Buddha of the West, or the Christ in his Second Appearance) is always portrayed in this position (or standing upright).

The child of Adam-II in each of us, is strongly oriented toward sex and sexual expression. The child of the Elohim in each of us is even more strongly oriented toward spiritual pursuits, towards the functions of the head or Divine Mind.

So the seed of the woman of Jehovah's Adam in each one of us bruises (hurts, harms, inhibits, or otherwise painfully hampers) the head (mental and spiritual functions) of the seed of the serpent people. On the other hand, preoccupation with the things of the spirit bruises (painfully inhibits and frustrates) the heel or sexual inclinations of the seed (or genetic inheritance) of animal chemical humanity.

This basic enmity or difference is responsible for a tremendous amount of the domestic difficulty experienced by married people.

There are a couple of comments in the prophecy of the Jehovah to the serpent and the woman that will bear a second look and some brief discussion. Some scholars consider this to be a very mysterious series of statements, which indeed it is, unless the foregoing portions of the narrative have been read aright.

The Jehovah foresaw that the seed or descendants of the serpent people would mingle with and eventually intermarry with the seed or descendants of the second Adamic population.

It was obvious that this circumstance could bring very little good to either side of the bargain and might cause no end of harm.

So perhaps the words spoken to the Serpent in Genesis iii. 14, were spoken more in sorrow than in anger.

In the fifteenth verse, the Jehovah is made to say a very strange thing that countless readers have used as an excuse to fear and kill ordinary little snakes. 'I will put enmity ... etc.'

This refers to some of the psychic and psychological consequences of the intermingling of the types which was about to take place. It is a little catalogue of some of the basic difficulties the mixed (crossed) race was going to encounter while trying to live with itself as well as with the other races. Here, we are not trying to be Freudian. Freud, whether he knew it or not, was trying to be Biblical.

This enmity is compounded of physical attraction and misapplication of the generative act, along with an actual difference in the intensity of need for and impulse toward it. Students of psychology have recognised the resulting animosity and have done their best to explain it along broad and general lines, mistaking at the same time, the result for a cause. But without a knowledge of how it began and what caused it in the first place, they have floundered rather badly.

The seed of the woman represents the genetic inheritance from the Adam-II animal mankind that was put into the garden. Through this heritage came the tendencies toward an animal life as an end in itself, orientation toward the body and its functions, and above all, the absence of the telepathic ability inherent in Galactic man. This telepathic ability was not (and still is not) possessed by Adam-II hu-manity.

Where cross-man is concerned, many have discovered and remarked that the possession of too much heavy chemical mass, too many gross atoms, or coarse vibrations as they are sometimes called, in the body, quite submerges any latent telepathic faculty.

It is through Eve, the mother of all living Adam-II humanity, that we inherit this tendency toward a bruised head; the crossed type is, for the most part, two-eyed, or non-telepathic, and from the point of view of a Galactic individual, a person who is deprived of the clairvoyant-telepathic ability is definitely hurt. He is a cripple. And the seat of the receptive (fem. Polarity) side of these functions, is in the head. So, in the cross, the seed of Galactic Man (the serpent people) has been bruised in his head. There is a further consequence of basic difference in genetic inheritance that comes up in the field of hu-man relationships, but the actual physiological consequence, as described, is at the root of it.

'And thou shalt bruise his heel'. This is a very strange phrase until it is understood that the word heel in the old language of the Bible means organs of generation, or generative function.

If we read on into the sixteenth verse, we see that this statement is further elucidated. 'Unto the woman he said, I will greatly multiply thy conception; etc.'

The effect of the hu-man genetic cross was to be one that is often observed in crosses in the animal world; a great stimulus to fertility. These people became more than ordinarily prolific. Later on we read that the children who were born between the Sons of God and the Daughters of Men were larger than ordinary children. They grew up to be Giants, in more ways than one.

There were giants in the earth in those days; and also after that, when the Sons of God came in unto the daughters of men, and they bare children to them, and the same became mighty men which were of old, men of renown.

—Genesis vi. 4.

It is interesting to note that the human body is still born big, considering the machinery that produces it. This was even more the case in those early days of the cross. So the women who mated with the Sons of the Serpent suffered intensely in bringing forth their more than ordinarily numerous children.

Because these women were members of Adam-II humanity, oriented toward the body and its animal functions, they were pretty thoroughly concentrated upon the pleasures of that body, including those of sex, and so were compulsively subject to their husbands.

This attitude is typical of Adam-II (or, in our own times, Adam-II dominant) hu-manity, and it is true of individuals of both sexes. A person so oriented, whether a male or a female, becomes the emotional slave of his sexual object, as, in this particular reference, the woman was foretold to be ruled over by the husband toward whom her desire would be directed.

As the cross became more firmly established, then, of course, either Type-I or Type-II could be dominant in either men or women. (Each one of us has his own particular cross, his own particular proportion and assembly of factors, to which he is nailed for the duration of any given lifetime.)

As a result of this proportional distribution of genetic factors there came to be men who were ruled over by their wives, men and women who tried to rule one another, but who were fighting it out on more or less equal ground, and, of course, women who were ruled by their husbands—all combinations, in fact, that we have with us today.

And the stories given us in the Bible illustrate every one of them.

The social order in which we find ourselves at this time is based on the statement in the sixteenth verse of Genesis iii—but quite without any understanding either of the statement itself or of the progress earth hu-manity has made since that statement was made.

This is certainly not to say that women ought to take over and rule the world, or that we stand in any real danger of their doing so. Men and women have equally valuable, but very different functions in any well-ordered society (which ours most certainly is not), and the society remains in good health only so long as these functions are recognised and remain relatively unmixed. This is no easy accomplishment in a society where the race itself is a mixture of two such different originals as Adam-I and Adam-II.

However, in the case of an Adam-I dominant woman, let us say, whose physical urges are far less compelling than those of the Adam-II dominant male to whom she may be married (or the other way round, the Adam-I man to an Adam-II dominant woman—same problem) even a little understanding of the basic causes of their emotional conflicts, and some attempt to give way a little on both sides, might go far toward keeping their marriage out of the divorce courts.

So the inheritors of Adam-II's strong physical impulses could not help but feel that their Adam-I mates were often cold and unresponsive. They were, and still are, hurt by this condition—hurt emotionally and mentally—in the psychological area referred to by the euphemistic writers of the scriptures as the heel.

There are certain psychological factors inherent in the very make-up and nature of the Adam-II type people. These factors arise from their physical and psychological structure in the same way that courage and tenacity, for example, are bred into the bulldog and are known characteristics of the breed.

Adam-II hu-manity is, first of all, non-telepathic except as a Receiver. An Adam-II individual is capable of receiving telepathic impressions but he is incapable of recognising them as such at the present time because he does not send out any band his fellow Adam-II individuals are capable of receiving.

In the much mixed population of the earth there are individuals (increasing in number) in whom the Adam-I or telepathic factor is dominant. These people can (a) receive telepathic impressions and they know them for what they are, and/or (b) transmit some form of telepathic impressions of their own origin. In other words, the Adam-II characteristic of inhibited telepathy is wearing out, and the race is quite rapidly reverting to the condition that is both original and natural for Man's organism, i.e. that of telepathic sender-receiver. That half of the brain commonly not used by Adam-II hu-manity is a switchboard for these functions (and others related to them). In individuals being born during about the last six hundred years, the genes controlling these functions are becoming dominant again, and this other half of the brain is coming back into use.

A great deal of this civilisation's progress up out of the dark ages can be traced to this revival in increasing numbers of individuals of this unused portion of the brain.

The Adam-II hu-man created by the Jehovah is beginning to disappear, and Cross-Man on earth is rapidly developing, by a process of not entirely unaided selection, into a type which will be capable of contact with and assimilation by the other races of the system and of the galaxy.

There is already conflict between the two types, and between national and religious groups in which one type or other is predominant. There will be increasing conflict between them until one or the other is victorious. The problem at hand is to prevent the Adam-II people from annihilating those of Adam-I category (and a similar catastrophe taking place as occurred in Atlantis), and the prospect for this prevention is very good, partly because the extraterrestrial peoples are taking a firm hand to see that the inherently paranoid, non-telepathic Adam-II animal hu-man does not gain control. Adam-II, as a type of hu-manity, is on the way out. He is approaching the end of his cycle, the consummation of his world. He was not a success, and there is small room for his type in a galactic civilisation.

This is no tragedy, although some Adam-II individuals, sensing the fact that their physical type of hu-manity is one of Nature's blind alleys and so faced with either extinction or drastic change, have exhibited the inherent paranoia of their kind and have fought bitterly against the idea.

They appear to be incapable of accepting consolation in the fact that the physical regeneration of their type will release the tremendous spiritual potential that has built up during their long and difficult connection with it.

But they are fighting a losing battle; Adam-II, as a physical type, is on his way out of the race, to join the Dodo and the Dinosaur. Even his religions, which are full of mummified scientific facts, tell him this, but with typical paranoid projection he extends the circumstances to include all of hu-manity everywhere.

It may seem unkind to brand an entire hu-man group as paranoid, but unfortunately this is a datum we cannot escape if the type is observed objectively, dispassionately and with accuracy.

Why is the Adam-II type paranoid? There are several reasons, but the most important reason is his lack of the telepathic faculty. Along with this very serious inhibition goes his complete dependence upon vocal speech to exchange ideas.

Communication is the very important factor in the mental health of any human being, whatever his type. It could be said to be the prime factor in that mental health. A person in good communication with his fellow beings is a person in good communication with his environment, and such a person is inevitably and always healthy in both mind and body. He is capable of handling his problems as they arise; he is capable of creating for himself manifold future possibilities, capable of planning and executing those plans, or changing them quickly to suit new circumstances. He is at peace with himself and with his environment, knows he can cope with it, and if need be, control it to meet both his own needs and the requirements of hu-manity.

On the other hand, the person who is uncertain of his possible communication with either people or with his environment (and the two go together, inseparably) becomes sick in mind and body. He becomes, to some degree, paranoid. In time he replaces the uncertainties and unreality of his life with illusions and delusions because he feels he has some definite and predictable control over these (which he subtly recognises as creations of his own), whereas the actual environment and other people present to him only mysterious and incalculable

LEGACY OF THE SKY PEOPLE

forces beyond his power to control. And control he must, because he feels he cannot be a cause. He comes to distrust his fellow man, because, using only vocal speech, that fellow man can (and often does) deceive him.

Further, deprived of what should be his natural ability to observe the energies of his physical environment, and to manipulate those energies with the marvellous instruments of his own mind and body (which are equipped to do this to a very high degree, in the normal Adam-I type man), he cannot escape a deep sense of inadequacy and helplessness. He attempts to compensate for this in different ways. One way is through alliance with beings more capable and powerful than himself. This is a very natural reliance, if not, indeed, the most natural. Adam-II was created to be and to remain under the care, direction, and constant supervision of the Jehovah.

But, in Adam-II, what should be an alliance along constructive lines becomes one perverted to the inhibiting and even destructive motive of control, producing conflict, antagonism, struggle, restriction and death. The prayers going up to any God to 'destroy the enemy' must fall strangely indeed upon Galactic ears.

The paranoid condition of Adam-II hu-manity is a piece of known fact that has been mummified into the religions of the world and appears now in the doctrine of Original Sin. Paranoia is the sin or lack inherited by all the children of that Adam—one and all, as inhibited telepaths and therefore obviously inadequate to handle their environment on their own, they are incipient paranoiacs. There is original sin, inherent inadequacy, inherent tendency to abnormal behaviour, in Adam-II, but it is doubtful that the application of a little water and recitation of a few ritual words can do much to repair the defect-however much they may symbolise to the knowing eye.

Brad takes photo of Sherry contemplating the energy, on the site the Native Peruvians call the Naval of the World —a most important Vortex of energy, located in Cuzco, Peru.

Sherry on the Hitching Post of the Sun. Machu Pichu, Peru.

Both photos from the private collection of Brad and Sherry Steiger.

LEGACY OF THE SKY PEOPLE

CHAPTER VIII

THREE GLORIOUS SUNS

There are more things in heaven and earth Horatio, than are dreamt of in your philosophy.

—Hamlet.

Stories of the Space People coming to Earth in their golden sky chariots in past ages emanate not only from Greece and the Biblical Lands, but from everywhere on the planet.

The Red Indians of North America have many such traditions. The poet Longfellow made a lifelong hobby of gathering the finest Indian legends, many of which came to him from the lips of famous tribal chiefs of his day, such as Black Hawk and Kahge-ga-ga-bowh. In his famous epic Hiawatha, a well-blended compilation of such traditions, perhaps the most outstanding allusion to the Sky People is found in story twelve, **The Son of the Evening Star**. If you are not already familiar with this enchanting little space tale then you may be surprised at how much science remains in the legends. Here are the first few lines:

> Can it be the sun descending
> O'er the level plain of water?
> Or the Red Swan floating, flying,
> Wounded by the magic arrow,
> Staining all the waves with crimson,
> With the crimson of its life-blood.
> Filling all the air with splendour,
> With the splendour of its plumage?
> Yes; it is the sun descending,
> Sinking down into the water;
> All the sky is stained with purple,
> All the water flushed with crimson!

The Hopi Indians of Arizona hold the famous Niman Ceremony each year and the culmination is the picturesque and beautiful Home Dance. The purpose of the Ceremony is to invoke Divine help for their crops and to ask the Creator to send rain.

LEGACY OF THE SKY PEOPLE

Many white visitors attend the Home Dance, which is very enjoyable to watch, and the Hopis are a most friendly and spiritual people.

The Kachinas, a clan who live behind a sacred mountain, come and dance in the Hopi villages and are traditionally a heaven sent people. The significance attached to the Hopi's friends, the Kachinas, is most important. The Kachinas believe they originated from the skies. Sometimes alluded to as demigods, these beloved helpers symbolically relate, through dance, ritual and costuming, the story of who they are, whence they came, and what gifts, tangible and spiritual, they bring to Earth.

Incidentally, the Russian astronomer, Gavriil Tikhof, says his observations have led him to deduce that on Mars are flora, including moss and juniper trees, similar to our own in northern mountain regions. Among the Hopi regions, where the juniper and spruce grow together, the spruce is held sacred, as having been brought a gift to the Hopi, by their Kachina friends.

The Kachinas wear a most resplendent costume for the dance, complete with mask, headboard, feathers, plumes, all in colours symbolising some important point of their beliefs. On their upper torsos, which are painted greyish-brown, appears the symbol of friendship for all men. This consists of two pairs of half-crescent moons.

A correspondent in the United States writes that an Indian friend has on the wall of her living room, in place of the usual picture, these same crescent moons, in the same relative positions, with a star centered between them.

If the Hopis and Kachinas had a link long ago with Mars, could the Kachinas today in their ritual and dancing still wear the symbol of the two Martian satellites?

George Hunt Williamson, in **Road in the Sky**, devotes considerable space to the remarkable Hopi tribe and makes some very interesting comments on their connection with space people.

The Mormons, who were founded in 1830 by Joseph Smith in New York, have their own scripture, the Book of Mormon, which was written on plates.

Here are some verses taken from the plates of Nephi,

1 Nephi, xvi.

And thus my father had fulfilled all the commandments of the Lord which had been given unto him. And also, I, Nephi, had been blessed of the Lord exceedingly.

And it came to pass that the voice of the Lord spake unto my father by night, and commanded him that on the morrow he should take his journey into the wilderness.

And it came to pass that as my father arose in the morning, and went forth to the tent door, to his great astonishment he beheld upon the ground a round ball of curious workmanship; and it was of fine brass. And within the ball were two spindles; and the one pointed the way whither we should go into the wilderness.

And it came to pass that we did gather together whatsoever things we should carry into the wilderness, and all the remainder of our provisions which the Lord had given unto us; and we did take seed of every kind that we might carry into the wilderness.

15. And it came to pass that we did travel for the space of many days, slaying food by the way with our bows and arrows and our stones and our slings.

16. *And we did follow the directions of the ball, which led us in the more fertile parts of the wilderness.*

This seems similar in many respects to the story of the Israelites' journey through the wilderness guided by a pillar of a cloud by day and a pillar of fire by night.

One of the earliest known records of a fleet of flying saucers, written on a papyrus, long, long ago in Ancient Egypt, was found damaged, with many gaps in the hieroglyphics, among the papers of the late Professor Alberto Tulli, former director of the Egyptian Museum at the Vatican.

Prince Boris de Rachewiltz subsequently translated the papyrus. He stated that the original was part of the Annals of Thutmose III, circa 1504-1450 b.c. There are many broken sections.

In the year 22, of the 3rd month of winter, sixth hour of the day . . . the scribes of the House of Life found it was a circle of fire that was coming in the sky . . . it had no head, the breath of its mouth had a foul odour. Its body one rod long and one rod wide. It had no voice. Their hearts became confused through it: then they laid themselves on their bellies. . . . They went to the Pharaoh to report it. His Majesty ordered . . . has been examined . . . as to all which is written in the papyrus rolls of the House of Life. His Majesty was meditating upon what happened. Now after some days had passed, these things became more numerous in the skies than ever. They shone more in the sky than the brightness of the sun, and extended to the limits of the four supports of the heavens. . . . Powerful was the position of the fire circles. The army of the Pharaoh looked on with him in their midst. It was after supper. Thereupon, these fire circles ascended higher in the sky towards the south. Fishes and volatiles fell down from the sky. A marvel never before known since the foundation of their land. And the Pharaoh caused incense to be brought to make peace on the hearth. . . . And what happened was ordered by the Pharaoh to be written in the annals of the House of Life . . . so that it be remembered forever.

These ancient Egyptians called the saucers 'Fire circles'. This is a very good description. Most modern sightings of flying saucers are of circular objects brighter than the stars. The Bible, too, referred to them as fiery chariots.

Desmond Leslie, who did some excellent research for his book, **Flying Saucers Have Landed**, quoted from two famous Hindu classics, Ramayana and the Maha Bharata, to support his contention that Ancient India knew the secrets of space ships. Here is his quotation from Ramayana, and translated from the Sanscrit.

The Puspaku Car, that resembles the sun and belongs to my brother, was brought by the powerful Ravan; that aerial and excellent car, going everywhere at will, is ready for thee. That car, resembling a *bright cloud* in the sky, is in the city of Lanka.

The two words 'bright cloud' are, indeed, interesting, in view of the many references to clouds, connected with space ships in the Bible, discussed earlier. Yes, all over the world, in North, Central and South America, Egypt, India and, in fact, everywhere civilisation has existed, there are legends and tales, many dimly remembered, of our friends the Sky people; of their wondrous Star Ships looking like suns, fiery chariots or fire circles.

Even William Shakespeare, perhaps inadvertently, recorded a saucer sighting! At any rate, the lines written below do not sound like the pure imagination of the famous playwright.

They are taken from King Henry VI, Part III, Act II, Scene I.

A Plain Near Mortimey's Cross-Herefordshire

Edward: Dazzle mine eyes, or do I see three suns?

Richard: Three glorious suns, each a perfect sun,

Not separated with the racking clouds,

But sever'd in a pale clear shining sky.

See, See! they join, embrace and seem to kiss,

As if they vowed some league inviolable:

Now they are one lamp, one light, one sun,

In this the heaven figures some event.

Edward: Tis wondrous strange, the like yet never heard of.

LEGACY OF THE SKY PEOPLE

I think it cites us, brother to the field,

That we the sons of brave Plantagenet

Each one already blazing by our meeds,

Should notwithstanding join our lights together

And overshine the earth as this the world.

Whate'er it bodes, henceforward will I bear

Upon my target three fair shining suns.

Many modern accounts of flying saucers have testified to disc-shaped objects entering a parent craft and becoming as if 'one lamp, one light, one sun'.

Brad and Sherry Steiger with "Grandmother Twylah" the Repositor of Seneca Wisdom. All the Native American tribes had legends of the Sky People and the Star People. Brad was adopted into the Wolf Clan of the Seneca in 1974, and both Brad and Sherry are members of the Wolf Clan Teaching Lodge. From the private collection of Brad and Sherry Steiger.

LEGACY OF THE SKY PEOPLE

CHAPTER IX

SPACE SHIPS GALORE

A Sophist approached one of the wise men of Ancient Greece—he was a Sage of Miletus. He asked: What is the greatest of all things? Answer: Space because it contains all that has been created.

There were many reports of space ship activity in Roman times a century or so before the era of Jesus. In 222 b.c. it was recorded 'there shone a great light, like... three moons (that) appeared in quarters of the sky distant from each other, over the town of Ariminium.

'A round shield' was sighted over Arpi, 180 miles east of Rome in 216 b.c., and according to a report in the Dublin Evening Press of June 16, 1959, Mr. Railsback of Moline, Illinois, came across the sentence in one of the Roman historian Julius Obsequens' writings: At sunset a circular object like a shield was seen to sweep across the sky from west to east.' Mr. Railsback said the object was reported in 100 b.c. near Tarquinia, north of Rome.

Here is another of Obsequens' reports: 'A globe of fire (aurea globis), at sunrise, appeared in the sky with terrific noise, and burning over the town of Spoletum, Umbria. This was in 90 b.c. 'This globe... golden in colour fell to earth from the sky and was seen to gyrate.' Later it rose 'from the earth, was borne east, and obscured the disc of the sun with its magnitude'.

In the nearly two thousand years that have passed since Jesus's time, space ships have continued periodically to visit the earth.

Desmond Leslie described in **Flying Saucers Have Landed**, how a 'large round silver thing like a disc flew slowly over Byland Abbey, Yorkshire, in a.d. 1290'. He related that an old manuscript was found at Ampleforth Abbey in 1953 describing the occurrence.

For copious reports in the sixteenth, seventeenth and eighteenth centuries, Charles Fort's four famous books, **The Book of the Damned, New Lands, Lo!,** and **Wild Talents**, are invaluable. They are now published in one volume, entitled, **The Books of Charles Fort,** published for the Fortean Society by Henry Holt & Co., New York, 1941.

In 1897, a mysterious cigar-shaped airship was seen over various parts of

LEGACY OF THE SKY PEOPLE

the United States. This was five years before the Wright Brothers made their historic flight! Thousands of people saw this airship, which the authorities tried to explain away as the planet Venus. They still try to do that today when faced with sighting reports that do not measure up to a rational explanation.

And so to the twentieth century. Max B. Miller, in his book **Flying Saucers—Fact or Fiction?** records an unusual sighting.

Artist and explorer Nicholas Roerich, while travelling in Mongolia, was one of such few to observe the virtually ever-prevalent circular-airfoil—*the flying saucer*.

At 9:30, a.m. on August 5, 1920, several of his expedition were watching a remarkable 'bird', when suddenly one of the group spotted 'something far above the bird'.

'We all saw,' wrote Roerich in **Attai Himalaya** in 1921, '... something big and shining, reflecting the sun like a huge oval moving at great speed. Crossing our camp, this thing changed direction from south to southwest.

'Through binoculars,' he continued, 'they saw quite distinctly an oval form with shining surface, one side of which was brilliant in the sun.'

During World War II the 'Foo Fighters', as they were termed by pilots, were seen. They were small remote-controlled 'eyes' craft about a foot in diameter, which dived and flew around bomber formations. Both sides thought that they were a secret weapon belonging to the enemy and little knew they were being watched from a mother ship high up in the heavens above them.

We have only considered so far in this chapter just a few reports of space craft seen in the last few centuries prior to 1947. There are records of very many more. How did the term 'flying saucer' come about? For the benefit of those readers who are not 'blue stocking' saucer researchers, the spate of flying saucer reports in modern times could really be said to date from June 24, 1947. On that date, an American businessman, Kenneth Arnold, was flying his own plane near the Cascade Mountain Range in the State of Washington, when he spotted between his plane and the peaks nine huge gleaming objects flying at an estimated 1,200 miles per hour. Upon landing Arnold described the motion of these objects as like 'saucers skimming over water'. The Press headlined them as flying saucers and the name stuck ever since. Many people regard it as an unfortunate appellation which has helped to cast ridicule on the subject. However, it could be a blessing in disguise. As we have seen, studying the subject in depth in this book, people are at various stages of development and understanding. Some people, without being gullible, are prepared to accept anything as possible under God and to adapt themselves to change, new outlooks and ideas. They are truly the stuff that

LEGACY OF THE SKY PEOPLE

Galactics are made of.

Others, even highly trained, so-called scientific experts, are prejudiced to either their own preconceived ideas, or to the dogmas and teachings of both orthodox science and religion.

The common man, neither a scientist nor one of the clergy, has in the past been accustomed to taking his cue from these authorities and for hundreds of years has been educated that the earth was the centre of the universe. Even up to very recently, he was told that there was no life on the planets, but let us hope he is noticing that the scientists are beginning to change their ideas.

Many scientists now are beginning to have a broader outlook. Professor Hermann Oberth, the father of rocketry, has repeatedly stated in public that this planet is being watched by intelligent beings from outer space. Here is one of the most exciting saucer accounts ever recorded, taken from the May/June 1958 issue of *Flying Saucer Review*.

'On the night of September 4, 1957, there took off from Ota Air Base, Portugal, a flight of four jet fighter-bombers, F-84s of American design, belonging to the Portuguese Air Force. The pilots involved were three sergeants, Alberto Gomes Covas, Salvador Alberto Oliveria, Manual Neves Marcelino, with Captain Jose Lemos Ferreira, acting as flight commander. The mission was a routine practice night navigation flight at 25,000 feet between Ota Air Base, the Spanish town of Granada, the Portuguese town of Portalegre, and finally to the Portuguese village of Coruche.

Captain Ferreira stated in an interview at Ota Air Base with Senor Marciano Alves, Flying Saucer Review's Lisbon correspondent:

'After we reached Granada, at 2006 hours, and started a port turn to change course to Portalegre I noticed on my left and above the horizon a very unusual source of light. We completed the turn and still I continued to be very interested in that light. I may add that after three or four minutes of close observation I decided to report it to the other pilots. At that time the pilot flying on my right wing told me he had already noticed it. The other two pilots flying on my left wing had not yet seen it. Together we started exchanging comments over the radio about our discovery and we tried several solutions but none seemed to be a reasonable explanation for the thing we were observing at the moment. The thing looked like a very bright star unusually big and scintillating with a coloured nucleus which changed colour constantly, going from deep green to blue, passing through yellowish and reddish colorations.

At first one would think it was some kind of a star, perhaps Venus, although we could not confuse any other star visible in the sky with the thing we were discussing. But soon we repudiated the Venus hypothesis because we already had surely identified that planet. Then, after running out of solutions, such as balloons, aircraft, celestial bodies, etc., without finding an answer we were almost apt to forget the case when all of sudden, the thing grew very rapidly, assuming five or six times its initial volume, becoming quite a spectacle to see. Before our surprise had time to expand, the thing fast as it had grown, decided to shrink, almost disappearing on the horizon, becoming just a visible, small yellow point. These expansions and contractions happened several times, but without becoming periodic and always having a pause, longer or shorter, before modifying volume. The relative position between us and the thing was still the same, that is about 40º on our left, and we could not determine if the changing dimensions were due to very fast approaches and retreats on the same vector or if the modifying took place stationary. If the first case was the reality the speed would be tremendous and out of all proportion for any aircraft we have seen or heard of. After about seven or eight minutes of this the thing had gradually been getting down below the horizon and dislocated itself- for a position about 90º. to our left. A little before reaching the town of Portalegre, at 2038 hours, I decided to abandon the mission and to make a port turn in the general direction of Coruche since nobody was paying any attention to the exercise. We turned about 50º to port but still this thing maintained its position of 90º to our left, which could not be possible with a stationary object. By now the phenomenon was well below our level of 25,000 feet and apparently quite near, presenting a bright red and looking like a curved shell of beans at an arm's length. After several minutes on our new course we discovered a small circle of yellow light apparently coming out of the thing and before our surprise elapsed we detected three other identical circles on the right of thing. The whole was moving with their relative positions changing constantly and sometimes very rapidly.

Still we could not estimate the distance between us and them although they were below us and apparently very near. In any case, the big 'thing!' looked ten to fifteen times greater than the yellow circles and apparently was the director of operations since the others were moving round it. As we were near Coruche the "big thing' suddenly and very rapidly made what looked like a dive, followed by a climb in our direction. Then everybody went wild and almost broke formation in the process of crossing over and ahead of the UFO.* We were all very excited and I had a hard time to calm things down. As soon as we crossed over everything disappeared in a few seconds and later we landed without further incident. Since the first moment we detected the UFO to the final show a registered time of forty minutes had elapsed, and during it we had ample opportunity to verify every possible explanation for the phenomenon. We got no conclusions, except that after this do not give us the old routine of Venus, balloons, aircraft and the like which has been given as a general panacea for almost every case of UFOs.'

LEGACY OF THE SKY PEOPLE

* UFO = Unidentified Flying Object. This is the term used by the U.S, Air Force to cover anything in the sky they cannot identify: The term has over the years become interchangeable with flying saucer.

The Lisbon Diario llustrado stated that the Coimbra Meteorological Observatory registered extraordinary variations in the magnetic field at the same time that Captain Ferreira and his squadron were observing the space ships. According to the Lisbon paper, this can be verified by diagrams at the observatory.

Yes, today, the Sky People are back with us again! Since 1947, literally thousands of their space ships have been seen in every part of the world. They have been photographed, filmed and recorded frequently on radar. Many people, too, have claimed actual physical contact with the occupants of these ships of light. Once more the Sky People are mingling with mortals!

Here are a few more sighting highlights from the last three years, culled from *Flying Saucer Review*.

The launching of the Sputniks, especially Sputnik 2 in 1957, heralded the greatest saucer show ever, topping even the previous best in 1952. For a dramatic and objective account of that astounding year 1952, including the amazing Washington Airport 'saucer flap', read Major Donald E. Keyhoe's *Flying Saucers from Outer Space*.

Sightings on November 1957 were indeed reported from all over the world. The United States Army stated that a huge, oval object 'nearly as bright as the sun' was spotted on November 3, at White Sands Proving Grounds, New Mexico, hovering near bunkers used in the first atom bomb explosion on July 16, 1945. Two sightings of the object were made by two different patrols of military police, seventeen hours apart.

On November 5, at 5:21 a.m., came a most objective and dramatic sighting! The U.S. Coast Guard cutter Sebago, cruising in the Gulf of Mexico, reported a brilliant flying object in the sky about 200 miles south of the Mississippi River. The object was tracked on the vessel's radar for twenty-seven minutes. It flitted off the screen several times. Radar trackings showed the object reached speeds of up to 1,000 m.p.h. The crew saw the UFO also visually for a brief period of a few seconds. The commander described it as resembling a brilliant planet speeding through the sky. It finally disappeared into a cloud bank at about 2,000 feet. It moved in concentric circles around the ship at great speed and was last tracked 175 miles from the vessel.

Saucer reports were by no means limited to the United States during the November flap. Reports came in from Australia, France, Great Britain, Egypt, Japan and indeed, from all over the world. Here are a couple of rather amusing ones taken from *Flying Saucer Review*.

The crew of the Fleetwood trawler Ella Hewett, which was off the northeast of the island (Isle of Man-Author) saw the object. Bos'un Hugh Smith gave this description: A massive glow surrounded the ship, an eerie something all about us. There was no vibration, no explosion, in fact, no sensation at all.

Then the skipper, Fred Sutton, radioed from the Atlantic: A funny thing happened to me last night. The whole paint on the front of the bridge vanished.

'The paint was definitely there before I went to bed. This morning only the red lead undercoat was left. I have been scratching my head all day about it, and now you can scratch yours.' The next day another brief radio message from the ship (owners: Hewett Fishing Co. Ltd.) said: 'Yesterday bridge pink, today normal white. The white paint on the bridge had returned!'

An account of a similar occurrence which took place in Norway during 1956 was given by Carl Olsen, writing in *Flying Saucer Review*.

A Mr. Trygve Jansen, a master-painter, was returning by car to his home at Ski, after having supervised work in Oslo. He was accompanied by a lady, Mrs. Buflot a neighbour to whom he was giving a lift.

Mr. Jansen had travelled this road daily for several years. It should be explained that the road runs for a considerable distance by the side of a long, narrow lake called Gjersjoen.

At Gjersjoen bridge they first observed the phenomenon, an object came with great speed from behind a hill, made a swing out over the lake, and back to the road.

Jansen was keeping his eyes on the road, and therefore did not look closely at the object. He thought at first that it was caused by some kind of light reflexes, or perhaps by a large bird.

After a time, however, he became aware that the light seemed to follow the car. It circled the car again and again, and occasionally made great wide sweeps. Both driver and passenger soon got the feeling that they were pursued. Six or seven times during the run beside the lake the object was close to the car, and the occupants had a feeling of unrest.

Just after having passed the lake, when they were on a level stretch of road, the object flew in front of the car and stopped above the centre of the road. Mr. Jansen felt as if he was compelled to stop the car, and he finally did so when the object started coming down towards it.

When it was straight in front of the car, the object stopped again and stood completely still. Both occupants of the car had a distinct feeling of being scrutinized. Suddenly the object took-off straight upwards, and then disappeared with great speed behind the car. While the object was standing in front of the car, both witnesses felt a prickly sensation in their faces; it was as if they were exposed to a strong beam of some kind. And most curious of all, Mr. Jansen's watch, which had kept perfect time for years, stopped at that moment. The watch later had to undergo a very expensive repair, and the watchmaker said that it had been exposed to a strong magnetic current. When Mr. Jansen arrived at his home, his wife came running out and asked him if he had bought a new car. 'No,' said Mr. Jansen, 'why do you think so?' 'Well, see for yourself,' said his wife, pointing to the vehicle.

The car which had been of a dull beige colour, was now shiny, and the colour more nearly green.

There were many witnesses to this change of colour, and they all saw it before Mr. Jansen or Mrs. Buflot had said a word about their adventure. The next day the car had resumed its normal colour.

The Jansens had a party that evening, but Mr. Jansen could not manage to swallow the least bit of food. He wasn't exactly ill, but felt unwell. His skin was still prickly, as if he had been sitting too long before an ultra-violet lamp. He did not feel normal again before the next evening. Mrs. Buflot had exactly the same experience. Both witnesses had ample opportunity to study the saucer closely, and they say that it looked like a shining disc with wings. The disc seemed to rotate, and on the top it had what they described as a kind of cockpit. The light that emanated from the saucer was quite strong, and of a greenish-white colour. It often seemed to come in waves and at times lit up the whole forest.

Both these stories once again indicate how strong the force field of a flying saucer can be and some of its effects.

On January 16, 1958, the Brazilian Navy ship Almirante Saldanha was taking part in research for the international Geophysical Year programme and was near to the island of Trinidad. (Not the island in the West Indies, but the one off Brazil.) A flying saucer flew over the island from the sea and several good photographs of it were taken by the cameraman on the deck of the naval ship. The Rio de Janeiro newspaper Correio da Manha published six photographs of the object, together with an account of this occurrence, on the front page of its February 21, 1958, issue. The Brazilian Navy stated these photographs were authentic. Two well-authenticated sightings involving airliners which took place thousands of miles from each other occurred during 1959. Here are condensed extracts from the two accounts as I wrote them in *Flying Saucer Review*.

Thirty-five passengers watched in wonder as three illuminated flying saucers escorted their American Airlines four-engine DC-6 airliner for forty-five minutes! Captain Peter Killian, a pilot of twenty years experience, with a total of more than four million miles to his credit, was at the controls. The co-pilot and First Officer was another experienced flier, John Dee.

The airliner had left Newark airport at 7:10 p.m. on February 24, 1959, on a non-stop flight to Detroit. It was 8:45 p.m. over Pennsylvania when Captain Killian first spotted the three yellowish lights in a single line formation. He pointed them out to his co-pilot, John Dee, the other crew members and the passengers. The crew assured him he was not seeing things. Killian even radioed two other American Airlines planes flying in the vicinity to make sure he wasn't 'seeing lightning bugs in the cockpit'. Both other captains called Killian back to assure him he wasn't—they saw the saucers too.

Among the passengers was Mr. N. D. Puscas, general manufacturing manager of Curtis-Wright Division at Utica. He said the strange objects were in 'precise formation' and seemed to dance in the sky. 'They were roundlike, and every now and then one would glow brighter than the others, as if it had moved closer to the plane.'

To enable the passengers to have a better view of the saucers, the stewardesses, Edna Lagate and Beverly Pingree, turned out the cabin lights and everyone watched the fantastic 'out of this world' spectacle for the next forty minutes.

Captain Killian radioed a report of the incident to American Airlines communications at Detroit Airport before coming in to land. The three objects became lost in a low altitude haze.

In addition to the crew and thirty-five passengers of his own plane and the two other American Airlines planes he had contacted by radio while in flight, the three UFOs had also been sighted by the crews of three United Airlines planes! All the pilots and flight engineers agreed that the lights were on separate vehicles which were in formation.

According to a report published by NICAP, Lieutenant-Colonel Lee B. James, an army missile expert associated with Wernher von Braun, in the Army Ordnance Missile Command, suggested that the objects came from outer space! Speaking before the Michigan Society of Professional Engineers, Colonel James stated that the objects seen by the various airline crews were quite possibly spaceships.

'I know they are not from here,' said the missile expert, 'and they are not coming from Russia, We in this civilisation are not that advanced yet.

'If the crews and passengers really saw what was reported,' Colonel James said, the objects 'would have to come from outer space—a civilisation decades ahead of ours.'

LEGACY OF THE SKY PEOPLE

Far away from Pennsylvania where Captain Killian's airliner was escorted by saucers, another amazing sighting involving five more airliners and five more saucers took place about 1,000 miles east of Honolulu on Saturday, July 11, 1959.

The most detailed report available to the public was that of Captain George Wilson, forty-three-year-old Pan-American Airways pilot with nineteen years flying experience. He was flying from San Francisco to Honolulu. He said: 'At 3:02 a.m. Hawaii time I saw one intensely bright white light followed by four smaller lights.'

Captain Wilson, visibly shaken by his experience, went on: 'My co-pilot, Richard Lorenzen, of Los Altos, California, and flight engineer Robert Scott, stared open-mouthed as the light came towards us at an extremely high rate of speed.

'For at least ten seconds it maintained its course, which was on an opposite heading to us; and had it been another aircraft it would have passed well to our left.

'Suddenly the object made a sharp right turn at a speed inconceivable to any vehicle we know and the light suddenly disappeared. The smaller lights were evenly spaced and were either a part of the mysterious object, or this was an example of darned good formation flying.'

When he landed in Honolulu Captain Wilson said he had never seen anything like this in his nineteen years of flying. He added that he had never believed such foreign objects existed.

'I'm a believer now,' he said.

The other pilots who filed reports were Captain Lloyd Moffatt of Canadian Pacific Airways; First Officer Erwin Zedwick of Slick Airways; Captain Noble Sprunger, of Pan-American Airways, and Captain E. G. Kelley, also of Pan-American.

Captain Moffatt confirmed Captain Wilson's story. He said: 'You can take it from me they were there. I never saw anything like it in my life and there are five of us who saw the same thing at the same time.'

It is not the purpose of this book to recount saucer sighting after saucer sighting. That, with all due deference to the understanding occupants of the craft, would become tedious. Suffice it to say there are over one hundred books on the subject of flying saucers now, and many of these list more modern reports than appear in these pages.

The recent sightings included in this chapter have been selected to show how well authenticated some of these happenings can be. The Portuguese Air

LEGACY OF THE SKY PEOPLE

Force one, the photographs taken from the Brazilian Navy ship and the two amazing airliner sightings just related, were all observed by trained and experienced pilots or by service personnel, and in each case there were many witnesses.

Now to close this chapter, are two very important sightings which happened, at the time of writing, only a few months ago. In each case witnesses saw actual people in the spacecraft concerned.

The first made the front page of the Brisbane Sunday Mail for August 16, 1959. The report came from the Reverend Father W. B. Gill, of the Boianai Anglican Mission, Papua, New Guinea.

Here is an extract of this sensational sighting as reported in *Flying Saucer Review*, by its correspondent in Papua, the Reverend N. E. G. Crutwell. The data supplied by Mr. Gill to Mr. Crutwell is dated Saturday, June 27, 1959.

Large UFO first sighted at 6 p.m. in apparently same position as last night [there had been considerable saucer incidents over Papua just prior to this report-author] only seemed a little smaller.... I called one of the Mission boys and several others and we stood in the open to watch. Although the sun had set, it was quite light for the following fifteen minutes. We watched figures appear on top—four of them—no doubt they are human. Possibly the same object that I took to be the 'mother' ship last night. Two smaller UFOs were seen at the same time, stationary. One above the hills, west, another overhead. On the large one, two of the figures seemed to be doing something near the centre of the deck; were occasionally bending over and raising their arms as though adjusting or setting up something (not visible). One figure seemed to be standing, looking down at us (a group of about a dozen). I stretched my arm above my head and waved. To our surprise the figure did the same. One of the Mission boys waved both arms above his head, then the two outside figures did the same. There seemed to be no doubt that our movements were answered. All Mission boys made audible gasps (of either joy or surprise, perhaps both).

As dark was beginning to close in, I sent Eric Kodawa for a torch and directed a series of long dashes towards the UFO. After a minute or two of this, the UFO apparently acknowledged by making several wavering motions back and forth. Waving by us was repeated and this was followed by more flashes of the torch, then the UFO began slowly to become bigger, apparently coming in our direction. It ceased after perhaps half a minute and came on no farther. After a further two or three minutes the figures apparently lost interest in us for they disappeared below deck. At 6:25 p.m. two figures reappeared to carry on with whatever they were doing before the interruption. The blue spotlight came in for a few seconds twice in succession.

LEGACY OF THE SKY PEOPLE

The other two UFOs remained stationary and high up. . . .

Incidentally, the Brisbane Sunday Mail in its full account of this occurrence stressed the reliability of Father Gill, who graduated from St. Francis Theological College, Milton, in 1950. This sighting too, it should be noted, had about a dozen witnesses. The second recent case of people being seen in space craft occurred on Wednesday, September 23, 1959, and was front page news in the Dublin Evening Herald for that day. Here is the story:

The pilot of a Pan-American jet airliner, flying almost four miles high between New York and Paris this morning, reported that he had sighted what he believed was a space ship with people on board.

In a brief message to Shannon from the Clipper the pilot, Captain J. Cone, said it was visible for forty seconds only and that the object had vertical tail fins. It was travelling very fast in a southwesterly direction between the stars Elnath and Caston.

The object was sighted close to the D.E.W. line 'Dewiz', the distant early warning radar screen which protects the entire northwest coast of America and Canada from attack.

There were 111 people, including twelve crew members, on board the jetliner, which later landed at Paris.

It was flying at an altitude of 20,000 feet when the object was sighted. Other brief details given in the message give the object's position at 53°—40° west, which would be slightly northwest of Goose Bay, Labrador, Canada, about 2,000 miles west of Ireland. The report has set off considerable speculation in international circles studying space aeronautics.

The reports given here are but an infinitesimal number of those that have been recorded since 1947. Thousands and thousands of people in all countries have seen the saucers. Why are they coming back in such increasing numbers at this time? Why are they watching us so intently?

In the last one hundred and fifty years hu-mankind has made tremendous progress—the whole technology of this present civilisation has bounded forward from the horse and carriage which it had been in for centuries and the momentum of increasing knowledge is stepping up at an almost incredible rate. The steam engine, the motor car, the aeroplane, the radio, television, radar, the marvels of electronics, stereophonic sound, and nuclear fission. The list is unending and growing every day. Man has explored every part of the earth, reached the poles, the tops of the highest mountains, descended in bathyspheres to the uttermost depths of the ocean and now plans to 'conquer' outer space—first the moon, then the planets and finally, hopes to reach the stars.

LEGACY OF THE SKY PEOPLE

It is the ultimate destiny of hu-man to raise his status to that of real Man and live among the stars, enjoying the fellowship and respect of his fellow godlike Galactic Beings, but will hu-manity on earth be allowed out of quarantine yet?

We have seen how at the time of the building of the Tower of Babel, humanity tried to get back to their original home in the heavens, and how the Sky People scattered the people abroad over the face of the earth. Will something similar happen again? The trouble is that the world today is divided into two opposing camps and both sides have the means to end all life on this planet! Humanity has not yet learnt its lesson and will not be allowed to take its animal-man characteristics plus the violent atomic and other destructive forces at its disposal into outer space!

However, as has been indicated earlier, hope for hu-manity remains. Biblical prophecy (Matthew xxiv and Mark xiii) need not necessarily come to pass. Many prophecies do not mature for the simple reason that the pattern of events changes. At the time prophecies are made, the seers base them on an existing pattern which if carried right through will bring about a certain result. Today, thousands of Galactic dominant people in the world are working for peace and for the eventual exclusion of all nuclear weapons. Let us pray and hope they succeed in their work and change the pattern so that hu-manity will forsake the ways of violence and really accept both in word and deeds the old saying, 'Goodwill to all men'. Then they will be accepted on equal terms as friends, by our next of kin, among the stars!

CHAPTER X

THE PROBLEM OF ADAM-II

The man who never alters his opinions is like standing water, and breeds reptiles of the mind.

—William Blake.

XENOPHOBIA, irrational distrust of unfamiliar people and things, is an inevitable outgrowth of Adam-II's non-telepathic inadequacy.

If he must distrust his own kind—and he must, since he is never able to be sure of their motive or honesty—then how much more must he distrust the stranger, particularly if that stranger bears upon his bodily form the outward and visible marks of his difference, such as different hair colour or texture, or a different stature, or a different skin pigmentation? If his manner and customs are different, too, as they must almost always be, then the distrust is intensified—and when his vocal speech is found to be different, also, then indeed he is to be feared. It is always safer to fear, and to avoid—even, sometimes, to attack and to kill first. The basic impulse of paranoia is fear—a special kind of fear that arises out of an inability to predict control of someone or somebody. One of the manifestations of incipient paranoia is an obsessive desire to control everything and everybody in the environment at all times. When this becomes obviously impossible, compensation sets in: magic is born, gods and other supernatural agencies are invoked at a debased level of misunderstanding. War, destructive and other forms of wholesale enforcement of control are justified.

In Adam-II hu-manity, the energies that normally exist to be channelled through the telepathic and associated functions are diverted, instead, into feelings, into emotions and into the mechanisms of vocal expression, which is an emotional process.

This has resulted, as environmental stresses build up, in a large number and astonishing variety of mental and emotional insanities. While hu-manity is aware of this increase in what it calls mental disease, it remains unaware of the basic cause of the disorders and so has made very little headway in coping with them. Just how many Adam-I dominant natural telepaths are incarcerated right now in our mental institutions is a good subject for anybody's appalling guess. That number, however, must equal, at least, the number of Adam-II dominant indi-

LEGACY OF THE SKY PEOPLE

viduals who are there because their half-functioning brain-switchboards were simply unable to handle the load imposed upon them by an increasingly complex civilisation that clings stubbornly to archaic emotional taboos.

One of the most effective of these taboo-patterns, unfortunately, is the jumbled mass of relics and misinterpretations Adam-II sanctifies with the name of religion.

This statement is not to be construed as an attack upon Christianity or any other form of religion. In the first place it is impossible to give any adequate single definition of the term Christianity as it is presently applied in the world. Christianity as it exists is a bloc of mutually antagonistic cults whose only point of juncture is a terminology which each group defines differently. In addition to the teachings of the Jewish reformer, Jesus of Nazareth, as they have been handed down in the collection of books and letters known as the New Testament, there are remnants of almost every magical and religious rite, and of nearly every god, saint and hero, known to the planet Earth during the whole long history of hu-man. Instead of rejoicing in this preservation of ancient lore, the religionists have, upon adoption of these philosophical, scientific and historical mummifications, stoutly maintained that these items were either special revelations or True Christian Practices which had been 'anticipated' by the Devil and distorted to entice and to pervert mankind! Being the only right one or the sole possessor of the truth is typical of the paranoid's attempt to establish some sort of safe identity and inner security for himself.

Incidentally, when be realises this, it gives him a convenient lever for the rejection of any fact or statement he does not understand—obviously the other fellow is crazy. And, of course, it becomes equally obvious that anybody who points out the difficulties of Adam-II must be subject to those difficulties himself—and the squirrel cage is then in motion with everybody invalidating everybody else.

Nevertheless, in the interests of information, that pointing out needs to be done, for the sake of educating those persons in whom the inherent structure of Adam-I is, or can become, dominant. For it is those people and their descendants who shall survive the Judgment preached and promised by the religions of Adam-II. What are some of the mummified facts discoverable in the religions perpetuated by Adam-II hu-manity? First, the idea that Adam-II was a special Creation; and that he owes service to and is responsible to a definite local creative agency to whom he belongs in very fact. This cannot be argued. The question is: does it still apply? And, if so, does it still apply in the same manner and form in which it applied during the days of that Garden eastward in Eden?

The stock Adam-II answer is that it does, indeed. Adam-II, in his search for stability and reliability, in a universe full of never-ceasing motion and change, is very, very slow to admit otherwise. To him change simply means more uncertainty, and he has entirely too much of that as it is—so he struggles endlessly to keep things as they are, or even, preferably, as they were, and he resists all change with a passion. And this is entirely in keeping with his nature—he was originally created to be a Guardian and a Preserver of things as they were, and he has not changed in this respect. One of the built-in characteristics of Adam-II hu-manity is a factor that might be called the compulsion to report.

As caretaker and guardian of the garden area, reports were expected and demanded of Adam-II persons at regular intervals. A good man reported well and completely to the Jehovah.

Adam-II man first ran headlong into difficulties with this inherent compulsion when he failed to report his exogamous activities with the people of the Serpent.

It was only through observation of new ideas and different notions of morality and social propriety picked up from the people of the Serpent that the Jehovah discovered what had been happening to their project.

It was through an attempt to conceal his activities, against the strong inner promptings of his compulsion to report, that Adam-II man first experienced the feeling of guilt. It is still the chief source of this feeling in Adam-II man—the attempt to conceal some fact, particularly the infraction of some rule or regulation he has accepted as being authoritative, against the pull of his compulsion to report everything that happens.

This is a very serious difficulty in Adam-II, and the more he tangles up his life with inherited regulations, taboos, and religious injunctions, to say nothing of contradictory, often archaic and inapplicable civil laws, the worse off he finds himself.

So, he is at once, a chosen person, important, special, and, at the same time, he sees himself as a moral delinquent—and one more vast source of conflict comes into his life.

Some attempt to cope with this difficulty was made by the Christian Church when it installed the practices of confession and oral testimony. Present day psychology has attempted the same kind of cure for the condition with its free-association, stream of consciousness, and other active, verbal processes of the couch.

Both systems have brought about a certain amount of relief for a fraction of the population, but again there was ignorance of the basic factor causing the disturbance, and so the effect was only partial. In most cases the individual, having unloaded his reports to date, simply went out and accumulated more, and after a while found himself right back where he started from—burdened with a surplus weight of unreported incident. The cure proved to be only a temporary alleviation of a symptom and left the causative disease untouched.

So-called Angels, Man-like beings who are capable of flight and who live somewhere in the sky, are another religious idea with a concrete basis in fact. Angels, or Messengers, are space people, messengers of the Jehovah and upon certain occasions, if we are to believe the Scriptures, some of the Jehovah themselves.

They certainly do have powers and abilities beyond those of Adam-II humanity—and, therefore, to that egocentric type of being, they are supernatural. The paranoid personality must always be at the top of the heap, in order to hide from himself the fact that he is not, in actual truth, as capable as somebody else. The present population of the planet Earth is mixed. In some individuals the Adam-I telepathic inheritance is dominant. In others it is either absent or suppressed. The mere fact that some individual protests that he is completely without any kind of telepathic tendencies is no reliable basis upon which to judge his actual condition. As a matter of fact, such a protest may well mean that somewhere in the process of his growing up he discovered he did have a faculty not possessed by other people in his environment, ran into the suspicion and disapproval his possession of that faculty brought down upon him, decided it would be distinctly non-survival to advertise his possession of such a tail, and thereafter suppressed all manifestations of it—even to himself. This happens over and over again with children who actually carry the Adam-I gene dominant.

In later adult life we often find this person dramatising the character who is the careful researcher, the not inconceivable skeptic, the quiet, very way over backward tolerant person. In short, he is dramatising in his own life all the qualities he wishes people had displayed toward him and his freak talent. Acceptance of the Adam-II norm and adherence to it under social pressure can also cause a person with a dominant Adam-I inheritance to go through life without suspecting his own potentials. Of course, he will have certain experiences involving telepathy and its related functions, but these he will tend to suppress and to explain away, often by distinctly Adam-II means, like angelic visitations, the voice of God, and so on.

It is distinctly non-survival to be different in any way from Adam-II if you have to live with him and he is in the saddle, or at all influential in your environment. The possessor of any extraordinary faculty or talent is immediately strange, and therefore suspect, feared, shamed, or considered ill. He is a green monkey and the other monkeys will proceed to tear him to pieces without any further reason or provocation. This is merely a known fact, and it is recorded here without emotion, contempt, or judgement. The bee has a sting which she will use when disturbed. Adam-II has certain characteristic reactions which he displays—and

LEGACY OF THE SKY PEOPLE

it is a good thing to be able to recognise them, for we have to live with a multitude of his kind in this world. His judgment day is still in the future.

Many writers and philosophers have talked about the coming of a New Race. In one sense only is this coming race new, and that is in the fact that it will be a mixed race, carrying the old Adam-I factors dominant. Its newness will lie in its physical structure and the consequent liberation and development of spiritual potentials that regenerated structure will make possible. It will retain the characteristics which adapt it to Earth life, such as the more massive character of the cells, the higher percentage of water in the cell structure, greater weight per cubic inch—to adapt it to the higher gravity of Earth—and resultant strength and hardihood under the conditions native to Earth.

Most of this will be unwelcome, and therefore unbelievable, information to nearly everybody. Nevertheless, the ideas are being presented to a number of people all over the world and they are getting into circulation. It matters very little that in each case the circulation may necessarily be a small one. The Adam-I dominant type is a telepath. One strongly telepathic individual in an area, thinking about these ideas, is also-broadcasting them. Although most of the Adam-I dominants in his area will be receiving them at a level of conscious operation they do not commonly use, still they are receiving them, and the fact that the ideas are present somewhere in their mental sphere will influence their behaviour and increase their usefulness to progress and to peace.

The process of waking up all the Adam-I dominants to their latent potentialities is a long, slow, deliberate enterprise. It is, however, possible, and it is being speeded up. Some of the slowness of the operation, even though intensified, may be gathered if it is remembered that the speedup was begun only about a century and a quarter ago.

Spaceships, broadcasting information, now patrol the skies of earth on regular schedules. Contacts have been made, where possible, with Adam-I dominant people. By far the greater part of the information, however, will continue to arrive for some time yet as inspiration, or that occasional hunch obtained and used in some way by some Adam-I dominant individual who has captured it.

Some people know exactly where their information comes from. These people must be extraordinarily careful either in their trying to use or to disseminate whatever they have learnt. The difficulties involved and the risks run under present circumstances of opinion and practice are obvious and well known.

Yet no information is ever wasted, even if no word of it is ever transmitted by way of vocal speech. Just now it is most important to get ideas into the mental and emotional atmosphere, and by sheer repetition of impact to accustom the

LEGACY OF THE SKY PEOPLE

Adam-I dominants in the population to the reception of ideas by telepathic means.

Obviously this is not an idea that will appeal to Adam-II individuals. Their first suspicion would be, 'Somebody is going to try to control me!' This would be followed by fear, antagonism, resistance and the whole attempt at an educational programme would fall through. It would be quite beyond the grasp of Adam-II humanity that anybody more powerful or more intelligent would want to do anything with that power and intelligence except to effect some kind of personal control. Adam-II would insist upon control. He would not feel safe otherwise.

So the plain facts of life boil down to the circumstance that the Adam-II portion of the population is not ready for outer space, and, because of certain factors inherent in his psychological and physical constitution he never will be, at least in his present body. He was not created for space. He was created to live planetside. The only way he will ever get into space is to be taken there by people with fully developed Adam-I dominant abilities—an impossibility for any individual with the Adam-II inheritance still dominant.

There is a niche in the universe for Adam-II as long as he survives. No attempt is being made, or will be made, by anybody except himself, to exterminate him, despite his fears.

Nevertheless, he will not survive for ever as a type, and as long as he does survive there will be trouble with him. He is an incipient paranoid, an xenophobe, and a fighter by both breeding and inclination,

He needs to be tamed as one would tame an animal with the same characteristics—and this is no easy thing to do. Indeed, Adam-II represents in many ways a regression in hu-man types and not an advance. He was formed much closer to the animals than Galactic Man——or, as he himself puts it, a little lower than the angels.

He is very definitely a galactic hot potato, but unlike the hot potato of the proverb, he cannot be dropped. He must be educated and tamed, willy-nilly-galactic tradition frowns upon deliberate extermination of any human or even semi-human types. The philosophy maintains that every surviving thing has some kind of use, although upon occasion it may over extend its capabilities and temporarily upset the ideal balance of order.

And so, the planet Earth might be said to be under a kind of quarantine. The people of space (so called) will not step in overtly until hu-man actually projects himself into space so effectively as to become a threat to systemic or galactic order. The really adult and developed individuals of Earth must be allowed to achieve that status with as little overt direction and manipulation as possible within the limits of accelerated progress. They must learn to cope with, and to tame, Adam-

LEGACY OF THE SKY PEOPLE

II under the same conditions.

In the earlier days of history, one great final war between the two types of hu-manity on Earth was foreseen as an unavoidable probability. References to it are to be found in various prophetic statements, some of which are included in the Bible.

Now, however, it is considered that such an ultimate conflict may well be avoided. Several factors have contributed to this, not the least of which has been the deliberate and calculated inclusion of people from off Earth into the population, where they have worked, married and contributed children to the race who are definitely and selectively and above all, vitally-Adam-I dominant.

The mechanics of this accomplishment are not for discussion here, but it is by no means difficult to do, and it is being done constantly. It forms an important part of the programme for the salvation, or salvage, to be more exact, of the Earth.

Adam-II would, however, be distressed to know about any such operation, except, perhaps, in the vaguest and most general terms. He is, in his purest type, egocentric to a psychotic degree, and would resent any such activity as tampering and interference with all the vehement antagonism of the fearfully insecure.

Being insecure within himself he dares not consider the possibility that beings exist who are more intelligent, more mature, and generally more capable than himself—unless he defies them and puts them (a) out of his reach, and (b) well out of direct communication with himself. He is afraid of his own inadequacy. He would be even more afraid of their adequacy!

This, coupled with his inherent propensity to fight anything and everything in any way different from himself, makes him a dangerous creature. Indeed, the mental health of an Adam- II individual can be measured fairly accurately by the degree to which he feels himself to be dangerous to his environment! Many of his potentials remain undeveloped because of his instability and the lack of assistance he has had in coping with it. Adam-II may yet learn to live with himself and accept his place in the universe, but it will not be an easy thing for him to do, nor will he achieve it quickly. When he does, however, he will be mature, and whatever can be done to help him reach that maturity is being done, and will continue to be done.

In the meantime, those individuals with Adam-I dominant patterns continue to 'increase and multiply' as was intended, and to fill the earth and subdue it. It may well be that they will have to subdue Adam-II hu-manity in the process, as the old prophets foresaw. However, if this eventuality can be avoided in any way, it will be.

LEGACY OF THE SKY PEOPLE

A much larger percentage of the people of this planet are now telepathic or have potential telepathic powers not awakened than previously. The swing toward the side of the Angels should be increasingly rapid from now on. Before much longer the snowball effect will begin to make itself felt very definitely.

However, at the same time, the effect of this condition upon Adam-II humanity will be to increase its feelings of inadequacy and desperation. This is already noticeable in the growing return to a religious philosophy of fundamentalist theism. There will be more and more pressure applied to enforce, even by means of legislation, primitive religious beliefs. This tendency has been influenced by steering the idea of Jehovah-as-God into a merger with the idea of One Universal Creative Intelligence, but the Creator, for Adam-II, will never be anything but a god who is a projection of his own psychological make-up—his own personality. Any other idea is beyond his depth.

This presents some major difficulties to any educational programme, but they are not entirely beyond solution.

The greatest difficulty here remains the necessity to maintain enough religious freedom to ensure Adam-I humanity the right to entertain different ideas. Adam-II hu-man did not turn out to be a very inventive creature. On the other hand, it may not be quite fair to consider this in a too regretful light, since Adam-II was never intended to be a particularly creative type. He was deliberately produced to be a farmer, to maintain an agricultural under direct supervision of the Jehovah; and to be a soldier whenever it might be necessary to defend the farms. He was created and organised both mentally and physically to take orders, and because of this fact he has never been capable of solving his own problems very well.

He is inclined to depend upon authority, either natural (strong men and heroes) or supernatural (gods, angels, demons and other spirits), to tell him what to do, and when and how to do it. He simply does not feel either safe or secure unless he has someone or some spirit to take the responsibility for decisions and to take a paternal interest in the preservation of his life and goods. This is no criticism of Adam-II; this is just the way he was made.

Adam-II was deliberately formed to be non-telepathic. Any organism living can be impressed by some kind of mental suggestion. This, however, is not what is meant by telepathic communication. It is not a complete communication just to impress an organism. The recipient of such a one-way impression is unaware, in most cases, that it is receiving an impulse from outside itself, and is incapable of formulating and returning a reply on the same terms, using the same forms of energy, and directing that reply back to the sender of the impression it has received. Adam-II type hu-manity can neither receive impressions consistently nor can it transmit them consciously and deliberately.

The chief result of this non-telepathic condition has been that Adam-II hu-manity is forced to depend upon articulate speech for its communication with its own kind. So, articulate language has developed to its present stage of complexity.

Incidentally, it is difficult for this type of hu-manity to imagine the existence of a civilised culture that does not possess some kind of complicated vocal speech. For him, the two are quite inseparable.

Adam-II hu-manity formed, very early, the habit of articulating replies to the Jehovah, who impressed him with orders—their suggestions. This situation gave rise to the idea of communication with higher or more powerful and puissant beings who could be invisible—elsewhere. Since these beings were more capable than hu-man, and since Adam-II has always measured Nature and what is natural by his own abilities and impulses, he soon assumed that these sometimes invisible beings were in some way supernatural. And, so, hu-man invented gods, spirits, demons and other supernatural entities.

Because certain of the Jehovah were in charge of definite and separate operations, Adam-II hu-man identified them with these operations, and so arose his belief in gods and goddesses of agriculture, tribal groups, particular areas and settlements, and later on, since hu-man decided that absolutely everything that happened must be under the directions of the supernatural beings, just as he was himself, so came gods of the weather and other natural phenomena-including volcanoes, like the one in Moab, where Jethro, the father-in-law of Moses, was priest.

This latter idea, contrary to much respected anthropological opinion, came along at a much later date than modern scholars suppose, and it is actually a degeneration of Adam-II's earlier notions concerning the state of his affairs.

Still later, certain Adam-II people specialised in thinking about such matters (and in telling other people what ought to be thought about them), and it came to be supposed that every hu-man being was under the special supervision of a certain angel or daemon, who was assigned to him. From this point in Adam-II's thinking, it was only one more step to complete identification of this angel as a heavenly part of himself, living in a heavenly home—or, temporarily separated from that home during a brief residence here on earth—somewhere in the sky-world, and the idea of Man-as-a-body somehow connected with a separate, supernatural part of man that was not quite his actual spiritual identity arose-the soul was formed.

Adam-II has been philosophising about this schizoid tour-de-force ever since, and from there on theology developed into its present complicated struc-

LEGACY OF THE SKY PEOPLE

ture.

In the Polynesian system these angels were called Aumakuas and it was supposed that there were two in charge of each person born into the world. These were spoken of as the dual high self which was almost but not quite a part of the symbiosis called man. Man's own consciousness was thought of as a middle self.

Apparently this middle self, the actual hu-man entity, did not amount to much, but existed as a kind of servant and collector of energy for the high selves who, in return, offered their hu-man beings a certain amount of care and protection as long as the mana-psychic energy-arrived on schedule and in full quota. So do historical ideas achieve a kind of immortality in a transformed state.

Still later, an additional self (sic) was added to the list, splitting Adam-II's idea of his individuality three ways in a marvellous kind of compound schizophrenia. This third self was called the low self and was identified with all man's irrational, instinctive and suppressed impulses and reactions—also, of course, it was this low self that was made responsible for Adam-II's disobedience to orders. In his desire to avoid responsibility both for decision and for blame man became a corporation. In other parts of the world, the Elohim came to be identified with the non-physical, sky-dwelling part of man which would survive his bodily death, and which man would become in some mystical manner.. The third self, however, remained a separate entity, a sort of anti-god or devil who is supposed to specialise in tempting man to transgress the divine laws of the Elohim.

So, it can be seen how hu-manity's interpretations of his own Self have been completely distorted.* It was Apollo, many, many thousands of years ago, who originally said, 'Man know thyself'. Cross hu-manity, with very few exceptions, has not followed that sage advice yet. It can be seen, too, how hu-manity's ideas about the Sky People have at the same time been misinterpreted through a combination of ignorance, dogma and traditional acceptances. Since the development of Adam-II type hu-manity, exceptional individuals capable of understanding and existing in a galactic culture have been taken to other places than the earth. This circumstance gave rise to the idea that if a person was good and obeyed all the divine laws, he would be taken to heaven by the gods—a very primitive and oversimplified interpretation of an actual event. After it became less common for the Sons of God to associate so directly with Adam-II hu-manity, the idea arose that the taking to heaven occurred after physical death.

Perhaps it should be noted that all such analyses of mankind's structure can be utilised as roads back to understanding as long as they suggest eventual reunification of the supposedly separated parts of man.

This idea, in the hands of the self-elected priesthood, became a powerful whip by means of which to establish and hold political control over large groups of hu-man beings. The priesthood was, of course, no more in contact with the Sons of God than the rest of hu-manity, but they claimed to be, and they enforced their claim with the fear of an everlasting punishment or outright annihilation if their orders were not obeyed.

The priests found it outrageously easy to enforce such orders of their own upon a people who had, since the time of their actual beginnings, been under the paternal supervision of an extraterrestrial race. The chance to take control into their own hands was too obvious to be missed by the priests, and take control they did. While the hands off policy that prepared the way for all this to happen was a necessary step in the racial maturing of Adam-II, as Cross-Man, it had led to complications and suffering.

Incapable of offering the kind of supervision given by the Sons of God, the priests could interpret such a relationship only in terms of control, and that, unfortunately, has been the basis of socio-religious pattern ever since. Only here and there, and very recently, have other ideas been allowed to appear and to develop to national proportions.

The Universal Teaching too has become so distorted from the original truth, that there are now hundreds of sects and cults under the umbrella of one major world religion alone-Christianity.

Now let us look for a moment at Astronomy, a science which deals with the Universe. Astronomy is an awkward science. Astronomers struggle against the same difficulties a group of scientific frogs would encounter if they chose to study the atmospheric world from the bottom of a pond. It is one of their sorrowful frustrations that their best telescopes must look out through a contaminated and forever agitated puddle of air. Theory-building in the face of all the unknown factors introduced by this one problem is a very risky business, but they do their best. And they try to remain alert to better explanations, fond though they may be of their favourite theories.

It might be to our advantage to be able to see clearly through our murky atmosphere and to be able to verify some of the strange information, fantastic or magical as it would probably appear to be, that claimants of riders in flying saucers have brought back to Earth.

Some people would still not believe the claimants, even if the astronomers' observations backed them up. Some savages never realise there isn't a tiny man imprisoned in a record player. It *is* talking and singing, isn't it? And that savage knows all the facts—*his facts*.

Nevertheless, if scientists got their mental hands on enough of this evidence,

LEGACY OF THE SKY PEOPLE

some genius among us might be able to put together a new theory of the universe.

There is some evidence in the Scriptures of the world that such a theory once existed, was somehow lost, and its dismembered and dehydrated remains were mummified in ritual and religion. This is not a very efficient means of preservation and we could do with a fresh start.

LEGACY OF THE SKY PEOPLE

CHAPTER XI

COMMUNICATION

Professor Charles A. Maney, head of the Department of Physics at Defiance College, Defiance, Ohio, has contributed several scholarly and scientific articles to *Flying Saucer Review*. His contribution in the November-December 1959 issue was written with his usual flair, but one passage, referring to people who have claimed contact with extraterrestrials, must be challenged.

Could not one expect astonishing revelations of information of one kind and another from these representatives of an order of civilisation or life centuries beyond us in advancement in fields of science, arts, and modes of living? When and if the human race ever becomes introduced to such knowledge one could well judge it as being truly out of this world.

Why?—to both his question and his statement. Also: How?

If we grant that these extraterrestrials do exist, and if we grant that they are meddling in the affairs of men-on-earth, why is Professor Maney apparently so sure he is not already enjoying the fruits of 'many astonishing revelations of one kind and another'? Does he really believe the human race, after coasting along for thousands of years without much change in its fundamental way of life, suddenly jumped off its laurels, and within a few short decades produced (all by itself) the technology surrounding him? What evidence exists, in all of human history as it is known to us, that this intellectual explosion was a natural, normal, logical, and to be expected event in the development of our humanity?

Tinkering with one culture can be a ticklish business. What, then, about tinkering with a complex of cultures, with a planet? Consider the effect some of the new technological discoveries have had upon the stability of nations, social groups, religions, political ideas, economics—to name a few areas. The sudden introduction of sweeping changes makes the manufacture of nitroglycerine look like the paddling of a two-year-old in a mud pie.

A reformation of an inadequate morality, with all the necessary readjustment of values that sort of missionary activity would entail, might be an even more trying task.

It could not happen overnight unless the meddlers were willing to settle for a planet full of slaves. If they are even a little way ahead of us, they are probably

LEGACY OF THE SKY PEOPLE

wise enough not to desire such a liability.

If the inhabitants of the earth are, indeed, to receive authority to become Children of God as they have been notified by seers and prophets both before and after the appearance of John the Baptist, they may need time to grow in grace and strength. People are not cattle, and it may be that they will be required to appear as brethren—not as sheep—when the Day Be With Us rolls around. This would imply the opposite of dependence upon their benefactors, and its achievement could call for their reshuffling many of the ideas now held sacred, or at least, profitable.

Unless the mission of the extraterrestrials is to destroy the integrity of earth humanity, any necessary reorientations here will need to be self-recognised and self-imposed. Again, this isn't going to happen between any two days.

If the extraterrestrials wish to astonish us with either their science or their accumulated wisdom, they have already given abundant evidence that they could do so, and easily, if it would serve their purposes or ours.

This does not appear to be the case.

However, the science Earthman has and upon which he congratulates himself so freely is a gift, and not, as he supposes, an accomplishment.

Impressionable people, with strongly dominant Adam-I characteristics, have been made the recipients of ideas which they have developed and presented to the world. The really great steps forward have been the work of comparatively few such men and women. Thomas Edison was such a person. In another field, Luther Burbank also performed 'miracles'. I do not believe in miracles. The definition of a miracle is a setting aside of the laws of Nature. Only I do believe in unsuspected natural laws of which we know little or nothing. Whether or not such people knew where their ideas were coming from is an intriguing conjecture. Certainly, if they did know they would have appeared even more outlandish and strange in the eyes of their fellow men than their inventions already made them. They even have been declared insane, confined to institutions, and the numerous advantages of their work lost to mankind. Earth, for millennia, has remained a primitive and backward planet, actually in a state of quarantine. Occasionally, however, it has been possible to make contact with some human being in whom the original Adam_I characteristics were dominant, and the result has been some great contribution to civilised progress. Sometimes, on the other hand, the result of an attempted contact has been increased instability or outright madness.

The notebooks of Leonardo Da Vinci bear evidence of his having been, in addition to such an outstanding Galactic Dominant, a much-contacted person. Some of his notes read like quite literal assignments for his study, and the enormous

LEGACY OF THE SKY PEOPLE

number, variety and practicability of his inventions reward close investigations.

Near to our own times, the man who stands out as an exceptional Galactic person and who, in his way of life, exemplified this status to a high degree, was Nikola Tesla. He was in constant contact with the Sky People.

This amazing tall, handsome superman spoke fluently eight languages, besides being telepathic. He was the discoverer of the rotating magnetic field and of alternating current. A few of his other achievements were putting Niagara Falls in harness; operating a boat by remote control in 1898; and creating an earthquake in New York City.

Tesla refused to accept the Nobel Prize and tore up the agreement giving him royalties on his most money-making invention as a gesture of friendship. The fascinating story of this remarkable man is told by the late John J. O'Neill, Science Editor of the New York Herald Tribune, in his book **Prodigal Genuis**.

Today, the Sky People are contacting Cross-Man on earth frequently. Arthur H. Matthews, and his father, now passed on, both worked with Tesla during the latter's lifetime. Mr. Matthews, who lives in Canada, knows of at least 1,200 Tesla inventions. He claims that periodically the Sky People land in their ships on his property to see how he is getting on with building the Tesla anti-war machine.

Communications can be impressed by extraterrestrials in earth people in more than one way.

Just how these communications are finally shaped into words depends upon the manner in which they were impressed upon the person receiving them, and his own personal machinery for expressing the impression.

Some methods of impression are:

1. Direct dictation. The receiver is given actual words which he repeats or writes down. This is not control. It is a form of direct telepathic communication, and can be used for anybody who has at least one channel clear.

2. Dictation and paraphrase. The recipient hears the communication in words but cannot recall, but having got the gist of the statement, he then puts it into his own words. Communications put through in this manner are sometimes very peculiarly worded, or the language is distorted in some way, due to mental or emotional characteristics of the recipient.

3. Symbolic communication. The recipient is shown a symbol which will affect his mental machinery like a punched card fed into a computer, and he more or less automatically delivers the message. In this case, the more fully automatic the delivery, the more likely it is to get through without its being garbled.

4. Emotional impact. This works in much the same way as symbolic communication, but utilises emotional patterns instead of the memory circuits. While this is the only possible way to get a communication through to some recipients, it is the least reliable of all, due to the constantly shifting patterns possible to emotion. It is only reliable when the recipient is either an emotionally stable individual or temporarily experiencing a stable emotional state. Under any other circumstances the results of this kind of communication are liable to be fantastic, to say the least.

5. Conceptual communication. This is achieved by implanting a whole concept in the mind of the recipient, at a level just above that at which he normally functions. He may or may not be aware, immediately, of his having received an impression. He may get a peculiar feeling. He may be completely unaware that anything has happened to him. Then, later, when his mind is not busy with something else, the concept will register at his ordinary level of conscious awareness. It will come to him in a flash, but he may need many words to express it. Here again, the recipient will express the concept either in his own ordinary language, or he will adopt some more or less unusual form of speech, depending upon where he believes the concept came from and his own personal emotions, attitudes and acceptances.

This fifth method is at once the highest and lowest form of telepathic communication. It is the surest way with clear-channel well-trained minds, and the fastest. On the other hand, it is the only way with the completely undeveloped.

Galactic Man is telepathic and, indeed, so are all Cross-Men (galactic dominant) either actively or potentially. A Galactic communicates without the necessary inclusion of vocal speech. Vocalisation is an emotional process. Galactic Man does not communicate at the emotional level. His communications go from mind to mind and are, therefore, less subject to distortion than communications expressed in vocal forms of emotional reaction.

Cross-Man (animal dominant) is a non-telepath. If enough mass is included by way of complex protein molecules as developed on Earth, the mind-to-mind communication function shuts down. Any mind-to-mind ability that any earth inhabitant has comes down to him through his genetic heritage from Galactic Man. Any lack of inhibition of that function is strictly characteristic of Adam-II man.

Sometimes mysterious visitors from Space have contacted earth people, and after the visitors have gone away the visited are amazed to realise that, although they now have a headful of new ideas, not one single vocal word was uttered by either party! What the visited person gets, and gives, out of such a contact depends, of course, upon the method of communication used, and to what degree the recipient is able to react to, and to complete, that method with accuracy.

LEGACY OF THE SKY PEOPLE

We should never be too critical, then, of any message anyone receives. If the person is honest and has done his best to deliver the communication, we can usually recognise the method that was used to give him the ideas by examining the form of his expression of them. Knowing this, it is then possible to extract the meat of the message in almost every case. And this applies even when, to the recipient himself, he has been conversing with monstrous devils wearing hoofs and horns. The point that real mind-to-mind communication is not control of any kind cannot be stressed too strongly or repeated too often.

Control, as in the function of ordinary mediumship, is a brutal method, actually, of getting a message through. It involves tremendous effort on the part of both the sender and the receiver, and is comparable to smashing the communication through with a bulldozer. It is never considered optimum because it can be harmful, and it leaves the sender under very great obligation to the medium. If he is at all ethical, the control must literally adopt his medium and look after him or her as he would care for his own child.

Less and less need for controlled communication through the medium will arise in the future as more and more sleepers—Galactic dominant earth people—are awakened to their telepathic powers.

The effect of a contact by an extraterrestrial on a human earth person cannot always be safely gauged. In the present expanding programme of contacting people who are Galactic dominant, those contacted are not always stable enough to follow through and may even colour the message they receive and sooner or later become a prophet. In a widescale programme of this nature, the Sky people have to take a chance with some of those contacted. If the recipient of the message proves unstable, then contact is withdrawn.

What makes a prophet? This is a basic problem that has confronted extraterrestrial intelligence since the world began. It is doubtful if any Galactic intelligence ever really wanted a prophet on his hands after communication with some earth person. Not, at least, as we are accustomed to understand prophets in the light of ordinary experience with them. Under existing circumstances, however, a prophet is what rises up once an earth-type human being is thoroughly convinced he has received a communication from Above. Not always, but all too often. Prophets have their uses, and perhaps the persistently communicative extraterrestrials are resigned to their appearance. From a wider view, the plan may have room enough in it for all of them, from the syrupy salvationists to the junior Jeremiahs. At any rate, communication is still attempted, and Prophets, Seers and precursors continue to spring up like field mushrooms in the pasture grass, in circle after circle. The phenomenon is so monotonous it arouses suspicion that it may be mechanical. On these grounds, it would appear to be perfectly legitimate to inquire: 'What makes it?'

Because we live with our fellow man from day to day, cope with him with some success, and he doesn't ordinarily break into our private preserves, strip the pantry, and melt away into the night with the family plate; we usually think of him as being sane.

But is he? If he is more of the planet earth than he is a Galactic, by virtue of his heritage, he most certainly is not entirely sane. Not, at least, by any Galactic standard. He is born burdened with the original sin of the Second Adam-a hearty tendency towards paranoia.

Two of the outstanding symptoms of this rather complex malfunction of the emotions are familiar to every parlour psychologist. They are: delusions of persecution, and delusions of grandeur. Paranoia is a contradictory malady, based upon contradiction, and thriving upon contradiction and conflict.

Very often the delusions of persecution appear first, to be followed in time, as the disease progresses, by the delusions of grandeur until a typical attitude builds up: 'The world doesn't recognise my greatness, but, of course, I do, and the fact I must live among such fools may add to my sorrows, but it will never shake my firm conviction of my own innate superiority.'

This feeling may never grow great enough to appear on the surface of the overlaid social training an individual receives from those around him. Nevertheless it is there to some degree, and at one time or another it appears in nearly everybody on this planet.

The first problem facing a would-be communicator, then, is to select an individual in whom these tendencies are relatively nonexistent, or submerged.

Unless an extended, deliberate and detailed training programme is successfully applied to the contactee before he is sent out to bring the Good News to the Gentiles, he is all too prone to colour it up a bit with footnotes, explanations, personal references and addenda out of his own private spider collection. And so we have Prophets of the New Age in a variety of traditions, from H. P. Blavatsky to Jehovah Witnesses, with everything possible in between.

To speak only of the legitimate prophets, and ignore the opportunists who climb up on the bandwagon in the hope of making a fast buck, each one of these has received, either through a thin, faint voice, or some other mode of communication, a few true words, ideas, concepts, pictures, etc., according to his own peculiar native ability.

The sudden, often unheralded, receipt of so much positive certainty may trigger a kind of chain-reaction this hapless individual has stored up for a life or

LEGACY OF THE SKY PEOPLE

two.

If you are an extraterrestrial communicator this may be a hazard of the occupation, a chance you have to take. From the evidence available at this end, it is a chance communicators take so often it must be almost a matter of course with them.

If you have read the first part of Ezekiel's book as many people interested in flying saucers have learned to do, and observed that in the course of his visions, Ezekiel had a fifty-five mile ride in one of those amazing vehicles, and thereafter began to prophesy ... you will have a short textbook history of many another case in our own time. The syndrome, essentially the same today as it was by the river of Chebar, could very well be called the 'Ezekiel Complex'.

Contact, followed by disorientation, followed by an impulse to tell everybody what's wrong with him and his present way of life, and announcement of the inevitable doom lurking just round the corner if things are not put to rights according, of course, to the particular recipe the prophet has received from the lips of whatever god or semi-divinity he has been worshipping lately, is the natural order of events for the new prophet.

And, since it is all based upon words of truth, which the prophet remembers perfectly well—no matter how he chooses to display them, or how he decided to explain and to interpret them for the lesser beings he goes forth to save—it becomes, in any form, a particularly difficult argument to refute.

When a worldwide crop of prophets comes up within less than half a generation, the fog becomes thick enough to encourage anybody to reserve an upholstered suite in the nearest bedlam.

To himself, each one of these prophets is the Only One Who Knows the straight of whatever it is he has heard tell. Nobody ever said just this to him before, therefore, nobody ever said this to anybody before. And another saviour unties his apron full of nails, chucks his hammer and saw into the corner, and marches out on the missionary circuit to save the world.

Because there are so many of these right now, there is in progress a kind of Olympic Games in which the only event is One-Upmanship. Concentrating on the details, the embroidery, the gist of what is being said, the participants proceed to criticise, condemn and calumniate one another, 'She's just a medium': 'He's a fake'; 'I'm the sole and only chosen mouthpiece' 'Mine is the only Message for all the people of Earth'; and so on as long as your ears can function. And the Goat Song that rises behind the Chorus is, inevitably, freighted with one realisation: strip off the pictures, the dramatisations, the characters and their trappings, and the plot is clear and constant, always the same.

LEGACY OF THE SKY PEOPLE

Problem: How to get the people to pay attention to the plot when they are so wonderfully amused and entertained by the cast of characters, the scenery and all the props.

There is an old Chinese story, attributed to some Abbot of some monastery or other on some stock Chinese mountain. Concerning Truth, he is supposed to have said: Truth is like a spring gushing out of a rock. Anybody may carry away the water. And that man does not lie, who, having first strained the water through a filthy cloth, maintains what he brings down with him to be the True and Veritable Water From The Spring.

The symbolism of the Serpent Race observing as their Adam-I gardeners seek the truth of their creation is apparent in all modern depictions of Adam and Eve.

CHAPTER XII

TEKTITES AND SILICON

There are some rebels who hold the view that the sun is in reality a cool body and furthermore, inhabited. That distinguished astronomer the late Sir William Herschel was one.

Most people, taking their cue from orthodox astronomy consider the sun as a giant ball of burning fire, and that life on those planets nearest the solar orb would be untenable, because of the immense heat, and on those planets farthest away would be equally hopeless, because of the intense cold.

However, suppose we look at it another way. Some scientists concede that the sun has a tremendous electrical corona which causes its fiery appearance. Recently, the earth was discovered to have a corona too, and it has been named the Van Allen Radiation belt. This, of course, confirms biblical references to the Arc of the Firmament.

Do people realise that the corona around the sun is probably as far away from the sun as the earth is? Could it be that the rays of the sun are not in themselves heat? That heat is generated when the rays strike the atmosphere of a planet? Maybe it is the particles in the atmosphere when energised by the rays coming from the sun's corona that cause heat. W. Gordon Allen in his book, ***Spacecraft from Beyond Three Dimensions***, amplifies this concept further.

Now, in a town which gets its electricity supplied by a power station, it makes no difference whether a residence is in the centre of the place or on the outskirts, all the houses get the same treatment, the same amount of current.

I must, therefore, most certainly ask the question, do not all the planets in our solar system get their heat and light from a power station—the sun? In the same way that quite regardless of distance and how far they are away on the outskirts of a town, all the houses get their electricity, so too, quite irrespective of how many million miles they may seem to be away, surely do the planets on the fringe of our system, such as Pluto, get the same amount of rays from the sun. And, providing an atmosphere is present, heat will be the result.

If this theory could be seriously investigated by the scientific world, a big step forward would have been reached towards a realisation that intelligent life could exist on other planets.

W. R. Drake, in a brilliant article entitled *Is Our Sun Inhabited?* which appeared in the November-December 1959 issue of *Flying Saucer Review*, wrote:

We remember that all our astronomers once swore that the moon was an utterly dead, icy planet. Last November, however, a Russian perversely photographed an active volcano. If many of us associate volcanoes with heat, burning with oxygen, volcanic ash with fruitful soil, soil with people, people with civilisation, then we are soundly condemned for wild romanticism of the astronomers who grumble that it is just like the Russians to try to force them to revolutionise their preconceived conceptions. If the same astronomers sat on a lunar crater and peered at the earth with the same instruments they would declare that all the earth's atmosphere was unbreathable hydrogen, that earth had no heat of its own. They would report that telescopes showed not the slightest sign of human life.

It is a source of constant wonder that while our geologists admit their ignorance of the constitution of our earth, the astronomers claim direct unimpeachable knowledge of the centre of the far distant sun, 93 million miles away.

George Hunt Williamson, in *Other Tongues-Other Flesh*, stated that

... in 1543, a great comet came closer to the sun than any previous comet had and this was repeated by another comet in 1882. They actually entered the sun's corona which supposedly has a temperature of one million degrees absolute.

These comets travelled over one million kilometers through this blazing corona and emerged unscathed—and with no change in velocity or direction. If the sun is radiating heat, why weren't these comets instantly disintegrated upon entering a tremendous heat of one million absolute degrees? Surely nothing could survive such a treatment!

Is it possible that our astronomers will shortly be revising their ideas about the sun?

Incidentally, Williamson goes on to postulate that under the sun's photosphere are twelve planets not yet known to the scientific world.

Could it be that the solar system has a correspondence with the atom? The central nucleus of the atom corresponding to the sun and the electron rings to the planets. Williamson brings out the point that in atomic structure the electrons are balanced by an equal number of protons within the nucleus, thus making a balanced system. Therefore, the sun, too, should have both twelve inner and twelve outer planets.

LEGACY OF THE SKY PEOPLE

The time is coming when the whole theory of life in this solar system may have to be revised. If heat is generated by rays from the sun's corona—not the sun itself—striking particles in a planet's atmosphere, then it is highly possible that intelligent life may exist not only on all the planets in this system, but also on the sun.

Personally, I have always thought that there is a pattern of order and intelligence in the universe. You have only to look at the skies on a clear night and consider the infinite number of stars (suns) that can be seen with the naked eye (remembering, of course, there are myriads more that are invisible, but can be viewed through a telescope) to realise the infinite organisation behind it all. Mariners since time immemorial have navigated by the positions of the stars. Even in our own comparatively little system the planets keep on their courses with clockwork precision.

If there is all this law and order in the universe and in our own system, surely it is nothing short of arrogance and egocentrism for a continuance of the centuries-old view held by scientists that there is no intelligent life on the planets? However, there are signs that a breakthrough is on the way. Many people on this planet, eminent in science and public life, are beginning to have quite a different view.

The distinguished former President of the Royal Aeronautical Society, Mr. Peter Masefield, wrote in the Sunday Express, on January 10, 1960:

And by sending first of all scientifc instruments deep into outer space, we may discover—and in the next ten years—whether Man is alone in the Universe.

Almost certainly he is not. The first contacts with other life in outer space will be the greatest news since civilisation began.

However, it is good to see that at least one famous scientist is concerned about the way humanity will behave in outer space. Professor A. C. B. Lovell, who is in charge of the Jodrell Bank Radio Telescope in Cheshire, concluding his lecture, *'The Exploration of Space'*, on February 24, 1960, before the Royal Society of Arts in London, pleaded that exploration of the planets should not be made haphazardly for the purposes of showmanship. Unless the greatest care was used, space ships might well contaminate the planets and their atmospheres with macromolecules which have developed on Earth.

The professor urged that space exploration should be promoted for peaceful purposes only. It was an innocent mind which did not see how space probes and radio telescopes had emerged from the cataclysm of war and that today they remain close relations of the defensive devices of nations.

The danger is not the aspects of research which I have discussed will lack support, but that they will be supported extravagantly for the wrong purposes.

LEGACY OF THE SKY PEOPLE

The devices of the scientist who is concerned with the exploration of outer space are double-edged. It would be an inconceivable disaster if they are built up and organized in such a way that they can too readily be switched in support of national jingoism at this crucial moment of the inquiry into the fundamental nature of life and the Universe.

If Man exists in other parts of the Universe, as has been postulated in this book, how are his space ships propelled?

A well-known French aircraft manufacturer, Louis Breguet, considers that 'discs use a means of propulsion different from ours. There is no other possible explanation—flying saucers come from another world'.

What is this mode of propulsion?* Scattered in various localised and circumscribed areas on the earth's surface are smooth, glassy lumps of curious shapes.

These objects, called Tektites, are found strewn in fixed areas called 'Tektite strewn fields' covering several miles. The chief ones so far discovered are in Iraq, Lebanon, the Dead Sea area, Libya, Bohemia, Texas, Mexico, Peru, Central Australia and elsewhere. These strange objects have been the subject of sharp scientific controversy for many years.

These notes on Tektites were supplied by Dr. Bernard E. Finch and subsequently appeared in July-August 1960 issue of Flying Saucer Review.

On examining tektites one is first struck by their smooth aerodynamic form suggesting they have travelled rapidly through the air in a softened state. Again, they are chemically different from meteorites and their appearance in localised fields demands special explanation.

The second striking feature of tektites is their chemical composition. The glasslike substances are found to be composed of silica. Some contain varying quantities of radioactive isotopes of aluminium and beryllium; some are pure silicon; others resemble quartz, glass or flint, and contain varying quantities of boron. The interesting thing about these silicon masses is that they are powerful insulators of electromagnetic forces such as gravity. Therefore, all the evidence associated with tektites, their locations and properties, points to their extraterrestrial origin. By examining large quantities of tektites and their distribution on the 'strewn field' one clearly notices the resemblances of the remains of a burnt-out air crash or missile. Some areas contain tektites resembling quartz, others pure silicon, and others, radioactive beryllium. Perhaps, these other locations are the remains of parts of a burnt-out disintegrated space ship, the glass control room, the hull, the drive and so on.

That the tektites are not due to the effect of lightning on sand, as was once

LEGACY OF THE SKY PEOPLE

thought, is evident by the discovery at various times of a mysterious substance floating on the sea in different parts of the world. This substance was found some months ago near the Pitcairn Islands. It was described as light honey coloured, soft and of a silky consistency. Examination showed it to be of pure silicon. Hence again, we have evidence of extraterrestrial objects reaching the Earth.

Finally, recent research work has shown that silicon is affected by light waves. When sunlight or the light of stars falls on a wafer of silicon and mica, an electric current flows. If the sunlight is concentrated by a quartz lens, large voltage differences are produced. The result is solar energy.

Recently, an antique car, a Baker, was renovated by the International Rectifier Corporation of El Segundo, and ran around at a speed of twenty-five miles per hour through the power of solar energy. An account of this event was published in the ***Evening Outlook***, of Santa Monica, California, on March 7, 1964.

Dr. C. A. Escoffery, a member of the firm's staff, said it was decided to use the Baker for the conversion because its roof was ideal for supporting a solar cell panel, stated the newspaper.

The car is believed to be the first in the world utilising the rays of the sun and employs the same type of solar cells used in space satellites.

More than 10,000 silicon solar cells are mounted on the roof of the automobile in a detachable twenty-six square foot panel which company engineers believe is the largest single photovoltaic panel for conversion of solar energy built in the world to date.

The panel has been named the Solar King.

The sunlight energizes electrons in the cells, which are wired together in a circuit, and puts them to work charging the car's seventy-two-volt battery system. The car then works off the batteries. The cells are similar in function to cells used to open automatic doors and in camera light meters, except that they are made of silicon instead of selenium.

From all this evidence one can now deduce for the first time that flying saucers may be made of silicon and its compounds and the antigravity effect is produced and controlled by electric power flowing in the hull and activated by sunlight which is concentrated by a quartz lens on top—the electrical energy may be stored in silicon batteries. The silicon body of the saucer acts an insulator to gravity and other electromagnetic waves and an alternating current passed through the hull of silicon or through quartz crystals produces a Piezo-Electric effect or high frequency ultrasonic waves which may be associated with propulsion.

From this point of view it is interesting to note the recent experiments in laboratories in different parts of the world, using ultrasonic waves, causing the air to become ionised typical of the Aurora Borealis, which glows from a dull red at low frequencies to a bluish white at high frequencies throughout the range of the spectrum. The air became ionised acting as a plasma conducting electricity and magnetism.

Hundreds of saucer reports have testified to changes of colour, red, blue, green, orange and indeed the whole range of the spectrum, on the part of these objects as they passed through the skies. This new concept of saucer propulsion has been gained from the careful study of flying saucer reports and satisfies all the known criteria of sightings.

There are other concepts which might be considered. Here on our own planet, vehicular propulsion has emerged along certain definite mechanical and electronic lines. That there exist other possible areas of development is clear from some of the more modern research now going on in the fields of magnetism and light. It has been suggested seriously that spaceships of the future may be propelled by the energy of light itself. Certain developments in satellite research show this to be no impossible dream.

It would be only logical to suppose that another civilisation already capable of space travel might have based its technology upon the development of universal energies still unknown to our men of science. To pursue this idea still further and include a so-called etheric universe increases the range of imaginable possibilities even more.

Our own chemical metals, for instance, may have more life in them than we suppose. Under conditions of stress, metals behave in a manner suggesting fatigue, and physicists have found no better word to describe this condition. From another point of view, it is well known that many metaphysical authorities have maintained consistently that there is no such thing as dead matter.

In an etheric universe which might well have a less complicated fundamental structure than our own chemicals show, the processes we recognise and associate with life may continue farther on down the scale toward the simpler molecules and even to the atoms themselves.

If this were true, machines—or their etheric equivalent—could be produced by some process more akin to growth than to manufacture. As a result of this combination of circumstances we should expect such machines to exhibit some of the characteristics of sentient life—and indeed they often do. Reports of sightings have included statements referring to the peculiar motion of the objects observed, such as: 'They behaved as if they were alive.'

Some people have gone so far as to suppose the saucers, or some of them,

LEGACY OF THE SKY PEOPLE

at least, are actually animal life-forms inhabiting the fringes of outer space. This idea need not be particularly startling to us if we consider the everyday fact that, to a fish who lives in water, a relatively dense medium, air-breathing animals appear to exist in an uninhabitable vacuum!

Could it not be, then, that the owners and operators of sentient machines have, upon occasion, left their living vehicles to rest and to refresh themselves under favourable circumstances, much after the manner that we ourselves leave faithful horses to frolic in the fields? When they have regained their strength and vigour, might not their owners call them back again into their usual service?

Viewed in this light, such living vehicles would fall somewhere in between an advanced machine and an uncomplicated animal. Such an alert but still mechanically reactive construction might be very sensitive to telepathic impulse, controlled and directed by the very thought-processes of its rider, and capable of rudimentary but immediate and accurate response-judgments based upon environmental data. Although apparently aimless and irresponsible in their actions when alone and unaccompanied by their operators, such animal machines might easily show the same sort of strange curiosity and apparent playfulness attributed to some of the unidentified flying objects that have been reported.

On the other hand, when they are under the full control of their owners, we could expect to observe the more patterned and purposeful behaviour characteristic of what is by far the majority of sightings.

To speculate upon the possible mode of propulsion utilised by flying saucers without considering, at least, the possibility of their being planned and produced from some more advanced and possibly very different basic structure would be to put a limit on our thinking. Without further exact data, not yet forthcoming, such thinking cannot be anything but restricted, and confined to logical extrapolation from our own experience. Let us then beware of dismissing too summarily and out of hand what may at first appear to us to be quite astonishing notions concerning the possible way in which UFOs are made, what they do, and how they do it. In so doing we may let some important datum slip away, and find ourselves no nearer to a solution of the mystery.

When the Scythians rode their horses into Greece, the Greek people, who were unfamiliar with such an arrangement between man and beast, mistook the combination for a single extraordinary animal and believed in Centaurs. The Indians in Mexico made a similar error in judgment concerning the Conquistadores and their horses, assuming that the saddle and all the other elaborate Spanish trappings were a part of the animal, and that the men in armour were actually metal men,

LEGACY OF THE SKY PEOPLE

Would it not be wise, on our part, for us to watch our own judgments rather carefully when we try to determine from available data the nature and modes of action of the UFO? We are dealing here with something from well beyond the range of our own immediate experience. We are trying to think creatively and to analyse far out into the framework of the unfamiliar. If we are to understand it at all, we must be able to stretch our minds to include certain logical, but not so easily imagined, perhaps, possibilities.

Not the least of these is the suggestion that etheric minerals may be more fundamentally alive than our familiar chemicals, that vehicles produced from them actually may be self-propelling, that they furnish their own energy and motive power, and that, like our own domesticated horses, they can be controlled and directed by the mind of man.

However, lest we be caught in restrictive error as were the ancient Greeks and the Mexican Indians, we ought to be prepared to add in the significant datum from beyond our own personal experience, which will provide the true and valid answer to our question: How are the flying saucers propelled? This significant datum may have little to do, directly, with the saucers themselves, but may have its roots in the very foundations of the world from which they come. If we fail to consider this possibility we may continue to interpret as merely mechanical what may well be sentient living creatures, perhaps not capable of what we would recognise as thought, but easily responsive to telepathic impulse from the mind of the being in control.

LEGACY OF THE SKY PEOPLE

CHAPTER XIII

THE SERPENT PEOPLE

Be ye wise as serpents. -Jesus to his initiated disciples.

There is nothing new in stories of the Serpent or Sky People coming to Earth in their ships of light. At least, nothing new to many an ancient race, but the idea may seem strange to those living in this twentieth-century material civilisation.

Why are they called the Serpent People? Well, the serpent in the folklore and traditions of nearly all cultures has always been the symbol of Wisdom, Science and Knowledge.

Braghine wrote in **The Shadow of Atlantis**:

The source of light, the sun, was often symbolized by the Toltecs, Mayas and Aztecs in the image of a more or less conventionalised feathered serpent. Quetzalcoatl and Cuculcan, the enlighteners of Central America' were also often symbolised by winged serpents. . . .

The yogis speak of Kundalini, the serpent fire which moves up the spinal column awakening Man's psychic nerve centres. When the serpent fire of the Kundalini is turned upward then the man becomes a sage or seer.

Churchward wrote of Narayana, the Seven-Headed Serpent who was the symbol of the Creator and Creation. Nara means Divine One; Yana-Creator of all things.

Thoth of Egypt, known also as Hermes in Greece, brought the people Wisdom—the balancing of good and evil. He showed that matter is a reflection of spirit. As above, so below. Hermes, like many other Messengers, carried the Caduceus, a divine rod. This was a staff, symbolical of the Staff of Life, around which two serpents intertwined in opposite directions. One serpent represents the negative, receptive or female, and is given activity by the positive, projective and male opposite. Neither can manifest without motion. The Staff of Life is polarised and is the neutral centre around which the two opposite forces intertwine (spiral) in their eternal progression of recreation.

Similar 'magic' wands or rods were also given to Moses by the Jehovah, and both Moses and Aaron used them in front of the Pharaoh. Consternation was caused when their Serpent rods proved superior to those of the Magi at the Egyptian Court.

LEGACY OF THE SKY PEOPLE

Athena, favourite daughter of Zeus, was often depicted wearing a helmet surmounted by a representation of a serpent.

There are many stories about the birth of Athena. In Crete it was said that the Goddess had been hidden in a cloud and that Zeus had struck it with his head, thus causing Athena to appear.

The cloud is interesting because of the remarkable number of incidents in the Bible mentioning clouds in relation to visitations by the Sky People.

Yes, indeed, the serpent was the sign of a Being who had balanced the two opposing forces of good and evil, and risen above them to Galactic Manhood.

It is only through experience of the knowledge of good and evil that humanity can learn discrimination and wisdom. When animal hu-man was helpless in the Garden of Eden, it was through the compassion of the Serpent people and their subsequent help as educators that Jehovah's creation found their self-determinism and began their spiralling journey to Godhood.

There have been many such visitors. Every so often, the Serpent People come to Earth and the consciousness of the world is raised an octave or two. Then, after the Wise One has departed, his sayings eventually become distorted, a religion is initiated and the particular Celestial Messenger worshipped as a supernatural Being.

When civilisation hits a new low ebb once more, another Avatar or Messenger from Out There arrives with his special message. Strangely enough, each Messenger brings the knowledge, or rather awakens humanity and draws out the knowledge, needed for that particular Age.

This time the response may bring that civilisation up to a much higher level, surpassing even that under the influence of the previous Visitor. So, once again, a spiral presents itself. Hu-manity goes up a little, then down, and next time up higher than before. Thus, there is a definite spiralling effect.

When the race goes down, a lesson has to be learnt and is the cause of a strong upward surge afterwards.

This spiral can be likened to the symbol of the serpent—gliding like sticky clay—undulating in a movement found both in the land and in the water.

The Magi with their wands described this original natural spiral form. They made the same design as that created by the serpent crawling across the Earth. They traced this pattern in the sand to evoke their magic.

The Mayas of Mexico, in Central America, tell of a mysterious white man who came to them from the East. He had a high forehead and flowing beard. The

LEGACY OF THE SKY PEOPLE

American Indians do not have beards. This white man, Quetzalcoatl, was dressed in a long white garment, on which were numerous red crosses.

His name, Quetzalcoatl, meant feathered serpent. Nobody saw him arrive in Mexico. He led a most ascetic life and strongly condemned all animal sacrifices, which Adam-II man is so fond of making.

Quetzalcoatl's work closely paralleled that of Osiris in Egypt, in that he introduced into Mexico better conditions and taught the natives many arts. He invented the Mexican calendar.

Like Osiris, he was against all violence, and is reported to have 'stopped his ears with his fingers' when the subject of war or fighting was brought up' He is said to have finally sailed away to the east in a canoe made of serpent skins. To the ancients eastward was synonymous with 'sunward'.

Subsequently Quetzalcoatl became the chief god of the Toltecs. His images often depict him with the solar disc. Colonel Braghine relates in **The Shadow of Atlantis** an interesting account about another, bearded white man, who came to the Chibcha race in Colombia.

Many millenniums ago, when the moon did not yet exist, there suddenly came to Colombia from the us old man with a long white beard. He had three names: Socnica, Zukha, and Nemketaba. His handsome wife had also three names: Chia, Huitaca, and Ubecaihuara. Both came riding camels. Chia was a very wicked enchantress, a true contrast to her infinitely kindhearted husband: she tried to hinder him in everything that he undertook to help his people. At one time she created a dreadful inundation: obeying her charms, the Funza river came out of its bed and inundated the whole Bogota valley. A multitude of Chibchas perished and only those who succeeded in climbing the mountains in time remained safe. Bochica became very angry with his handsome wife Chia for such a misdeed, and threw her heavenwards, transforming her into the moon. After that Bochica destroyed the rocks which impeded the flow of the Funza and drained the Bogota valley.

Bochica enlightened the Bogota upland tribes, organised their government, ordered them to build cities, introduced the solar cult, and appointed two rulers: one religious with the title of Zaké, and one civil, subordinated to the first. According to the legend the first Zaké ruled the Chibchas for 250 years. His mission fulfilled, Bochica retired to a lonely place named Eraca, where he lived for 2,000 years under the name of the anchorite Idacansas. During all this period he fasted and prayed for his beloved people. The end of Bochica was as mysterious as his arrival in Colombia: he disappeared. Later on he was transformed into the sun-god.

LEGACY OF THE SKY PEOPLE

H. T. Wilkins states that the Muyscas Indians called Bochica sua, or sun, and when the bearded Spaniards arrived in the sixteenth century, the Muyscas, who were still surviving as a tribe, called them 'children of the sun'. This implied, wrote Wilkins, that Bochica was a white bearded man.

Another bearded white man suddenly appeared from nowhere in Peru. The Incas called him Ayar Manco Capac. But he was also known as Viracocha. He, too, brought great benefits to the Incas, as well as spiritual assistance, including the solar cult. Before Viracocha left he set up a great cross on a mountain. He told those left behind that he would send messengers to protect them and to renew their knowledge.

Viracocha, like Jesus, was a healer and is also credited with walking on the waters.

Yes, these Wise Men who mysteriously came and went in days long ago, Apollo of the Sun, Hermes, Osiris, Quetzalcoatl, Bochica, Viracocha and many others, have always been known as the Serpent People. They introduced the solar cult. Those who took part in pure sun worship used the sun, the means of light and heat, to symbolise the fountain of light and knowledge; the Christos or Logos. They did not actually consider the sun itself as a deity, but as symbolical of the Godhead, and indeed, the sun in turn was only the symbol and representative of a far greater Central Sun.

LEGACY OF THE SKY PEOPLE

CHAPTER XIV

THE WORLD WILL NOT END TOMORROW!

Nothing in life is to be feared. It is only to be understood. -Marie Curie.

Although the Sky People have always been with us, it was no mere coincidence that the space ships were seen so often soon after the first atom bomb was exploded in 1945. When that bomb went off over Japan the Space People knew hu-manity had at its disposal the means to destroy itself. They came in increasing numbers to observe and study physical reactions on the Earth's surface after nuclear tests, especially along fault lines—weak spots, where earthquakes are prone to occur.

They were to some extent concerned because of Earth's rapidly growing technology and that its inhabitants might eventually have the means to carry these newly-found nuclear toys into outer space, But, their own attainments were more than sufficient to deal with any ill-considered and wrongly inspired sortie with nuclear warheads outside the planet.

To a much greater degree, they were coping with the possibility that humanity, pursuing its playing with fire policy to a point of no return, might destroy the world. There is a legend that another planet once orbited in our solar system where the Asteroid belt is now between Mars and Jupiter.

These asteroids, numbering thousands, are said to be the remains of a planet, significantly called Lucifer, which blew itself up.

The Sky People wish to preserve Earth, which, leaving aside slums, smog and strife, can be a very beautiful place, for future races of Mankind. No individual is expected to commit suicide, let alone a planet. All God's mansions were meant to be lived in, neither to become floating cemeteries nor to be disintegrated at the whim of some animal man's sadistic fancy. To play around with nuclear weapons is the act of planetary delinquents. Therefore, in a sense, the Sky People are here as Solar policemen. If earthmen start a nuclear conflagration, it is more than likely the Sons of God will intervene, put out the fire and salvage their own kind.

Cross-Man is no longer in the bow and arrow stage where the only damage he can do is to destroy his fellows. He has now discovered the fundamental building blocks of the Universe. Until the animal in him is eradicated entirely he is not to be trusted with such a cosmic secret.

However, there will be no open intervention unless humanity goes too far. Hu-manity has the divine gift of free will to make decisions. The Serpent People in their wisdom, like good parents, have allowed the children to grow up in the nursery, and have not interfered. If the children are naughty and set fire to the house, the grown-ups will come upstairs with fire extinguishers.

Up to now the grown-ups have been way-showers and throughout history have come among hu-manity leaving a little more wisdom and then have withdrawn to see what Cross-Man did with this knowledge. The unalterable fact is Man must learn for himself. He must discover and apply Truth himself. No one can do it for him.

This planet will not be allowed to blow itself up—the world will not end tomorrow! Whatever the prophets of Doom may say, the elder brothers will not permit this to happen. There is every hope that a nuclear war will not occur. Foreseeing hu-manity's technological advances, large numbers of extraterrestrials have come back to help at this critical period of Earth's history. They have reincarnated in human bodies. Numerous Cross-Men, too, are now Galactic dominant. Many of them are still 'sleepers', not yet or only partially awakened, but soon they will be aware of their potentialities.

Additionally, many people have claimed contact with actual space people who have landed here. Although not human, like earth men are, the visitors with their ability to manipulate chemical matter can load up sufficiently with chemicals to appear here as solid earth people. Indeed, they look more physical than the average inhabitant of this planet. They come here on missions and after a short stay return to their own planets, since a prolonged visit loaded with earth chemicals is a definite strain.

To some, this is probably very startling information, but even if one cannot accept the actual visits to this planet of the Sky People—although the Bible indicates only too clearly that 'Angels' appeared in those ancient times who ate food, washed and mingled with mortals—then we can appreciate that many people in the world today are 'broadcasting' through prayer and thought the concept of Peace. These people are Galactic dominants.

The world will not end tomorrow, but the Age of Iron (Materialism) is drawing to a close and a New Era of Enlightenment—a spiritual renaissance—is about to dawn. There will be many changes in the days to come!

This is what I wrote in the September-October 1959 issue of *Flying Saucer Review*:

LEGACY OF THE SKY PEOPLE

There is a general quickening up in the tempo of living on this planet. New discoveries in electronics, physics, astronomy, medicine and other fields are being developed at an astonishing rate. In the realms of metaphysics, religion and philosophy, concepts have broadened and more people have a deeper understanding than hitherto. A definite spiritual renaissance is taking place alongside these scientific and technological advances. It will soon be seen that religion and science are really one. The laws of life are scientific and scientific laws are fundamentally spiritual.

Some may ask why is there such an outpouring of fresh knowledge and new ideas at this moment? Change seems to be in the air. Not only that. There is a general feeling of expectancy abroad—a kind of inner knowing that big events are pending. This is the time when everything shall be revealed and all things made new. There shall be a new heaven and a new earth. The old world of prejudice, exclusiveness, narrowmindedness and materialism is on the way out and the new era of spiritual and scientific enlightenment is on the way in.

Changes are coming not only in our thinking but outwardly. Physical changes are, of course, a result of our thinking. They are the effects.

According to Professor Earling Dorft of Princeton University warmer temperatures have already had effect in some various parts of the world. Records of sea levels indicate the oceans have been rising at the rate of two feet per 100 years since 1920 due to melting glaciers. The North pole is tipping towards the south in the western hemisphere. The Magnetic North Pole is now some nine to eleven degrees away from where it should be. Paradoxically, the bed of the Atlantic Ocean is rising. This may be something to do with the way the pole is tipping. An article, *The Lost Empire of Atlantis*, by Richard Clavering, in the February 1937 issue of the *Reader's Digest* states: '. That great movement has taken place in the bed of the Atlantic and is still taking place, none can doubt. In August 1923, a vessel was sent out to search for a lost cable which had been laid about twenty-five years before. Soundings taken at the exact spot revealed that the bed of the ocean had risen nearly two and a quarter miles during that short period.

It is a fact, too, that the Gulf Stream has changed its position recently. British national newspapers carried the news that the Americans are attempting to trace its new course by injecting a colour dye and a perfume as near to its northern course as possible. Yes, change is not only in the air, but on land and in the seas. Changes, too, are occurring within us. Many people are aware of the significance of these changes and coming events. As we enter these crucial days it is worth noting that there is a gathering together all over the world of groups studying these trends and preparing themselves for the days ahead!

Many members of these groups have been led together as if by some strange force.

LEGACY OF THE SKY PEOPLE

Another indication of the times we live in is the fantastic number of sightings of flying saucers all over the world since 1945, 'I will show signs in the heavens.' The evidence for the existence of spacecraft from other worlds continues to accumulate to phenomenal proportions. The truth cannot be kept from the public much longer. Everything will be revealed. The people are awakening!

Since I wrote those words last year the tempo of scientific progress has continued and there have been serious land disturbances on the planet, including those at Agadir in North Africa, South Persia and in Chile.

The Earth is now starting to go through a process that can be likened to the cleansing of a bottle full of dirty water. The filth has to be removed before the bottle can be filled with clean, clear water. This is what is happening now. But have no fear. These outward manifestations are the outward result of negative thinking. If Cross-Man will put his individual mind in order and in tune with the Divine Mind, then he will ride out triumphantly any physical storms and upheavals.

There is a greater reason why the space ships are present in such numbers. The time is approaching when wonderful events are destined to take place here. The Sky People are the vanguard for One who comes to rule over his kingdom on Earth. Before the Ruler of this Solar System comes to claim his own—it is later than you think—the hope and longing of all the Serpent People is that the largest possible number of hu-mans will reach Manhood status. Those that do will be like Galactic Commandos, for undoubtedly this planet Earth is a very tough training school. This world, when it does pass out its trainees, produces only the finest blades, capable of facing any resistance.

In this chemical world Progress is impossible without some resistance; motion is impossible without friction. It is the action or reaction of the organism in the presence of this resistance, this friction, that determines the form and kind of associated activity.

Man is capable of addressing himself to this resistance, this friction, with conscious thought, will (discriminative decision) and planned activity. To use this combination of faculties is, from one point of view, to be a MAN.

To react to this resistance, this friction, with a more or less randomly acquired set of emotional defences, instincts and pre-established patterns of automatic action is to behave like an animal—to be an animal.

There are on this earth two basic schools of thought on the subject of what makes a hu-man being more human or less human.

The more vocal of these two groups is, as is usual in such cases, the less wise. It is the sentimental, over-emotionally heroic antagonistic school which measures mankind's humanity by the degree to which he is controlled by his own feelings, the feelings of others, and automatic or preestablished reactions to environmental pressures. These are the advocates of War, self-created struggle, the imposition of pointless restrictions in the name of Discipline, and the stubborn maintenance of pastoral codes in the face of technological advancement. Their view is that man will become soft, listless and bored if he ceases to stir up emotional conflict with his fellow man. They preach peace, but always at the cost of War. Peace, as it is defined in their mode of speech, is actually a synonym for armed truce.

The vocabulary of their religious expression is the vocabulary of war, and in their daily life there is no difference that is not described or approached as a fight, battle, war, conflict—with clouds of repellent emotion attached. This group does not recognise the environment in which it exists as a legitimate environment. Consequently, it cannot recognise itself as a legitimate inhabitant of that environment. So far, so good. But taken at the level of antagonism, this recognition becomes destructive. Philosophers influenced by antagonism tend to glorify struggle at the level of negative emotion, or to escape entirely into high-flown heavens of transcendental mysticism and ignore their wives and children.

Theologians who are similarly affected fix a great gulf between God and Nature, Nature and Man, Man and Woman, Man and Man—wherever they are able to perceive a difference in the world—declaring war between each pair they are able to recognise, assuming them to be always opposites.

Because this group recognises antagonism as the highest possible emotion, it maintains that any higher forms of emotion are either some form of antagonism or belong to another world, or another plane of being than their own. For them, in any case, the higher forms of emotion have no reality here on earth. They may even maintain that when such emotions as love, pure enthusiasm and serenity are experienced here that they occur by accident, or are bestowed by grace—that unpredictable whim of a capricious god. Love is not an emotion. Love arouses emotions: affinity, empathy, affection.

But Love itself is of the Self, a creative acceptance of another Being, another Self, and is a divine attribute of the essential Self of Man.

The more clearly an individual exhibits truly Manlike behaviour, the more loudly these people proclaim him to be inhuman, cold or alien.

The overcoming of fear through anger, the establishment of an antagonisitis now you know who's boss relationship—or, in the event of failure, grief, apathy and voluntary death, or its dramatic simulation—this, they cry, is the proper scale of human values. Anything beyond it, particularly anything constructive, strips, so they say, man of his essential humanity, which is their definition for whatever

LEGACY OF THE SKY PEOPLE

identifies man as an animal.

The notion of constructive cooperation through recognition of and employment of emotional states higher on the scale than antagonism was first introduced into Western civilisation through secret orders. Members of the orders—Rosicrucians and Masons—became influential in politics and in religion, and the notion gradually spread abroad among the people, at least as an ideal.

One result of this has been the establishment of a strange sort of double standard in ethical, moral and religious fields where there exist two forms of proper behaviour for nearly every situation. At the familiar level and at the emotional level the old code and scale of sheer animal antagonism are accepted and employed. An individual is expected, nay taught, to strive with his siblings and to develop a hearty Oedipus complex, to have contempt for foreigners, and to go forth and slaughter them with bravado if not with gusto at the command of the State.

There are many points in between at which the code of antagonism meets and crosses over the code of cooperation. The location of these cross-over points is dependent in each personal case upon the structure of which ever local form of the codes is recognised and accepted. These cross-over points create patterns of stress within the culture. The hu-man world is plunged into a quandary of 'Right v. Wrong' with no clear or reliable definition of either.

In the cooperative hu-man view—which is not 'communist,' by the way, and has nothing whatever to do with 'communism', since the communist attitude is merely another form of the antagonistic code, full of misapplied and wrongly defined tag-words and blanket ideas, i.e. 'either you cooperate with the directives as they are issued, or you can cooperate with a firing squad'—the natural environment furnishes man with sufficient friction and resistance. Once man has taken proper notice of that natural environment and has set himself to explore and to subdue it, it is capable of providing him with all the resistance and friction he needs to assure his progress to and beyond that godhead promised him by the Messiahs.

Man cannot progress through struggling with man. Unless he learns to do better he will inevitably destroy himself. Progress in this chemical world is impossible without some resistance, motion is impossible without friction. But the truly manlike being seeks the resistance supplied him by the natural environment, and finds adequate friction for his motions in that environment. He refrains from the creation of artificial emotional tensions and conflicts with his fellow human beings, because he is able to recognise them not as just a part of the inert, nonliving, chemical environment, but as living, breathing, real and functioning extensions of himself.

LEGACY OF THE SKY PEOPLE

At what is usually called the spiritual level, he sees mankind—MAN—as a single organism, but an organism in which no part is subservient to the whole or to any other part.

Rather, each part is responsible for the creation and perfection of the whole, even as each and every stone in a true arch must be perfect according to its own design.

Blind antagonism, whether directed by the voice and vote of its participants or by the dictates of a tyrant, can achieve only the destruction of the Temple, never its rebuilding. A hu-man being can become MAN only insofar as he deliberately refuses to remain a beast.

CHAPTER XV
WHAT COLOUR ARE SPACE PEOPLE?

Many people have asked, what colour are the Space People? Are they black, brown, red, yellow or white? Well, that is an interesting and pertinent question.

However, colour is a delicate and vexed problem. One glance, at the time of writing, at South Africa should indicate my meaning.

First, it must be emphasised that any race superimposing itself by means of force over another is revolting, not only to many evolved people in this world, but to Galactic (Adam-I dominant) standards. What has been happening in South Africa and, to some extent, in other parts of the world, is animal (Adam-II) behaviour.

Every hu-man has the potential spark of Godhood in him, whatever his race, colour, earthly status, religion, political party, views, social position or education. Every hu-man being is entitled to every other hu-man being's respect as an equal partner,

This does not necessarily mean that we will all be Einsteins, Schweitzers or Shakespeares in this life. We probably will not. But, potentially, everyone, whatever his colour, and however undeveloped he may be now, is a god. It may take a thousand life spans, but sometime the entity wearing that black, red, white, yellow or brown suit of clothes will one day rule a Solar System or a Galaxy. The sooner everyone realises their potentialities the better. When that happens, mankind will behave towards their fellows with more respect and less bestiality.

Any violence by white people towards coloured peoples in any part of the world is to be abhorred. And, of course, vice versa. Whites, Redskins, Black, Brown, Yellow and any other coloured peoples should receive friendly, courteous and helpful treatment from all other races. Each should help the other.

However, there are problems to be faced in this colour business. Everyone knows only too well that if whites and blacks go to school or university or work together, then sooner or later white girl meets black boy. The inevitable sparks fly between them and hey presto! they are in love and wedded. Fine so far, but then their children arrive, white or black. A few generations later there may be a throwback.

LEGACY OF THE SKY PEOPLE

There are, of course, other problems too.

I know of a man in Honolulu who, among his other accomplishments, was quite an authority on land snails. It became an absorbing hobby with him. He roamed all round the planet, literally, looking for them, and being of a liberal mind he decided to set up an experiment to prove once and for all that the whole idea of segregation was a lot of nonsense and against Nature.

Behind his house, in Honolulu, lay the perfect environment—a lovely canyon which he had partially cleared out, and in which he grew orchids—thousands of them—another hobby.

So, Our Man in Honolulu took a large number of land snails from all over everywhere, scrambled them all up thoroughly, and set them free in the canyon in this mixed-up condition. Now, he thought, we will have a whole lot of crossbred snails never seen before anywhere—and he looked forward to their mixed matings and piebald offspring most hopefully and with great enthusiasm.

A couple of years rolled by, and our friend went happily out to examine the fruits of his somewhat Jehovistic experiment.

Know what he found? The snails had peacefully divided up the canyon. The Samoans had their corner; the Hawaiians theirs; the Mainlanders theirs, and so on right down the list—and not one single, solitary, lonesome crossbreed could he find, anywhere! So segregation is unnatural? One wonders, perhaps it is one of the fundamental basic necessities of evolution and natural selection. However, the way segregation is worked at present is entirely wrong and against the fundamental rights of Man. There should be no question of superiority or inferiority, supremacy or subjugation. There should, indeed, be equal opportunity for all—but not necessarily under the same roof.

Even within the limits of one race there are such vast differences between people—mental ability, emotional orientation and subcultural acceptances—that they cannot all be expected to share the same rules for living.

The only thing wrong with caste and class is that after a time the purpose is forgotten and the limits become rigid and enforced. What everybody knows in one generation, nobody takes care to teach the next generation—so the essential data are lost. Add to this actual differences in body structure, then stir with a too democratic spoon, and employment in a nitroglycerine factory is a good insurance risk compared to what comes of that!

Bodies are highly specialised instruments. In their details of construction they differ enormously, even though, at a gross (size-wise; not evaluation) level, sex, they can interbreed. But when it happens between very different body struc-

LEGACY OF THE SKY PEOPLE

tures something is always lost on both sides.

Now, I like my typewriter. A girl I know likes her sewing machine. Both are invaluable to us in our work. But if my typewriter needs a part to repair it, I don't try to find that part in the sewing machine.

It is a small planet, but it should be possible to divide it up equitably, as the land snails divided up the canyon, and still work out some way to live together. People are trying, but they are working from wrong premises. They confuse equality with equivalence—equal opportunity with identical activity, identical possessions, identical acceptance—and these are grave confusions, indeed. Confusion always leads to conflict and finally to violence.

One day we will see that violence achieves nothing. There are bigger and better reasons for giving everybody his own world. And this is the big difference that moves the whole question over from violence and control to fraternity and freedom. For one thing, it abolishes the question of supremacy. It permits cooperation because it leaves Everyman his own integrity, be he white, black, red, brown or yellow.

Now, let us get back to the question at the beginning of this chapter: What colour are space people? First take a look at our own planet Earth. Why so many colours on one small mud-ball? In the natural course of events, Earth is subject to an inordinate amount of radiation-producing mutation—and in the past this may have been even more intense than it is now. In addition to this natural radiation, Mankind has, if we are to believe available evidence and tradition, too, subjected Man to a good dose of artificial irradiation—and more than once.

Then along comes Jehovah and invents white people. Add it all up, and right there are several possible sources of variation. No, actually Jehovah's children were red. And the white variety arrived as a mutation some 25,000 years ago, after the sinking of the main portion of Atlantis.

But, all through the ages more and more people have been arriving from extraterrestrial sources on this planet. The Chinese are convinced their first ancestors arrived on the back of a Fiery Dragon from the direction of the Moon. A lot of modern cigar-shaped objects could be compared with a Fiery Dragon. The Japanese say they are descended from people who came from the Sun. Their Emperors were known as Sons of Heaven. The Egyptians learned their civilisation from Divine kings whose symbol is a disc with wings: the Sun Kings. Perhaps this doesn't mean these people actually came from the Moon or the Sun but those two objects are the most conspicuous articles up there, and when the elders pointed up, as Gypsies do when you inquire of them, *'Where Do The Gypsies Come From?'* it would seem natural for the youngsters to assume the sun or moon was meant.

LEGACY OF THE SKY PEOPLE

The scientific differentiation of races which we accept because we learned it from our textbooks, is neither completely accurate nor completely reasonable. Earth-man is a migratory creature, and he has mixed himself together with far more enthusiasm than the land-snails ever did. Whole segments of hu-manity are accepted into the so-called white race by scientists when, in reality, they belong in categories that haven't been invented. The Mediterranean peoples, for instance, are not strictly white. They are hybrids with a good portion of Asia Minor and North Africa in their basic recipe. The whitest-looking people in Europe, the Scandinavians, are fundamentally a Mongolian people. If you ignore the pigmentation and look at the bone-structure this shows up. It has historical validation, if you accept as history the evident remnants in their Sagas and in their language—there is a lot of Chinese embedded in Norwegian and Swedish—and besides, there is the interesting fact that the Norskies build Pagodas with Dragons on them: the old Stave Churches! They used dragons elsewhere, too, on boats. The Finns are rather different. They arrived where they are, apparently, from a Middle-European source, and are not true Scandinavians.

Pigmentation therefore isn't always a sure guide to racial origins. And it varies with locality. However, the acceptance of pigmentation as a visual aid to natural selection has produced an unimaginably complicated mixture of original stocks.

The Atlanteans of 25,000 years ago were what we should call a white race. Their nearest living relatives on the planet still among us, are the Basques, the Berbers of North Africa, the Celts (Scottish Highlands, Ireland, Wales, and part of the North of France), and a very, very few of some of the so-called Indians of both Americas. There is also a small area in the South of France, around Carcasonne and Toulouse, where the Old Blood is still going strong. Greece once had its share, but that has been mostly replaced by invasions from elsewhere so there is very little left nowadays.

The Jews were originally a part of the Atlantean picture, of course, and there may be a few of them who are still representatives of the old blood—but not many. Jewish is now a religious, not a racial designation. There are Jews of all colours, races and sizes these days, including one nest of them somewhere in the middle of China. Their wandering habits have lost them in their racial purity. They happened to preserve some of the old religious notions better than most other peoples.

You will discover the majority of your really up-and coming Galactic dominants—the top ten per cent—among people whose genetic heritage links back into one or more of the above named areas, at least to some degree.

The original pigmentation was not a pasty-white, but what Ezekiel refers to as 'the colour of brass',—a faintly golden tint—not dark at all, just a recognisably

LEGACY OF THE SKY PEOPLE

different tinge, very faint under modern living conditions.

The old habit people have had for so long a time of plating the statues and images of their gods and heroes with gold is not a monetary evaluation at all, but a dim memory of something else entirely—the appearance of these gods and heroes. And this may have something to do with the extraordinary—and quite arbitrary value placed upon gold by earth-humanity.

It is a mistake to think of the Space people in our system as coloured. I submit that they are gold or sun coloured.

It is possible, nay, probable, that in other systems of the Galaxy, and, indeed, elsewhere, there may well be people with other colours, black, white, brown, red, yellow and, maybe, even green. There have been so many wisecracks about 'little green men from Mars', that I would not be surprised to see a green specimen of mankind. And why not? Surely it is egocentric to restrict God's universe to what is found on this little speck appearing in a vast infinite array of star systems and galaxies.

CHAPTER XVI

ONE DUTY

It will ever remain incomprehensible that our generation, so great in its achievements of discovery, could be so low spiritually as to give up thinking.

—Albert Schweitzer, Life and Thought.

All through the ages, as you have seen from this book, the Sky People have been visiting planet Earth and showing the way for hu-manity to realise its Manhood and potential Galactic status. Ever since hu-man beings were manufactured by the Jehovah to guard and till their Garden of Eden, the Sky or Serpent People have had compassion on them and have been coming here to help Earth Man know himself. It was Apollo of the Sun, whom many consider none other than Michael, also of the Sun, that was credited with the saying 'Man know thyself', and down the centuries other wise men have reiterated this statement.

Today, these extraterrestrial visitors are to be seen again in our skies in their traditional space ships. Some of them are here among us mingling with you in your offices and in your homes. Yes, the occupants of these craft have always been with you. They are with you now, although you pass them by in the street without noticing them. But it is a necessary factor of both the knowledge they bring and its application that it must be self-discovered. As a man must breathe and eat for himself, he must discover himself. His discovery can be validated by other men, but it must be made by each and every one. Man is an individual. This is one of the characteristics that makes him Man and not some other creature. A hu-man being is a pre-Man, with enough of manhood about him to be able to decide whether he will become Man or remain an animal. If he decides to become an animal, he will be subject to the animals, for they are animal-born, while he is only an adoption.

If he decides to become a Man, he will be subject to no being but Almighty God, the One Supreme, and then only at his own discretion, for God Himself, being alive, must grow.

The creative mind of Man is the highest created entity Man can ever know. Even a God he must take on faith, at the God's evaluation, and his own.

If he is to become Man, then he must recognise the thing that makes a Man—

LEGACY OF THE SKY PEOPLE

the creative mind and its power of constructive thought. The very name of Man comes from a root word that means to think. The Spirit of the Universe became God when he created Mind. Man is an entity in mind, and therefore, in his fulfillment, equal to God, but not equivalent. The theology of the world, no matter what the founder of any religion said out of his own mouth, degenerates in time into the philosophical hopes of those who have chosen to rejoin the animals. This degeneration is not accomplished overnight. It comes slowly, as an inward rot, the gnawing of termites in the body of an oak. The slow change is undetectable except to the observant. From one generation to any succeeding generation, it is almost indefinable. But skip a generation and it appears, and there can be no doubt, either of its existence or of its pernicious character.

In our populations here on earth, we have two kinds of people. We have the rich, who are rich in the things of this world—and I do not mean money or the things associated with money—this is another language, and another definition.

Pigs are the richest people in the world. 'They toil not, neither do they spin.' They grow fat because they are kept by their brothers. To be rich, in pig language, is to be well-provided for with sensation, emotion, conflict and pain, and above all, drama.

Jesus was an Initiate, and he spoke in the language of initiation, even to people who might not understand. Afterwards he had to explain what he had said to his own disciples.

On an earth, in a form in which he ought not to exist at all, burdened with chemical elements that do not belong to his natural structure, bereft of many of his legitimate faculties, and weighed down with the unnatural burden of undeserved and artificial guilt—a Man, a real Man, is the poorest, in spirit, of the poor.

Confronted with all those people who had followed him so far, after he had done his best to get away from them for a little rest and quiet, Jesus must have been most sharply aware of the difference between what he hoped his disciples would become, and the assembled multitude.

And out of his tired reflections, he spoke, in the language of the ear, that meditation we now call the Beatitudes. And the multitude applied his remarks to its own earthly aspirations. They heard him not. But there is a hint in the Bible that he went back to his disciples and tried to explain himself to them. The Beatitudes make a different kind of sense when you add 'Here on this earth' after every category mentioned.

They are very similar, then, to the ear-whispered doctrines passed on by diligent students under gurus, after they have finally attained Samahdi—and have given their instructors convincing evidence that they are neither deluded nor pre-

LEGACY OF THE SKY PEOPLE

tending.

Until Samahdi is taught, the student is under the impression he has been working to subjugate his mind. Samahdi is, he suddenly discovers, the realisation that there is nothing to subjugate, because the highest mind he is capable of reaching is his own eternal Self.

One does not subjugate one's Self, one does not conquer one's Self, one does not dominate, control, or otherwise act as if one's Self were another being—if one has realised Selfhood. This is the Revelation of Samahdi, and this is the test of whether or not someone has actually reached that state.

THE KING DOES NOT RULE THE KING. HE IS THE KING.

The only legitimately selfless creatures are the animals.

To offer a God who created a Self and commanded it to increase and multiply its kind the denial and annihilation of that Self, is an unforgivable affront to the Creator in whose very image that Self was made. It is unforgivable because there is nothing left to receive forgiveness. It is an affront because it implies that the King of the Universe would be pleased with the destruction of his children.

Jehovah, it is recorded, regretted his Creation, but he was not the King of the Universe, only a planetary Lord, and his creatures were not made even in his likeness, let alone the image and likeness of the Supreme Being. If you would be a selfless servant without will or individuality, then refuse the image and disclaim the likeness. You will become a flocking animal, fit for slaughter, and dedicated to sacrifice. Your reward may be great indeed, but you will never become a Man.

A Man is a being whose immortal Self was created to be made eternal in a universe of Creative Mind. He was made to think, and to be creative, productive, in and through his thought. In addition to this Godlike attribute, he was given the equally Godlike power to choose whether he would make use of it, or not. He can even deny it altogether, and annihilate himself as Man.

He can go into a far country, waste his inherited substance, and in the end find himself in charge of swine who demand of him only that he feed them constantly and protect them, day and night. As long as he does not believe himself to be a pig, he can walk out of even this degraded condition, return to his joyful Father, and be welcomed as a Man again.

But if he falls into the delusion that he is a selfless pig, or if he blames himself for knowing he is not and tries to behave like a pig anyhow, then he is lost indeed, until he regains enough of his senses to admit, at least, the bare existence of his individuality and then he will know his true breed. Joy will replace unfounded guilt and sacrificial shame.

LEGACY OF THE SKY PEOPLE

His liberated awareness of Self will expand under the impetus of that joy to embrace the Universe, and again he will know how the 'Father' and the 'I' are one.

To be harmless is to refrain from the initiation of violence. This goes deeper than not striking the first blow. Too wide acceptance, too suddenly, of extraterrestrial moral notions would initiate such violence in the world as it has never known. Hence they are carefully kept. Little bits of them are dangled on lengths of string in places people feel free to label inconspicuous. To enlighten and improve the concepts of ethics and morality without upsetting too many precarious equilibria is a delicate task and it will take time because it must proceed slowly and by stages.

It is acceptable to stand up and curse the world and the successful people in it and say it is all bad, but it is not acceptable to diagnose, particularly if our diagnosis is close to fact. We may do our cursing in generalities: 'The world is very evil,' 'Man must turn to Good' (undefined), or: 'Do as I say for my profit'. But if we point to the perverted morality that keeps human beings from becoming responsible Men, then all the beggars, leeches and others who are the natural products of that morality will rise up and seek to destroy us.

Definitions have been reversed, ideas inverted, and all with violence, bloodshed and endless war. The task is now to return definitions to their original meaning, to set up ideas in their original meaning and in their original frames of reference, without undue violence. Sometimes you will go to a lecture, and you will hear the people coming out of it saying: 'But he didn't say anything new.' People, even people who do not think much, or often, appear to have some vague inward feeling that if anything is to be done in this world toward its betterment, some sort of new revelation must be forthcoming. They betray this unformed judgment in their haste to go and listen to any self-styled prophet who comes along promising Truth. Their going, and their judgment of him, if he does not provide them with what they are looking for, reveals their distrust of the moral and ethical systems this world has offered them. Yet, someone suggested to them that the whole interpretation of morality and ethics ought to be turned right over, set up at an angle approaching 180 degrees, and completely retranslated.

These same earnest people would be outraged if, according to the current recipe for Salvation and Eternal Bliss, if you steadfastly refuse to think about your Self, turn away from it, deny it the very necessities of its life, make-believe you haven't got a Self, carefully discard any interest that appears, nip off any enthusiasm that looks in the least creative (if it would require your individual attention), and dispense with every pleasure, diligently kill out every joy; then GOD will be pleased with you, and your reward will be an eternity of Bliss. And the definition of Bliss, after a life like that would be, is usually—and not at all strangely—very close to the lay-Buddhist definition of Nirvana: for all practical purposes, *extinction*. Every ingredient in that recipe is in total opposition to the liberation and

LEGACY OF THE SKY PEOPLE

fulfillment of the very element that makes a human a Man. It is a short course in the most strenuous form of spiritual suicide ever devised.

Nobody sat down and put it all together in one go. It developed over centuries of experiments in the control and suppression of humanity. A Man cannot be controlled or suppressed. He may find himself restricted, but if he does he will cope with the situation. He will never become a blob, a nonentity.

People feel a need for some kind of difference in their thinking about one another and themselves. However, they have another feeling that is even stronger: their resistance to Change. 'We adored your lecture on Differential Equations, Professor. Now! Please tell us how to do it all with simple arithmetic—and for God's sake leave out the long division!'

Elbert Hubbard said: People who want milk should not seat themselves on a stool in the middle of a field and hope the cow will back up to them.

What is needed, then, to save the world situation is a new recipe, or at least a proper translation of the old one, and if believe, we can begin with that.

First, though, just memorising a recipe for bread will never bake a loaf. The materials must be gathered together, an environment prepared. The mix must be just right, and certain rules of preparation have to be followed. Precise rituals, even, must be observed in order to give the ingredients time to blend with one another, work together, and produce a dough. Then it must be raised again, and baked, before you can make an honest loaf. People without previous experience, without the ability to evaluate that experience, without certain useful technical knowledge of the laws of life, could listen to the Sky people's wisdom for a thousand years, and all they would get out of it would be a stiff shot of adrenalin from the anger it aroused in them. 'That is not what we want!'

They have been taught that if they make themselves helpless and, as miserable sinners, the more they can make themselves suffer, the more God will shower them with pleasure. However, if they become Men, then the God they worship will become jealous of them, and smite them with his wrath. The worst of it is they can point to their own Bible and prove it to you. And, if you dare indicate the status of their God, then, obviously you are wrong, and tampering with Scripture. So these heretical ideas are unpopular, and they will always be so with those who are looking for the easy, irresponsible, animal way.

There is only one service you bring to the Almighty Creator of the Universe. There is only one duty you owe to him or to any other being. They are one and the same: to make sure that one Man stands before his face, joyous and unafraid ... yourself. You cannot send a substitute. The Almighty accepts no proxies, and he is not pleased by human sacrifices.

LEGACY OF THE SKY PEOPLE

If it pleases you to have company on your journey into the Presence, then wake up other MEN, and invite them to go along with you. Do not, however, pretend that you have found their Selfhood, or that you are bringing this to its Divinity, when you know that you have not, and cannot.

You can only go together if each MAN goes as if he went alone.

Osiris was an earthly ruler, who was popular with his subjects. His brother, Set, was jealous of this popularity and plotted against Osiris. Set's plans to be rid of his brother began when he secretly obtained his brothers measurements and had a magnificent casket made to fit. This casket was in the form of a human shaped box. Set then organised a large feast to which Osiris and a number of others were invited. At the height of the festivities Set produced the casket and announced that it would be given to whomever it fitted. All the guests tried the casket for size, but none fitted until finally Osiris stepped into the casket. Set immediately slammed the lid closed and sealed the casket shut.

The sealed coffin was then thrown into the Nile. Isis was devastated at the loss of her husband and searched for the casket throughout Egypt and then overseas. She eventually found it where it had come to rest in the roots of a massive tree. Isis then returned the coffin to Egypt for a proper burial. For safe keeping she concealed it in the marshes beside the Nile. Unfortunately for Isis, Set found the casket while out hunting and was so enraged he chopped the body of Osiris into pieces, and scattered the parts throughout the land of Egypt. Poor Isis had to then set out again looking for the parts of her husband. Eventually she found all the parts except one and reassembled Osiris and wrapped him in bandages. In some accounts Isis breathed life back into Osiris' body and it was then that Horus was conceived. This was a more magical event than it seems, considering the one part of Osiris Isis couldn't find.

The similarity of the Christian legend of Moses is apparent.

LAST SONG

The God stood at the top of the stairway to Heaven and looked down to see who it was coming up at such an unaccustomed hour:

Coming with such a noise of singing, and coming, it would appear, quite alone—but rejoicing for all that.

Who is it who dares to climb by himself in the middle of the night, and to sing with such a loud voice?

The singer stopped singing, and laughed, and kept on climbing.

I am climbing because I know how, she said, and I am not alone. And I am singing because of the other who comes the way I have come, and believes that he comes alone.

So the God sat down with the woman at the top of the stairway to Heaven, and they sang together.

LEGACY OF THE SKY PEOPLE

BIBLIOGRAPHY

The Holy Bible.

Young's Analytical Concordance to the Bible.

The Short Bible, edited by J. M. Powis Smith and Edgar J. Goodspeed.
    University of Chicago Press.

The Bible in the Hands of its Creators, by Moses Guibbory.

The Interlinear Literal Translation of the Hebrew Old Testament.
    by George Ricker Berry. Wilcox & Follett, Chicago, 1951.

The Zohar.

The Book of Enoch, Translation by Canon R. H. Charles.
    Oxford University Press, 1912. S.P.C.K., London, 1952.

The Secret Doctrine, by Madame H. P. Blavatsky. Adyar Edition.
    Theosophical Publishing House, London, 1888.

The Book of El-Daoud.

The Encycopaedia Britannica.

World Book Encyclopedia. Field Enterprises Association, Chicago, 1960.

Larousse Encyclopaedia of Mythology. Batchworth Press, Ltd., London, 1959.

The Works of William Shakespeare.

The Poetical Works of Longfellow. Frederick Warner & Co., London.

Gulliver's Travels, by Jonathan Swift, 1726.

Dialogues of Plato, Timoeus and Critias.

The Age of Fable, by Thomas Bulfinch. J. M. Dent & Sons, London, 1912.

The Gods of the Greeks, by C. Kerenyi, Thames & Hudson, London, 1951.

The Homeric Gods, by Walter Otto, Thames & Hudson, London, 1955.

A Handbook of Greek Mythology, by H. S. Rose. Methuen & Co., London,

LEGACY OF THE SKY PEOPLE

The Muses' Pageant, by W. M. L. Hutchinson. J. M. Dent & Sons, London, 1908.

The White Goddess, by Robert Graves. Faber & Faber Ltd., London, 1912.

The Atlantis Myth, by H. S. Bellamy. Faber & Faber Ltd., London, 1958.

The Shadow of Atlantis, by Colonel A. Braghine. Rider & Co., London, 1946.

Atlantis, by Ignatius Donnelly. Sampson Low, Marston & Co. Ltd., London, 1938.

The Story of Atlantis and the Lost Lemuria, by W. Scott-Elliot.
  Theosophical Publishing House, London, 1910.

The Lost Continent of Mu, by Colonel James Churchward.
  Neville Spearman Ltd., London, 1959.

Mysteries of Ancient South America, by H. T. Wilkins. Rider & Co., London, 1946.

Secret Cities of South America, by H. T. Wilkins. Rider & Co., London, 1950.

Stories of Egyptian Gods and Heroes, by F. H. Brooksbank.
  George G. Harrap & Co., London, 1914.

Giants of Britain, by J. Foster Forbes. Thomas's Publications Ltd., Birmingham, 1945.

The Riddle of Prehistoric Britain, by Comyns Beaumont. Rider & Co., London, 1945.

Afrable Swages, by Francis Huxley. The Scientific Book Club, London.

Monk and Knight, by Frank W. Gunsaulus. A. C. McClurg & Co., Chicago, 1893.

Prodigal Genius, by John J. O'Neill. Ives Washburn Inc., New York, 1944.

The Books of Charles Fort. Henry Holt & Co., New York, 1941.

Flying Saucers Have Landed, by Desmond Leslie and George Adamski.
  T. Werner Laurie Ltd., London, 1953.

Flying Saucers-Fact or Fiction? by Max B. Miller.
  Trend Books Inc., Los Angeles, 1957.

LEGACY OF THE SKY PEOPLE

Flying Saucers From Outer Space, by Major Donald E. Keyhoe.

    Hutchinson & Co., London.

Spacecraft from Beyond Three Dimensions, by W. Gordon Allen.

    Exposition Press Inc., New York, 1959.

Other Tongues-Other Flesh, by George Hunt Williamson.

    Neville Spearman Ltd., London, 1958.

Road in the Sky, by George Hunt Williamson. Neville Spearman Ltd., London, 1959.

UFO and the Bible, by M. K. Jessup. The Citadel Press, New York, 1956.

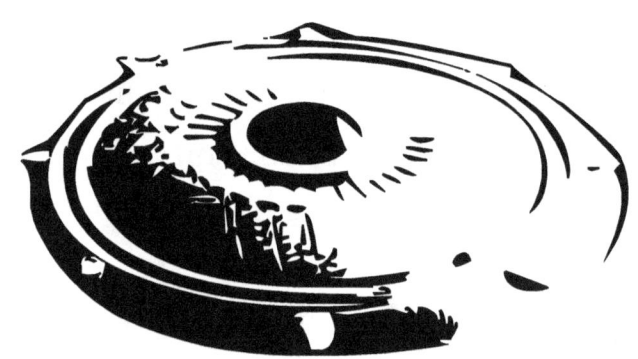

LEGACY OF THE SKY PEOPLE

THE CONTRIBUTORS

LEGACY OF THE SKY PEOPLE

SEAN CASTEEL began writing about UFOs, alien abduction and related topics in 1989 after reading Whitley Strieber's landmark book, "Communion." Prior to that, Casteel worked as a freelance journalist for various local newspapers and a smattering of national publications.

Since then, Casteel has written for "FATE Magazine," "Mysteries Magazine," and the now defunct "UFO Universe." He is currently a contributing editor to the newsstand publication "UFO Magazine" and a regular contributor to "The Conspiracy Journal" and "The Bizarre Bazaar" from Global Communications as well as "Open Minds Magazine." His articles have been published in the United Kingdom, Italy and Romania.

Casteel weighs in on the positive side of the UFO phenomenon, meaning that he feels what is happening currently with the UFO and alien abduction phenomena is a benevolent precursor to the Second Coming and the Battle of Armageddon, which will surely involve alien ships in combat for control of the planet. In other words, Christ will return in a UFO. This is of course somewhat of a minority opinion, but there it is.

Casteel's books include "UFOs, Prophecy and the End of Time," "Signs and Symbols of the Second Coming," "The Excluded Books of the Bible" and "Gone Forever In The Blink Of An Eye." All his books have been published by Inner Light/Global Communications and are available on Casteel's website at www.seancasteel.com and at Amazon.com

LEGACY OF THE SKY PEOPLE

NICK REDFERN works full-time as an author, lecturer and journalist. He focuses upon a wide range of unsolved mysteries, including the increasingly tedious Roswell affair of 1947, the macabre Men in Black, Bigfoot, UFOs, the Loch Ness Monster, alien encounters, and government conspiracies. He writes for UFO Magazine; Mysterious Universe; Fate; Cryptomundo; and Fortean Times. He also has a regular, weekly, cryptozoology-themed column at Mania.com entitled Lair of the Beasts.

His many previous books include Space Girl Dead on Spaghetti Junction; The FBI Files; Man-Monkey; Monsters of Texas (coauthored with Ken Gerhard); Cosmic Crashes; Final Events; On the Trail of the Saucer Spies; Keep Out!; There's Something in the Woods; Strange Secrets (with Andy Roberts); Memoirs of a Monster Hunter; Science Fiction Secrets; The NASA Conspiracies; A Covert Agenda; Celebrity Secrets; and The Real Men in Black.

Nick has appeared on numerous television shows, including VH1's Legend Hunters; the BBC's Out of this World; Fox News; History Channel's Ancient Aliens, Monster Quest, America's Book of Secrets; and UFO Hunters; National Geographic Channel's The Truth about UFOs and Paranatural; and SyFy Channel's Proof Positive, in which Nick and the Centre for Fortean Zoology's Jon Downes raced around Puerto Rico in a cool silver-coloured jeep in search of the blood-sucking nightmare known as the Chupacabra.

He lists his favourite things as late 1970s punk-rock and new-wave music, black t-shirts and black jeans, Carlsberg Special Brew, Tennents Super, zombies, chocolate, Family Guy, The Walking Dead, Night of the Demon, Terrorvision, the works of Jack Kerouac, the novels of Carlos Ruiz Zafon, Rammstein, Motorhead, Abby from NCIS, Oasis, a nice cup of tea with lots of milk and sugar, and burned toast with mountains of margarine.

Nick can be contacted at http://nickredfernfortean.blogspot.com

LEGACY OF THE SKY PEOPLE

TIMOTHY GREEN BECKLEY has been described as the Hunter Thompson of UFOlogy. Since an early age his life has more or less revolved around the paranormal. The house he was raised in was thought to be haunted. Tim saw his first of three UFOs when he was but ten, and has had two more sightings since – including an attempt to communicate with one of these objects. Tim grew up listening to the only all night talk show in the country that revolved around the strange and unexplained. Long John Nebel's guests included the early UFO contactees who claimed to have visited other planets and built time machines in the desert. Tim was fascinated by everything that went bump in the night – or even in the daylight for that matter. Over the years he has written over 25 books on everything from rock music to the secret MJ12 papers. He has been a stringer for the national tabloids such as the Enquirer and editor of over 30 different magazines (most of which never lasted more than a couple of issues). His longest running effort was the newsstand publication **UFO UNIVERSE** which went for 11 years. Today he is the president of *Inner Light/Global Communications* and editor of the *Conspiracy Journal* and *Bizarre Bazaar.*

He is one of the few Americans ever to be invited to speak before closed door meetings on UFOs presided over by the late Earl of Clancarty at the House of Lords in England. The Inner Light Publications and Global Communiations' catalog of books and video titles now number over 200, including the works of Tim Swartz, Sean Casteel, T. Lobsang Rampa, Commander X, Brad Steiger, John Keel, Tracy Twyman, Wendelle Stevens and a host of many other authors. He is also the host of numerous horror films under the moniker of Mr. Creepo.

LEGACY OF THE SKY PEOPLE

TIM R. SWARTZ is an Indiana native and Emmy-Award winning television producer/videographer. Tim is the author of a number of popular books including *The Lost Journals of Nikola Tesla, Time Travel: A How-To-Guide, Richard Shaver-Reality of the Inner Earth, Admiral Byrd's Secret Journey Beyond the Poles*. He is a contributing writer for: *Sir Arthur Conan Doyle: The First Ghostbuster*, and Brad Steiger's *Real Monsters, Gruesome Critters, and Beasts from the Darkside*. As a photojournalist, Tim has traveled extensively and investigated paranormal phenomena and other unusual mysteries from such diverse locations as the Great Pyramid in Egypt to the Great Wall in China. He has worked with television networks such as PBS, ABC, NBC, CBS, CNN, ESPN, Thames-TV and the BBC. His articles have been published in magazines such as *Mysteries, FATE, Strange, Atlantis Rising, UFO Universe, Flying Saucer Review, Renaissance*, and *Unsolved UFO Reports*. View his website at: www.conspiracyjournal.com

LEGACY OF THE SKY PEOPLE

BRAD AND SHERRY STEIGER –

The author/co-author of 170 books, Brad Steiger wrote the paperback bestseller *Strangers from the Skies* about UFOs. His edited work *Project Bluebook* was hailed by *Omni* magazine as one of the best UFO books of the century. Steiger was inducted into the Hypnosis Hall of Fame for his work with UFO contactees, abductees, and past life regression. In Minneapolis, he received the Lifetime Achievement Award at the National UFO and Unexplained Phenomena Conference.

The author/co-author of 43 books, Brad's wife, Sherry Steiger, an ordained minister with a special interest in UFOs in the Bible and world religions, began working closely in 1985 with Dr. J. Allen Hynek, official scientific advisor for the U.S. Air Force's twenty-year study of UFOs. Sherry served as his publicist, and confidante at his nonprofit UFO research organization in Phoenix until his death in 1986. This position made her privy to unpublished research and more than 80,000 documented cases from 161 countries.

For many decades, the Steigers have researched and investigated UFOs and their cultural impact throughout world history, and they have lectured and conducted seminars on the phenomenon throughout the United States and overseas. Sherry and Brad were featured in twenty-two episodes

LEGACY OF THE SKY PEOPLE

of the television series *Could It Be a Miracle?* Together, their television appearances and specials include: *The Joan Rivers Show, Entertainment Tonight, Inside Edition, Hard Copy, Hollywood Insider,* and specials on HBO, USA Network, The Learning Channel, The History Channel, and Arts and Entertainment (A&E), among others. They appear frequently as guests on numerous domestic and international radio talk shows.

LEGACY OF THE SKY PEOPLE

GIORGIO A. TSOUKALOS is Erich von Daniken's official representative in the United States and the rest of the English-speaking world. For over 10 years, Tsoukalos has been the Director of von Daniken's Center for Ancient Astronaut Research. He is also the publisher of "Legendary Times Magazine," the world's only definitive Ancient Astronaut research journal. He appears regularly on the History Channel program "Ancient Aliens."

Tsoukalos has been described as the real-life Indiana Jones and is a trailblazer changing the way the world thinks about the Ancient Astronaut Theory. He has traveled to 54 countries and is one of a few people who have actually visited and explored nearly all the mysterious places our planet has to offer. He is fluent in five languages: English, German, French, Italian and Greek. He lives in Oceanside, California..

LEGACY OF THE SKY PEOPLE

Send an email for a free subscription to our weekly Conspiracy Journal to –MRUFO8@hotmail.com

Web Sites: www.ConspiracyJournal.com www.TeslasSecretLab.Com

We publish many books, catalogs, audio CDs and DVDs on a wide variety of topics. Please contact us at above or thru the mail at

Global Communications
Box 753
New Brunswick, NJ 08903

LEGACY OF THE SKY PEOPLE

Send an email for a free subscription to our weekly Conspiracy Journal to –MRUFO8@hotmail.com

Web Sites: www.ConspiracyJournal.com www.TeslasSecretLab.Com

We publish many books, catalogs, audio CDs and DVDs on a wide variety of topics. Please contact us at above or thru the mail at

Global Communications
Box 753
New Brunswick, NJ 08903

Oahspe

Raymond A. Palmer Tribute Edition

WHAT IS OAHSPE?
THOUSANDS HAVE CALLED IT THE WONDER BOOK OF THE AGES.

Want To Know Just Where Is Heaven? What We Do When We Get There? Is There A Hell? Who "Manages" Earth, the Solar System, the Universe. . . and How?

OAHSPE reveals all this, and a thousand more answers to man's most difficult questions. Received from spirit in 1880 using one of the first typewriters at the unbelievable speed of 120 words per minute – a miracle in itself. In addition, much of the writing, along with the book's original drawings, was done in total darkness .

PRESENTED IN TWO VOLUMES, 1250 PAGES NEARLY A MILLION WORDS!

To many this work is one of the most astronomical ever presented. It is a book of Cosmology that could have been written by today's space scientists.

Do you think flying saucers are new? Then read OAHSPE! A whole panorama of aerial and special vessels are described as though from today's newspapers.

Do you wonder at Einstein's theories? Then read OAHSPE! He could have gotten his information from these pages!

Uncounted thousands of tons of meteorites fall to Earth each day, yet space is nearly empty of them. OAHSPE knew it in 1882!

Space is dark, say our daring astronauts. So did OAHSPE in 1882, and tells us why!

Archaeologists have claimed amazing discoveries of ancient races and dead cities and civilizations since 1882. They might have discovered them sooner had they read OAHSPE!

THIS EDITION IS DEDICATED TO THE LATE PUBLISHER, EDITOR AND RESEARCHER, RAY PALMER, WHO THOUGHT THIS ONE OF THE GREATEST WORKS EVER PENNED

Special: This is the only edition of OAHSPE to contain FULL COLOR PORTRAITS of the spirits responsible for dictating this amazing work to John Newbrough.

Over 1250 Pages - Two Volume Set - Color Plates - Retail Price $99.00
ISBN13: 9781606110676

PRICE REDUCED FROM $99.00 TO $79.95 FOR READERS OF THIS PUBLICATION ONLY!
Because of weight and size add $8.00 shipping/handling.
Copies shipped directly from the printer.

Order From: TIMOTHY G. BECKLEY · BOX 753 · NEW BRUNSWICK, NJ 08903

Age Old Questions

ARE YOU READY FOR THE RETURN OF THE ANCIENT WARRIORS?

SHOCKING TRUTHS REVEALED IN TWO NEW BOOKS THROUGH THE VALIANT RESEARCH EFFORTS OF "SIR" W. RAYMOND DRAKE

THEY HAVE BEEN HERE FROM THE BEGINNING OF TIME AND WILL SHOW THEMSELVES SOON! THEY ARE THE 'ANCIENT ASTRONAUTS" – THE ALIEN GODS OF OLD

Gods? Does The Weird Misshapen Skull Of A Strange "Star Child" Serve As Proof That Hybrids Do Exist And That Interbreeding Between Their Race And Ours Was A Fact? According To The Indigenous Prophets, What Events Are About To Lead Up To The Homecoming Of The Gods, And Who Will Be Accounted Worthy Of Reuniting With Them?

Join Our Group Of Expert Researchers Lead By W. Raymond Drake along with Tim Beckley, Sean Casteel, Joshua Shapiro, Brent Raynes and Angela Sangster, As They Question The Reality Of The Universe As We Know It – Things Are About To Change!

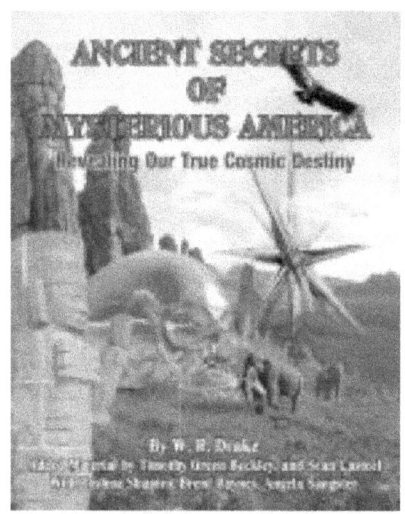

( ) Book One
ANCIENT SECRETS OF MYSTERIOUS AMERICA–REVEALING OUR TRUE COSMIC DESTINY —$22.00 (Over 300 pages)

DO STRANGE ALIEN ARTIFACTS DISCOVERED THROUGHOUT THE AMERICAS PROVE ANCIENT ASTRONAUTS ONCE WINGED TO EARTH AND SHARED THEIR WISDOM WITH EARLY HUMANS?

On Treasured Occasions Do Extraterrestrials Descend To Direct Through Chosen Initiates The Destinies Of Nations And Advance The Evolutionary Process? Did The Gods Mate With Virgins To Father Heroes Whose Wondrous Deeds Inspired Their People To New Glories? Does Tradition Tell Of Shadowy Figures, Not Born Of Woman, Flitting Down The Dusty Corridors Of Time To Preach Some New Philosophy Or Invent Some Novel Machine Revolutionizing Contemporary Culture? What Is The Evidence That The Mysterious Crystal Skulls Found Throughout Mexico And Central America Signify A Link With The Sky

( ) Book Two
ALIEN SPACE GODS OF ANCIENT GREECE AND ROME — REVELATIONS OF THE ORACLE OF DELPHI —$22.00 (Over 300 pages)

WAS THE MEDITERRANEAN REGION OF OUR PLANET VISITED BY A RACE OF "SUPER BEINGS" IN ANCIENT TIMES?

WAS THE ORACLE OF DELPHI A CONDUIT FOR PROPHETIC MESSAGES FROM OUTER SPACE – PERHAPS THE FIRST TELEPATHIC CHANNELER?

Did the giants of antiquity establish a UFO base atop picturesque Mount Olympus? Were they the gods and goddesses of "mythology" idolized and given names such as Apollo, Hades, Athena, Heda, Hermes, Zeus, Artemis, and Hestia?

Did the powerful deities of Greece help save Athens from being invaded by the mighty armies of Atlantis in 10,000 BC? Did the gods' intervene at Marathon and Salamis, sending flying shields to aid Alexander storming the walls of Tyre? Did a UFO encountered near Troy save the army of Loculus from destruction? Were omens observed in the sky just before the murder of Caesar? How does one explain the manifestation of mysterious voices and apparitions in the heavens as Hannibal ravaged Italy?

Super Special— Both Volumes $39.95 + $5.00 S/H
Order From: Timothy Beckley
Box 753 · New Brunswick, NJ 08903
PayPal: MRUFO8@hotmail.com

OTHER TONGUES OTHER FLESH REVISITED

By George Hunt Williamson - Edited by Timothy Green Beckley

"IN MY HOUSE THERE ARE MANY MANSIONS," JESUS STATED. NOW HERE IS THE PROOF!

"Evidence has accumulated that there are people on earth that don't really belong here!" George Hunt Williamson, author of *OTHER TONGUES OTHER FLESH* stated as early as 1955.

This doesn't mean they came here aboard a flying saucer, disembarked, put on a tweed suit, polished up their earthly languages and moved into the house next door. It does mean, however that there is a special class or order of beings in the Universe that are different from us because of the fact that they must wander from one world to another, and from one place to another. They are the "chimney sweeps" of creation. It is their specific job to be the "trash cans" of the Universe and aid their fellow man on these backward worlds."

They come in many disguises... Most are friendly. A few are NOT! They include: THE WANDERERS; THE MIGRANTS; THE PROPHETS; THE HARVESTERS; THE AGENTS; THE INTRUDERS; THE GUESSERS.

In *OTHER TONGUES OTHER FLESH REVISITED*, Williamson deciphers the strange symbols left from a depression of the bottom of the spaceman's shoes in the soil from which a plaster of paris cast was made on the spot. This is the famous George Adamski contact with Orthon in the desert of which Williamson was the primary witness.

Here are SECRETS concerning the creation of life and the evolution of humankind entrusted to only a handful. And, although Williamson has passed on, his legacy is vastly important. So much so that Alec Hidel in the Excluded Middle recently confided: "There can be no doubt that, by accident or design, Williamson and his various collaborators played an enormous part in shaping New Age thought in all its manifestations. Together they constituted the single most important occult group of the post-war era. Their influence is made all the more remarkable by the fact that it has seldom been acknowledged, or even perceived by other researchers in the field."

$24.00 + $5.00 s/h from:
Timothy Beckley • Box 753 • New Brunswick, NJ 08903
FREE SUBSCRIPTION www.ConspiracyJournal.Com